Advance (

How to Pl;

HOW TO
PLAY
THE
GAME

FOREWORD BY LEIGH STEINBERG

HOW TO PLAY THE GAME

WHAT EVERY
SPORTS ATTORNEY
NEEDS TO KNOW

DARREN A. HEITNER

Cover design by Elmarie Jara/ABA Publishing.

The materials contained herein represent the opinions of the authors and/or the editors, and should not be construed to be the views or opinions of the law firms or companies with whom such persons are in partnership with, associated with, or employed by, nor of the American Bar Association or the ABA Publishing unless adopted pursuant to the bylaws of the Association.

Nothing contained in this book is to be considered as the rendering of legal advice for specific cases, and readers are responsible for obtaining such advice from their own legal counsel. This book is intended for educational and informational purposes only.

Printed in the United States of America.

18 17 16 15 14   5 4 3 2 1

Library of Congress Cataloging-in-Publication Data

Heitner, Darren A., author.
  How to play the game : what every sports attorney needs to know / Darren A. Heitner.
     pages cm
  Includes bibliographical references and index.
  ISBN 978-1-61438-916-3 (alk. paper)
  1. Sports lawyers--United States. 2. Practice of law--United States. I. Title.
  KF299.S66H45 2014
  344.73'099--dc23

                         2014008460

Discounts are available for books ordered in bulk. Special consideration is given to state bars, CLE programs, and other bar-related organizations. Inquire at Book Publishing, ABA Publishing, American Bar Association, 321 N. Clark Street, Chicago, Illinois 60654-7598.

www.ShopABA.org

To Grandma Lottie—you are
my true inspiration.

Contents

Foreword

When I represented my first athlete Falcon Quarterback Steve Bartkowski. in 1975, there was no acknowledged concept of Sports Law. A general manager could respond to a phone call and say "we don't deal with agents." Had Rip Van Winkle fallen asleep in 1975 and awakened in 2014 he could hardly recognize the growth of collegiate and professional sports into a multi-billion dollar industry. The explosion in competing television networks created exponentially more actual games telecast, with analysis and highlights added to the mix. Sports television became a thriving growth sector and provided employment opportunities. The explosion in rights fees dramatically impacted franchise values and player compensation.

Social media and multiple platforms of content supply have led to experiences that draw fans closer to players and teams. An Oklahoma Land Rush race is going on to see which start-up business with a new sports idea can become tomorrow's Facebook or ESPN. Marketing, sponsorships, fantasy sports, stadia with premium seating, and video games all add to the growth. There are jobs for attorney's working for Leagues, Conferences, colleges, pro teams, and players' associations as well.

Sports can also serve as a powerful force to trigger imitative behavior promoting constructive problem solving. I asked each client to set up programs at the high school, collegiate and professional level. When Heavyweight Champion Lennox Lewis cut a public service announcement that proclaimed "Real Men Don't Hit Women" it did more to change attitudes in rebellious adolescents towards domestic violence than 1,000 authority figures ever could.

Sports Representation has become the "Golden Grail" of jobs for millions of students and professionals. I suppose *Jerry Maguire* triggered much of that.

But how does someone looking to enter the world of sports possibly discern the most effective way to have a career in sports?

Darren Heitner is the best and brightest of a younger generation who clearly see the multitude of sports possibilities in a holistic way. He is a young visionary who understands sports from the perspective of a former agent, current attorney, writer, inventor of a website, and teacher. He has written a compelling book which allows the reader to think of the issues facing sports. Anyone thinking of a career as a sports attorney must read this book first. Keep it handy as a powerful aide in navigating the often thorny issues in this career.

I first was acquainted with Darren through his brilliant analysis and writing on Forbes.com. He has the ability to provide a template of methodology that allows his readers to understand multiple issues in sports in a unique way. His understanding of the collective bargaining process, rules of amateurism, the challenge of agenting, marketing and endorsements is so insightful, it will give a reader a deeper understanding of how the sports business really works. So enjoy this book—it might change your life!

—Leigh Steinberg

Sports attorney, CEO of Steinberg Sports and Entertainment, and author of *The Agent*

Introduction

"[Sports Law] is largely an amalgam of interrelated legal disciplines involving such areas as contract, taxation, employment, competition and criminal law but dedicated legislation and case law has developed and will continue to do so. As an area of academic study and extensive practitioner involvement, the time is right to accept that a new legal area has been born—Sports Law."[1]
—Professor Simon Gardiner

Sports Law is a class taught at institutions of higher education across the world and is an attractive practice area at a variety of law firms. It is a discipline that I became fascinated with after serving as an intern at an Atlanta-based full-service sports and entertainment company between my sophomore and junior years at the University of Florida. At the time, I believed that my future rested in the realm of athlete representation. In fact, a couple of years later, I would create my own sports agency from scratch, an agency that existed for approximately four years before I decided to change the company's focus and direct the bulk of my attention to the practice of law. With a little bit of opportunity and a lot of preparation, I was able to build a robust practice. I have represented some of the best athletes, sports agents, media entities, managers, publicists, and other sports-related professionals and organizations, and doing so has allowed me to remain dedicated to the exciting and challenging world of Sports Law.

Sports Law is not limited to those who represent sports individuals and entities in their respective private practices. "Sports Lawyer" is also a label commonly attached to those who work in-house for professional and amateur sports organizations. Although Sports Law has grown into a distinct

---

1. Simon Gardiner et al., Sports Law 71, 74 (1998).

discipline, it amalgamates a variety of focuses, including but not limited to Contract Law, Torts, Intellectual Property, Criminal Law, Family Law, Trusts and Estates, Labor and Employment, and Antitrust. Further, evidentiary and civil procedure issues are commonplace in any Sports Law related litigation. Litigators must be familiar with the local, state, and federal rules of procedure, and transactional attorneys always have to be careful about sentence structure, key words, and punctuation. Paying attention to guidelines and detail is as important in Sports Law as it is in other legal disciplines.

The field of Sports Law has experienced aggrandizement in the recent past. According to Robert Denney Associates' 24th annual year-end market report released in December 2012 and highlighting "What's Hot and What's Not in the Legal Profession," Sports Law is considered to be a "Red Hot" practice area.[2] Although lawyers practicing Sports Law are expected to be experienced at applying general principles of law to sports-specific matters, the practitioner who prefers to procure sports-related clients can increase his or her chances of accomplishing such a goal by becoming familiar with the issues that have once concerned and continue to be an important component of Sports Law. This book provides specific examples of Sports Law litigation (finished and pending matters), statutes, and case law that have shaped the study of Sports Law, as well as sample documents with which any Sports Law professional should be familiar.

While writing this book, I came across a quotation that inspired me to push through and deliver a product that I hope will be enjoyed and used as a resource. Nelson Mandela once said: "Sport has the power to change the world ... it has the power to inspire. It has the power to unite people in a way that little else does. It speaks to youth in a language they understand. Sport can create hope where once there was only despair. It is more powerful than government in breaking down racial barriers."[3] Sport has become a part of my inner soul. It is something I cannot fathom living

---

2. *See* Bob Denney, *2012 What's Hot and What's Not*, ATTORNEYATWORK.COM, Nov. 27, 2012, *at* http://www.attorneyatwork.com/2012-whats-hot-and-whats-not/.

3. *See* Jay Busbee, *Nelson Mandela: 'Sport has the power to change the world,'* SPORTS. YAHOO.COM, Dec. 5, 2013, *at* http://sports.yahoo.com/blogs/the-turnstile/nelson-mandela-sport-power-change-world-215933270.html

without. My practice has been built on it, and my joy comes from watching it. Sport is the reason this book was created, and I hope it will be the impetus for future good.

Chapter 1

Collective Bargaining Agreements

The National Labor Relations Act of 1935 (NLRA),[1] also known as the Wagner Act, allows private sector employees to establish labor unions and engage in collective bargaining with their employers. The Wagner Act also served as the foundation for the National Labor Relations Board,[2] which has the authority to make, amend, and rescind rules and regulations contained therein.[3]

The government typically provides a lot of deference to the establishment and sanctity of bargaining units made up of employees. If the interests of a group of employees are dissimilar from those of another group, however, a single unit will likely be deemed appropriate. Certain factors to observe include the degree of function integration of the unit, the common supervision of the employee, the nature of the employee's skill and function, interchangeability and contact among employees, and commonality of work sites.

In the context of sport, it is easy to understand why collective bargaining tends to be the best fit, as the aforementioned factors typically reveal a strong community of interest with said interests unopposed to one another. Mandatory subjects within the bargaining process include wages (pay), rates of pay, hours, and other conditions of employment. It is illegal for

---

1. 29 U.S.C. § 151–169.
2. 29 U.S.C. § 153.
3. 29 U.S.C. § 156.

employees and employers to bargain concerning kickbacks and/or any type of unlawful support.

When irritated, sports-related unions have used a variety of tactics in an attempt to cause trouble for their employers, as will be evident to the reader in the discussion on union strikes. However, employers have also used collective bargaining to their advantage, as, for example, through lockouts or even in an effort to dismiss a bevy of concussion-related lawsuits filed by former National Football League (NFL) players and their spouses on the grounds that said individuals lacked jurisdiction because prior collective bargaining agreements stipulated that such disputes would be adjudicated outside of the judicial system. In some instances, both employer and employee do have a meeting of the minds and collectively bargain for systems that, although they may be amended in their structure from time to time, appear to have furthered the sports that they influence. An example of such a system is baseball's final-offer arbitration procedure, which will be explained in this chapter.

NFL Concussion Litigation

"A collective bargaining agreement is a powerful thing—so powerful that it can effectively slam the court door shut on the former players' claims against the National Football League."[4]
—Paul Anderson, Proprietor of NFLConcussionLitigation.com

Baseball may still be considered America's pastime, but football, in the form of the NFL, has become the biggest professional sports business in the United States, with annual revenues of roughly $9 billion.[5] The NFL has

---

4.   *See* Paul D. Anderson Consulting, LLC, *The Almighty CBA*, NFLConcussionLitigation.com, Aug. 30, 2012, *at* http://nflconcussionlitigation.com/ ?p=1080.

5.   *See* Judy Battista, N.F.L. *Commissioner Goodell Caught between Bad Calls and Owners*, N.Y. Times, Sept. 25, 2012, *at* http://www.nytimes.com/2012/09/26/sports/football/nfl-c ommissioner-goodell-caught-between-bad-calls-and-owners.html?pagewanted=all&_r=1&. (The author discussed the situation of the NFL officials and referee lockout and stated that

gone from a league raking in annual revenue of $6.5 billion in 2006 to its record-breaking revenue of $9.2 billion in 2012.[6] However, the long-term success of the NFL and the sanctity of that reservoir of money was put in serious jeopardy when a slew of former NFL players and their spouses filed complaints against the NFL and NFL Properties for the league's alleged mishandling of a lingering concussion problem that has had devastating consequences for the limbs and brains of those who played in the past.[7]

The very first NFL concussion-related lawsuit was filed on August 7, 2011, with seven former professional football players and their wives serving as the initial plaintiffs.[8] As of June 1, 2013, more than 4,800 former NFL players had become plaintiffs in over 240 concussion-related lawsuits spread across the United States.[9] Including said players' spouses, the number of plaintiffs increased to more than 5,800 altogether.[10]

Months prior to the first NFL concussion-related lawsuit being filed, I proposed to the managing partners at my former law firm that we should file a complaint against the NFL and expose the league to what I believed to be plausible liability. After creating a thorough outline and mastering my pitch, I was shot down. The partners were concerned about the long-term substantial costs of representing players on a contingency basis, with no guarantee of ever collecting a dime, against the behemoth of the NFL

---

at the time of the article, for the league to have met the union's demand and end the lockout, it would have taken "just 3.2 million annually," which is "a tiny fraction of the N.F.L.'s $9 billion in annual revenue.")

6. *See* Monte Burke, *Think the NFL Is in Decline Because of Head Trauma Issues? Think Again*, FORBES, Aug. 14, 2013, *at* http://www.forbes.com/sites/monteburke/2013/08/14/think -the-nfl-is-in-decline-because-of-head-trauma-issues-think-again/.

7. Nathan Fenno and Luke Rosiak of the *Washington Times* have compiled a constantly updated database (at http://www.washingtontimes.com/footballinjuries/) of former players who have filed a concussion-based lawsuit against the NFL. As of their December 20, 2013, update, 4,878 former players had pending litigation against the NFL based on head injuries sustained.

8. *See* Darren Heitner, *NFL Faces Tobacco-Like Damages Reaching Billions of Dollars in Concussion Litigation*, FORBES, June 12, 2012, *at* http://www.forbes.com/sites/darrenheitner /2012/06/12/nfl-faces-tobacco-like-damages-reaching-billions-of-dollars-in-concussion -litigation/.

9. *See* NFL Concussion Litigation, *Plaintiffs/Former Players*, NFLCONCUSSIONLITIGATION.COM, *at* http://nflconcussionlitigation.com/?page_id=274. ("As of June 1, 2013, there are more than 4,800 named player-plaintiffs in the 242 concussion-related lawsuits. Including the players' spouses, there are more than 5,800 plaintiffs, total.")

10. *Id.*

and its high-profile attorneys who would be paid whatever was necessary to defend the league so as to be able to continue to offer its product to the masses. It was an early experience in learning not only how to play the game, but the types of factors considered by those with decision-making power and the influence those factors have in determining whether certain issues are worthy for particular individuals to take on. Despite the potentially large windfall of money on the table for the law firm had they accepted the task of representing the damaged players, the firm weighed the risk versus reward and concluded that the litigation was not worth the cost and time commitment.

Although I did not become counsel for any of the former players who eventually attached their name to the NFL concussion litigation, many attorneys jumped at the opportunity. They saw it as a chance to represent the players who claimed that the NFL either should have known about the lingering harmful effects of multiple head injuries or knew about the ravaging significance of multiple blows to the head, all while making a concerted effort to feed players faulty information.[11] These attorneys looked to articles such as the one written by Bennet Omalu, who wrote in the peer-reviewed journal *Neurosurgery* that scientific evidence exists to prove that the type of repeated blows to the head that football players suffer while on the field could cause severe, debilitating brain damage.[12] Three scientists on the NFL's payroll, as members of the NFL's Mild Traumatic Brain Injury Committee, responded by making a concerted effort to have Omalu's

---

11. *See* Ken Belson, *N.F.L. Faces Retired Players in a High-Stakes Legal Battle*, N.Y. Times, Dec. 29, 2011, *at* http://www.nytimes.com/2011/12/30/sports/football /nfl-faces-retired-players-in-a-high-stakes-legal-battle.html. (The article quotes Larry Coben, who represents seven retirees in the action against the NFL, saying that "the N.F.L. knew or should have known" about the neurological problems, but failed to "take any active role in addressing the issue for the players.")

12. *See* Jeanne Marie Laskas, *Game Brain: Football Players and Concussions*, GQ.com, Oct. 2009, *at* http://www.gq.com/sports/profiles/200909/nfl-players-brain-dementia-study-mem ory-concussions?currentPage=2. (After months of extensive research on the topic, Omalu finally wrote a paper detailing his findings in an article he titled "Chronic Traumatic Encephalopathy in a National Football League Player," which was published in a "prestigious peer-reviewed journal" called *Neurosurgery*.)

article retracted.[13] They disagreed with the findings, said there were serious flaws with the study's conclusions, and even went as far as to claim, "We own this field. We are not going to bow to some no-name Nigerian with some bullshit theory."[14]

Omalu's article was published in July 2005. Two years later, the NFL released an outline concerning the steps it had taken to address the long-term effect of concussions.[15] The outline included an excerpt from a new "NFL Player Concussion Pamphlet" for players and their families to get a better understanding of the symptoms of concussions, and it outlined the ways to better detect when a player was suffering from a concussion.[16] Nestled near the bottom of that pamphlet were the statements "It is important to understand that there is no magic number for how many concussions is too many" and "Research is currently underway to determine if there are any long-term effects of concussions in NFL athletes."[17] Plaintiffs and their respective counsel pointed out that the independent studies had already provided insight in this particular area, yet those in power at the NFL chose to ignore the evidence that was right in front of them. Even worse, argued the plaintiffs, was that the NFL went the extra step by seeking to discredit the independent findings.

Two years after the release of the NFL's pamphlet and four years after Omalu's article was published in *Neurosurgery*, the Committee on the Judiciary in the U.S. House of Representatives held a hearing on the legal issues relating to football head injuries. At the hearing, NFL commissioner Roger Goodell reiterated what was said in his two-year-old pamphlet. Before the Committee, Goodell stated, "If I have had more than one concussion, am I at increased risks for another injury? Answer: Current research with

---

13. *Id.* (stating that three scientists on the NFL's payroll wrote a "lengthy letter" to the editor of *Neurosurgery* demanding the article be retracted). The three scientists, Casson, Pellman, and Viano, said that they disagreed with the article, alleging that it had "serious flaws" and was a "complete misunderstanding."

14. *Id.*

15. *See NFL Outlines for Players Steps Taken to Address Concussions*, NFL.COM, Aug. 14, 2007, *at* http://www.nfl.com/news/story/09000d5d8017cc67/article/nfl-outlines-for-players-steps-taken-to-address-concussions.

16. *Id.*

17. *Id.*

professional athletes has not shown that having more than one or two concussions leads to permanent problems if each injury is managed properly. It is important to understand that there is no magic number for how many concussions is too many."[18] The immediate response was one of concern, and it promptly raised the stakes based on the NFL's perceived actions (or lack thereof) regarding the lingering concussion problem. Representative Linda Sanchez of California compared the NFL's stance on concussions to that of the tobacco companies of the past that continually denied a link between smoking and damage to health.[19] Sanchez also urged the NFL to embrace that independent studies demonstrated a high correlation between number of blows to the head in football and cognitive impairment.[20] Goodell largely avoided responding directly to the representative's line of questioning.

Fast-forward to July 10, 2012. Many NFL concussion-related cases had already been filed, and New York Giants chief executive officer John Mara was still holding onto the notion that the NFL had no knowledge of the long-term effects of suffering multiple head blows during play, despite whatever independent research was available.[21] "But the notion in these lawsuits that we knew there were long-term effects and we withheld that information is ridiculous," said Mara.[22] "Is there some kind of cause and effect? I don't know, I'll let the medical experts tell you that; common sense would tell you that there is. But to say we knew it and withheld it, I really find that objectionable."[23]

The Omalu study, the "NFL Player Concussion Pamphlet," the Committee on the Judiciary in the U.S. House of Representatives hearing transcript, and the statements by Giants CEO Mara make up a small section of the plethora of documents and information that could have become available

---

18. *See Legal Issues Relating to Football Head Injuries (Part I & II)*, Committee on the Judiciary House of Representatives, Oct. 28, 2009, and Jan. 4, 2010, *at* http://judiciary .house.gov/hearings/printers/111th/111-82_53092.pdf.

19. *Id. See* Dave D'Alessandro, *Giants Owner John Mara Discusses NFL Brain Injuries*, NJ.com, July 10, 2012, *at* http://www.nj.com/ledger-dalessandro/index.ssf/2012/07/giants _owner_john_mara_discusses_nfl_brain_injuries.html.

20. *Id.*

21. *Id.*

22. *Id.*

23. *Id.*

if a discovery process had begun as part of the concussion litigation against the NFL. However, the plaintiffs had a major hurdle to pass before the discovery process was to begin. Most important was that the various lawsuits were consolidated into a master complaint in the Eastern District of Pennsylvania by a Case Management Order, which effectively turned the individual pending matters into multidistrict litigation for the purpose of handling pretrial procedures.[24]

On July 28, 2012, the NFL filed a motion to dismiss all the lawsuits filed by former players based on a claim that the collective bargaining agreement (CBA) signed between the NFL Management Council and the NFL Players Association (NFLPA) governed the players' concerns, which the NFL labeled as a "labor dispute."[25] If the court granted the NFL's motion, it would not have been the first time a court found that a complaint should have been dismissed for failure to make use of a grievance procedure established in a CBA or dismissed as preempted by Section 301 of the Labor Management Relations Act.[26] Granting the motion would have also largely erased much of the perceived gains that the plaintiffs' attorneys may have won up to that point in the litigation. Jurisdictional challenges are quite common for litigators in the practice of law and can be another significant bump in the road for practitioners who are attempting to successfully play the game.

In its filing, the NFL's undersigned attorneys wrote, "For almost 45 years, professional football players have played under CBAs, painstakingly negotiated through their union, that set forth the parties' understanding and agreement on how, among many other things, player health and safety will be protected,"[27] in an effort to persuade the court that it was not the proper jurisdiction to adjudicate the cases brought by the myriad plaintiffs. The NFL took the position that the grievance procedure (mandatory arbitra-

---

24. *See* Paul D. Anderson Consulting, LLC, *MDL Proceedings Are Set to Begin*, NJ.COM, Mar. 9, 2012, *at* http://nflconcussionlitigation.com/?p=316.

25. *See* NFL.com Wire Report, *NFL Asks Federal Judge to Dismiss Concussion Lawsuits*, NFL.COM, Aug. 30, 2012, *at* http://www.nfl.com/news/story/0ap1000000056716/article/nfl-asks-federal-judge-to-dismiss-concussion-lawsuits. (The article states that in its 40-page motion to dismiss, the NFL called the concussion litigation a "labor dispute.")

26. See Allis-Chalmers Corp. v. Lueck, 471 U.S. 202, 105 S. Ct. 1904, 85 L. Ed. 2d 206.

27. *Id.*

tion) was collectively bargained for; thus, former players had no right to bring their claims in state courts across the United States. The plaintiffs' attorneys countered that the players' claims were not subjected to the previously executed CBAs because the documents were signed while the NFL was fraudulently concealing the consequences of multiple blows to the skull.[28]

Judge Anita Brody, sitting in the Eastern District of Pennsylvania and selected to preside over the case, ordered the parties to mandatory mediation upon receipt of the parties' full briefing on the NFL's motion to dismiss "to determine if consensual resolution" was possible.[29] The mediation was to be controlled by former U.S. District Judge Layn Phillips, with the parties compelled to report back to Judge Brody with a progress report by September 3, a mere two days prior to the scheduled start of the 2013 NFL regular season.[30]

The NFL and the thousands of plaintiffs reached a proposed settlement five days prior to the parties' deadline to report back to Judge Brody.[31] A settlement effectively relieved Judge Brody from making a ruling on the NFL's motion to dismiss the lawsuits through its theories based on labor law. It also at least temporarily allowed the NFL to escape what could have been a very damaging discovery process should the court have denied its motion. Alternatively, by coming to terms on a proposed settlement, the plaintiffs may have been relieved from having to guess whether the NFL's eventual affirmative defenses, including but not limited to assumption of risk and causation, would be persuasive to a jury.

---

28. *See* Darren Rovell, *NFL Files Motion to Dismiss More Than 140 Concussion Lawsuits*, ESPN.com, Aug. 30, 2012, *at* http://espn.go.com/nfl/story/_/id/8314320/nfl-files-motion-dismiss-more-140-concussion-lawsuits (stating that the attorneys for the players argued that "the case belongs in the legal system because the collective bargaining agreement doesn't protect the league against the players' claim of fraudulently concealing the dangers of concussions, a charge the league denies").

29. *See* Jeff Blumenthal, *Judge Orders NFL, Ex-Players to Mediate Concussion Suits*, Philadelphia Bus. J., July 8, 2013, *at* http://www.bizjournals.com/philadelphia/news/2013/07/08/judge-orders-nfl-ex-players-to.html.

30. *Id.*

31. *See* Darren Heitner, *Breaking Down the Proposed $765 Million NFL Concussion Lawsuit Settlement*, Forbes, Aug. 29, 2013, *at* http://www.forbes.com/sites/darrenheitner/2013/08/29/breaking-down-the-proposed-765-million-nfl-concussion-lawsuit-settlement/.

The total sum of the proposed settlement was valued at $765 million, with $675 million of those funds being directed to compensate former players who have suffered cognitive injury or to their families.[32] If the settlement agreement goes forward, roughly 50 percent of the settlement proceeds will be distributed to the players and/or their families within three years and the remainder to be paid out over a span of 17 years.[33] All players who were retired by the time that Judge Brody granted preliminary approval of the settlement would be entitled to take a baseline medical exam (the funding for such exams to also be taken out of the total proceeds contemplated by the settlement) to determine whether they qualify for an award and how much that award would be based on the type of harm sustained.

As discussed, most of the attorneys for the former players who sought compensation from the NFL were working on a contingency basis, providing their services without compensation for a period of time, with a hope that a large settlement or verdict would line their pockets with millions of dollars.[34] Part of the settlement agreement included a provision that called for legal fees and litigation expenses to the plaintiffs' counsel, with amounts to be set by the District Court. While the proposed settlement agreement remained sitting in front of Judge Brody, a new issue arose concerning the payment of attorneys' fees to the plaintiffs' counsel. Judge Brody ended up appointing a special master to make a determination as to whether lawyers for the former NFL players were planning to "double-dip" by earning fees through a provision in the proposed settlement agreement in addition to a percentage of their clients' earnings via existing contingency fee retainer agreements.[35] The concern over double-dipping has led to squabbles between attorneys serving as counsel to a variety of former players in addition to causing a rift between many plaintiffs and their lawyers. The ultimate consequence is a delay in the potential resolution of highly contentious litigation with individuals who desperately

---

32. *Id.*

33. *Id.*

34. *See* Andrew Brandt, *The NFL's Concussion Conundrum*, ESPN.COM, Oct. 17, 2012, *at* http://espn.go.com/nfl/story/_/id/8513300/the-issue-concussions-nfl-not-going-away.

35. *See* Mark Fainaru-Wada and Steve Fainaru, *Concerns over Lawyer Pay in NFL Deal*, ABC NEWS, Dec. 16, 2013, *at* http://abcnews.go.com/Sports/concerns-lawyer-pay-nfl-deal/story?id=21235222.

need monetary assistance to cover medical bills and attorneys continuing to offer their services with the hope of an eventual payday. Meanwhile, the law firm of Paul, Weiss, Rifkind, Wharton & Garrison never risked entering the litigation without receiving payment for its services; the firm earned large sums of hourly fees based on the representation of the NFL in the dispute.[36]

Finally, the proposed settlement does not mark the end for the NFL when it comes to concussion litigation. The proposed settlement did not represent an admission by the NFL of liability or that the plaintiffs' injuries were caused by football and simply meant that the parties wished to compromise their claims and defenses rather than through litigation. However, it did not take the option of continuing to litigate against the NFL completely off the table. Players who were not yet retired by the time the settlement proposal was approved may still make claims for injuries sustained.[37] Further, any of the former players within the class represented may be able to opt out of the class and continue against the NFL if they believe that they will not be justly compensated for their particular claims.[38] George Washington University Law School Professor of Public Interest Law, John Banzhaf, says that he has been told that more than 2,000 retired NFL players may refuse to accept the proposed settlement, which may not only serve to prevent the proposed settlement from ever going into effect, but also renew the issue over whether the former players' claims are preempted by prior collective bargaining agreements between the players and NFL teams and once again cause the NFL to become concerned about the opening of a discovery period.[39] Further, new lawsuits continued to be filed by former

---

36. *See* Brian Baxter, *The Score: Dodgers' Fees, Concussion Suits, and Penn State Alums*, AM LAW DAILY, Feb. 12, 2012, *at* http://amlawdaily.typepad.com/amlawdaily/2012/02/the-score .html (stating that the NFL has "turned to lawyers led by Paul, Weiss, Rifkind, Wharton & Garrison chairman Brad Karp" to defend them in the concussion litigation).

37. *See* Daniel Fisher, *NFL Concussion Settlement Ends the Best Cases, but Not All of Them*, FORBES, Aug. 30, 2013, *at* http://www.forbes.com/sites/danielfisher/2013/08/30/nfl -concussion-settlement-ends-the-best-cases-but-not-all-of-them/.

38. *See* Matthew Futterman, *Deal in Concussion Suit Gives NFL a Big Victory*, WALL STREET J., Aug. 29, 2013, *at* http://online.wsj.com/article/SB10001424127887324463604579042980915590474.html.

39. *See* Darren Heitner, *NFL Concussion Lawsuit Settlement Agreement Stalled By Judicial Intervention*, FORBES, Dec. 17, 2013, *at* http://www.forbes.com/sites/darrenheitner/2013 /12/17/nfl-concussion-lawsuit-settlement-agreement-stalled-by-judicial-intervention/.

NFL players against the NFL despite the pending status of the settlement agreement. In late December 2013, 26 former NFL players filed a new lawsuit against the league, which purportedly included several players who had already opted out of the class of plaintiffs expected to be a part of the pending settlement agreement.[40]

Lockouts and Strikes

"Looking back at the history of collective bargaining in professional sports, a clear trend emerges: Significant work stoppages occur when one side is looking for a sea change in the relationship between the parties."[41]
—Gabe Feldman, law professor at Tulane Law School and director of the Tulane Sports Law Program

The words *strike* and *lockout* have become a part of the lexicon for sports enthusiasts of the most popular sports in the United States. In 2011, the National Basketball Association (NBA) team owners and the NFL team owners each locked out the respective players they employed from participating in any professional games until the owners were able to successfully negotiate new collective bargaining agreements with terms far more favorable to them than were the prior agreements that governed the working relationship between said entities. Similarly, in 2012, a labor dispute led to National Hockey League (NHL) owners locking out formerly signed hockey players until early 2013, when a new collective bargaining agreement was signed, which allowed a shortened season to begin thereafter. Only Major League Baseball (MLB) and the players recognized as being part of the bargaining unit by the MLB Players Association (MLBPA) were able to avoid a lockout (and a strike) between 2010 and 2013, successfully negotiating a

---

40. *See* David Barron, *Former NFL Players File Suit Against League*, HOUSTON CHRONICLE, Dec. 19, 2013, *at* http://blog.chron.com/sportsupdate/2013/12/former-nfl-players-file -suit-against-league/.

41. *See* Gabe Feldman, *NBA Lockout: The NBA's Nuclear Winter—Where Do We Go From Here?* TRIANGLE BLOG, Nov. 22, 2011, *at* http://grantland.com/the-triangle/nba-lock out-the-nbas-nuclear-winter-where-do-we-go-from-here/

new collective bargaining agreement without the involvement of any court of law, the National Labor Relations Board (NLRB), or a heralded mediator attempting to reconcile the players and owners.

The first collective bargaining agreement executed by players and owners, in any major American sport, was effectuated in 1968 by those within MLB.[42] The NFL quickly followed suit, and its players signed their first CBA within months; soon thereafter, the NBA and NHL joined as leagues governed by collective bargaining agreements.[43] The existence of CBAs in the major leagues along with a determination that the professional sports affect interstate commerce within the United States provided the NLRB the authority to govern unfair labor practice claims and the scope of bargaining, with an eye focused on the rules and regulations embodied within the NLRA.[44] However, the NLRB purposefully chooses to stay out of conflict between management and players until a stalemate is conclusively present. The Washington, D.C.–based Federal Mediation and Conciliation Service (FMCS), established by the Taft-Hartley Act of 1947, is called on first whenever there is a claim of unfair labor practices and typically when a party refuses to bargain.[45] After the NFL filed an action with the NLRB and claimed that the NFLPA would not bargain in good faith concerning the creation of a new collective bargaining agreement, the NFL and the NFLPA agreed to use an FMCS mediator.[46] The mediator was permitted to make suggestions and recommendations to the divergent parties, but could not force either side to settle on terms they did not approve. Similarly, in October 2011, an FMCS mediator was asked to step in to help with stalled

---

42. Berry Gould Staudohar, Labor Relations in Professional Sports 33 (1986).

43. *Id.*

44. Walter T. Champion Jr., Fundamentals of Sports Law 497, 495 (2d ed. 2004); *see also* Flood v. Kuhn, 407 U.S. 258, 282 (1972); Haywood v. Nat'l Basketball Ass'n, 401 U.S. 1204 (1971); Radovich v. Nat'l Football League, 352 U.S. 445, 453 (1957); Nassau Sports v. Peters, 352 F. Supp. 870 (E.D.N.Y. 1972); Ray Yasser et al., Sports Law: Cases and Materials 398 (5th ed. 2003).

45. Federal Mediation & Conciliation Service, *Who We Are, at* http://www.fmcs.gov/internet/itemDetail.asp?categoryID=21&itemID=15810 (last visited Dec. 11, 2013); CORNELL UNIVERSITY LAW SCHOOL, Collyer Doctrine, *at* http://www .law.cornell.edu/wex/collyer_doctrine (last visited Dec. 11, 2013).

46. *NFL, NFLPA Agree to Enter Mediation,* ESPN (Feb. 18, 2011, 10:39 a.m.), *at* http://sports.espn.go.com/nfl/news/story?id=6132690.

negotiations between NBA players and management.[47] The use of mediation as an alternative dispute resolution vehicle is a common practice for litigators who traditionally provide their services in connection with matters pending in front of judges. Mandatory mediation has become much more standard in recent years, and developing a skill-set suited to negotiating in good-faith toward a goal of acceptable settlement is valuable in all types of sports contexts.

Labor disputes are common in many types of labor and management relationships, but sport, in particular, appears to lend itself to an overflow of lockouts and strikes. For instance, since the creation of the first CBA governing the wages, working hours, training, health and safety, and so forth of NFL players, the players have instituted three strikes (in 1974, 1982, and 1987); in addition, as discussed previously, the owners locked the players out in 2011. The NBA has experienced four lockouts, all in a short period (between 1995 and 2011). NHL players put together a strike in 1992 and 1994, which was followed by two lockouts, and MLB, which is the only major U.S. sport to avoid a major labor battle since 2010, has had the most decorated history of strikes and lockouts. It survived lockouts in 1973, 1976, and 1990, and it endured strikes in 1980, 1981, 1985, and 1994.

Disparity in Baseball

"Most of the labor issues now being faced by players and owners were first addressed by Major League Baseball, which has had more work stoppages than any other sport. For better or worse, the MLB players association is the model for sports unions today."[48]
—James Dworkin, chancellor of Purdue University North Central and former associate dean of the Krannert School of Management

---

47. *Owners, Union to Meet with Mediator*, ESPN (Oct. 13, 2011), *at* http://espn.go.com /nba/story/_/id/7093566/nba-labor-owners-players-meet-federalmediator-week.
48. *See The Economy of Professional Sports—Difference Makers*, PURDUE UNIVERSITY, *at* http://www.purdue.edu/differencemakers/dworkin.html.

The MLBPA does not represent the vast number of players performing for their respective organizations' farm systems. However, the collective bargaining agreements (which have been negotiated and altered since the original 1968 Basic Agreement) do play a distinct role in the way that Minor League Baseball players operate. Ultimately, the interests of those Minor Leaguers without proper representation at the negotiating table are often disregarded or ignored when collective bargaining agreements are established.

Today's Minor League system is enormous; each MLB organization is represented by a club at every level of Minor League Baseball, which includes Rookie, Short-Season A, Single-A, Advanced Single-A, Double-A, and Triple-A.[49] MLB organizations pay the salaries of Minor League players, coaches, and managers even though the majority of Minor League teams are owned by individuals and companies independent of the Major League organizations.[50] The MLB club also makes the ultimate decision as to who is on what Minor League–level roster and determines which players to assign, promote, and release.[51] This scenario has resulted in a system in which MLB clubs will pay the least amount of money required to keep players within their farm systems, with the lowest players on the totem pole making just north of $1,000 per month. Meanwhile, Major League players continue to see their average salaries rise to amazing heights. In 1986, the minimum salary of an MLB player was $7,000.[52] In the 2013 MLB Championship season, the minimum player salary was $490,000.[53] That equates to 70 times the minimum salary offered only 27 years prior. Even older players beyond their peak years of performance are continuing to command lofty contracts. In December 2013, second baseman Robinson Cano agreed to a

---

49. *See* MiLB Clubs by MLB Affiliation, MiLB.com, *at* http://www.milb.com/milb/info/affiliations.jsp.

50. Josh Leventhal, 2010 Player Development Contract Chart, Baseball America (Oct. 6, 2010), *available at* http://www.baseballamerica.com/today/minors/business-beat/2010/2610422.html; Michael K. Ozanian, *Minor Leagues, Major Profits*, Forbes.com (Aug. 6, 2008), *at* http://www.forbes.com/2008/08/06/baseball-minors-sacramento-biz-sports-cz_mo_0806minors.html.

51. *MiLB.com Frequently Asked Questions*, MiLB.com, *at* http://www.milb.com/milb/info/faq.jsp?mc=business#3.

52. 1968 Basic Agreement, Schedule A.

53. *See Major League Baseball Players Association: Frequently Asked Questions*, MLB.com, *at* http://mlb.mlb.com/pa/info/faq.jsp.

10-year, $240 million contract with the Seattle Mariners, which included a full no-trade clause and would guarantee him $24 million per year beyond his 40th birthday.[54]

I distinctly recall the negotiations that took place between the agency that I formerly owned and the Washington Nationals concerning the Minor League Baseball contract of a pitcher named Dan Leatherman. It was March 2008 when I signed Leatherman to an agency contract after being told that he was released by the Minnesota Twins for what he claimed to be no real reason. Leatherman was an undrafted free agent signee of the Minnesota Twins organization in 2006 who earned a position on the team's rookie affiliate squad after impressing scouts at an open tryout. I was told by Leatherman that he was the only person selected among hundreds of players who paid a fee to the club for the opportunity to enter the open tryout. When I signed Leatherman to an agency contract, he was simply looking for work. He had been cut by the Twins organization and needed a new home. I first was able to negotiate a deal for Leatherman to play for the Winnipeg Goldeyes of the Northern League (an "independent league"). Soon thereafter, I began communicating with employees at the Washington Nationals and started to work out terms for a Minor League deal. Leatherman quickly became a member of the Washington Nationals organization, starting out at Class-A Hagerstown.

Life did not get any easier for Leatherman, however, even though he posted an impressive 2.68 earned run average that year, struck out 62 batters in 50 innings, and only walked ten batters on the season. Dan had a family to support and children to feed, and the Nationals did not want to offer him much money at all. In September 2008 the Nationals offered Leatherman a 2009 salary that would pay him $1,350 at the Class-A and Class High-A levels, $1,600 at Double-A and $2,200 at Triple-A. This offer was received while Leatherman was pitching in the playoffs for High-A Potomac. After some negotiation, wherein an executive from the Nationals wrote my agency, and said "You are obviously not satisfied with the

---

54. *See* Enrique Rojas, *Source: Robinson Cano, M's agree*, ESPNDEPORTES.COM, Dec. 6, 2013, *at* http://espn.go.com/new-york/mlb/story/_/id/10089241/robinson-cano-agrees-deal-seattle-mariners.

salary," Leatherman ended up leading his team to its first title since 1989 and accepting a deal that paid him $1,600 per month at the short-season Class-A and Class High-A levels, which increased to $1,800 per month at the Double-A level and a whopping $2,400 per month if Leatherman were to reach the Triple-A roster. Leatherman was barely able to continue to play the game he loved on that salary, and I quickly learned just how difficult it would be to play the game as a baseball agent representing Minor League players. However, I was blown away when Leatherman insisted that my agency receive a commission for negotiating his low-paying Minor League compensation despite our policy that we do not charge commission on Minor League deals. Leatherman was certainly an example of an athlete with integrity and professionalism.

Another lesson I learned as a young baseball agent is that to hedge inherent risks involved with being an agent, one must conduct as thorough due diligence as possible on the character and personality of potential clients. In January 2009, I received an e-mail from an independent contractor working for my agency who was excited about what appeared to be a strong likelihood that we would be signing a powerful first baseman in the Kansas City Royals organization who was upset with his agent at the time. The first baseman told us that he was not receiving help from his current agent in obtaining equipment. Equipment is like gold to Minor Leaguers performing on meager salaries. The player also told us that his agent was only calling him about once per month. He let us know that his agency contract was expiring and that he did not wish to renew it; instead, he wanted to sign with my agency. We signed up the slugger in the offseason, and at 24 years old, he began the next year with the Royals' Double-A affiliate. A year later, his former agent contacted me and provided his blessing with regards to my agency signing the player to a representation agreement. In that communication, the agent referred to the player as a decent guy.

The first baseman was drafted in the 25th round of the Major League Rule 4 Amateur Player Draft. He was not listed as a major prospect straight out of school and had to earn his way up the ranks of his organization. We wanted to do everything we could to help him each step of the way. We supplied him with cleats, turfs, and a glove, and we even brokered a deal with a company to provide him with enough bats and batting gloves for the season in addition to a healthy monetary stipend to endorse the company's products. A deal with a baseball equipment manufacturer containing a compensation clause for a 25th rounder who had yet to enter a Double-A batter's box was unheard of, but we pulled it off. This player went on to do the unthinkable. He earned Texas League All-Star honors in a year in which he recorded a 21-game hitting streak and led the Texas league in almost every offensive statistical category. November 19, 2010 was the deadline for MLB teams to protect qualified Minor League players on their 40-man rosters. Adding the player to the Royals' 40-man roster would protect him from being selected by a competitor in the Rule 5 Draft, which was not of utmost importance, since first basemen are rarely taken; however, not many first basemen have the year that this player accomplished. On November 19 we received the great news that the Royals rewarded the player by adding him to the club's 40-man roster. We were close to striking a major deal for him with New Balance, and then we received the type of message that every agent fears: We were asked to cease providing our services to the player. The game is tough not only for the Minor League Baseball player, but also for the hard-working agent.

Although the original Basic Agreement stated that the MLBPA contracts for and on behalf of the MLB players and individuals who may become MLB players during the term of the Agreement, it has been held that the clause only covers those players who are on an MLB team's 40-man roster.[55] However, even though the MLBPA is purportedly only concerned with items that affect Major League Baseball players, in subsequent CBAs it would also involve itself in the negotiation of provisions that affect the Major League Rule 4 Amateur Player Draft. Today, all players selected in the Rule 4 Amateur Player Draft must sign Minor League contracts. The most recent 2012 Basic Agreement altered the Rule 4 Amateur Player Draft through the formation of team aggregate signing bonus pools, in which every pick in the first ten rounds of the Draft is assigned a value and each club's signing bonus pool is the total of the established values of that club's

---

55. Silverman v. Major League Baseball Player Relations Comm., Inc., 880 F. Supp. 246, 250 (S.D.N.Y. 1995).

selection in the first ten rounds of the Draft.[56] The only way that a team's signing bonus pool is negatively affected after the first ten rounds is if it spends in excess of $100,000 on a drafted player between rounds 11 and 50.[57] Teams are taxed by the league if they exceed their allotted signing bonus pool ceilings.[58] The overall effect of the signing bonus pool system is a general decrease in team spending on signing bonuses, which is a major detriment to Minor League players who typically make below the federal minimum wage rate and often rely on their signing bonuses to survive the process of climbing the Minor League ladder. The 2012 Basic Agreement also instituted a signing bonus pool system for international signees who are not a part of the Rule 4 Amateur Player Draft.[59]

Baseball's Arbitration System

"[Baseball arbitration] is, indeed, one of the many 'games within the game' that continues to perplex and bemuse fans, while becoming a substantial part of the planning process for teams and players' representatives."
—Ed Edmonds, associate dean for Library and Information Technology and professor of law, Notre Dame Law School

MLB's final-offer salary arbitration process was first instituted in 1974.[60] An arbitration hearing with the Minnesota Twins on one side and pitcher Dick Woodson on the other was the first of its kind in professional baseball.[61] The split between the player's demand and the team's offer was much smaller than those common today. Woodson demanded $30,000, whereas

---

56. Summary of Major League Baseball Players Association–Major League Baseball Labor Agreement, MLB.COM, http://mlb.mlb.com/mlb/downloads/2011_CBA.pdf.

57. *Id.*

58. *Id.*

59. *Id.*

60. *See Major League Baseball Players Association: Frequently Asked Questions*, MLB .COM, *at* http://mlb.mlb.com/pa/info/faq.jsp.

61. Ed Edmonds, *A Most Interesting Part of Baseball's Monetary Structure—Salary Arbitration in Its Thirty-Fifth Year*, 20 MARQ. SPORTS L. REV. 1 (2009).

the Twins wanted to give him no more than $23,000.[62] Woodson prevailed and was awarded the $30,000 he requested.[63] From 1974 through 2012, however, MLB clubs succeeded in persuading a variety of arbitration panels that their salary valuations are more reasonable than the numbers advocated by players and their representatives. In fact, in that span, teams were victorious in 286 of the 500 salary arbitration cases that went all the way to a hearing. In 2013, for the first time since arbitration became a bargained-for system of determining players' contracts, no hearings were held.[64] All 133 arbitration-eligible players and their respective MLB organizations settled in advance of any scheduled hearing.[65]

Case Study

Pablo Sandoval, San Francisco Giants Third Baseman

In November 2011, the San Francisco Giants were determined to start the 2012 MLB season strong and finish with a World Series championship. Third baseman Pablo Sandoval may have dreamed of one day becoming the World Series Most Valuable Player (MVP), but back then, his main goal was to earn more money as an arbitration-eligible player. In preparation for an eventual exchange of what Sandoval believed to be his one-year value according to the various factors weighed in a salary arbitration analysis, Sandoval and his team of advisors created a preliminary report that compared him with other MLB players, looked at his defense, highlighted the Giants' attendance, and even diagnosed his ability to perform in "clutch" situations.[66] Sandoval and his team of advisors retained the services of a professor at Southern New Hampshire University

---

62. *Id.*

63. *Id.*

64. *See MLB Set to Have No Arbitration Hearings This Year*, SPORTINGNEWS.COM, Feb. 17, 2013, *at* http://www.sportingnews.com/mlb/story/2013-02-16/mlb-set-to-have-no-arbitration-hearings-this-year.

65. *Id.*

66. The full Pablo Sandoval Preliminary Report dated November 5, 2011, is attached herein in Appendix D.

Graduate School of Business to assist in preparing same, focusing on performance criteria that was a strength of Sandoval's and checking to ensure that it could be demonstrated that there was a historical correlation of that criteria to compensation. As is the case with the vast majority of arbitration-eligible players, Sandoval was able to come to an agreement with the San Francisco Giants instead of appearing at a hearing. On January 17, 2012, he signed a three-year, $17.15 million contract with the Giants, which will pay him a base salary of $8,250,000 in 2014.[67] He just so happened to also win the World Series MVP in 2012.[68]

When salary arbitration cases reach hearings, the matters are resolved by a panel of three arbitrators.[69] Players who have logged between three and six years of MLB experience are eligible for salary arbitration, as are players classified as "super-twos," defined by MLB's CBA to be players who have less than three years but more than two years of MLB service time and rank within the top 22 percent of all two-year players in terms of MLB service time.[70] Additionally, a player with more than six years of MLB service time may go to salary arbitration if his team consents to same.[71]

Super-two players have the unique opportunity to take advantage of baseball's final-offer arbitration a total of four times (instead of the standard three opportunities) if they are fortunate enough to have such a lasting

---

67. *See Pablo Sandoval Contracts, Salaries, Cap Hits, & Transactions*, Spotrac.com, *at* http://www.spotrac.com/mlb/san-francisco-giants/pablo-sandoval/.

68. *See* Anthony Castrovince, *M-V-Panda: Sandoval Takes Home Series Hardware*, MLB.com, Oct. 29, 2012, *at* http://mlb.mlb.com/news/article.jsp?ymd=20121028&content_id=40107150&vkey=news_mlb&c_id=mlb.

69. *See* Darren Heitner, *A Deep Look into Baseball's Salary Arbitration System*, Sports Agent Blog, Apr. 8, 2010, *at* http://www.sportsagentblog.com/2010/04/08/a-deep-look-into-baseballs-salary-arbitration-system/.

70. *See Super Two*, Fangraphs.com, *at* http://www.fangraphs.com/library/business/super-two/.

71. See David Ortiz, *Red Sox Agree to Deal*, ESPN.com (Feb. 13, 2012, 6:39 p.m.), *at* http://espn.go.com/boston/mlb/story/_/id/7570133/david-ortizboston-red-sox-agree-deal-arbitration. (David Ortiz and the Boston Red Sox avoided the arbitration hearing by settling on a one-year deal that paid Ortiz $14.575 million.)

career in the sport and opt against signing a long-term contract that may exclude them from the arbitration process during their "arbitration years." The fear of an extra year of possible arbitration has led to many teams holding back their premier prospects from being called up to the organization's 40-man roster until a point in time within the regular season when it is safe to say that the player will not achieve super-two status. The alluded-to practice of punishing players for their potential was a major reason the MLBPA pushed for an increase in super-two players in the most recent collective bargaining discussions.

MLB's salary arbitration system is a form of final-offer arbitration, which means that if a case goes to a hearing, the panel of arbitrators must either select the player's or the team's valuation of the player. There is no middle ground; however, the midpoint between the numbers submitted by the parties is typically a starting ground for negotiations conducted prior to a hearing. The arbitrators are permitted to take into consideration the following items: (1) the player's "contribution to his Club (including but not limited to his overall performance, special qualities of leadership and public appeal)"[72] in his prior season (commonly referred to as the player's "platform year"); (2) the player's "career contribution"; (3) the player's prior compensation; (4) the compensation received by comparable players;[73] (5) any "physical or mental defects" suffered by the player; and (6) the team's recent on-field performance, which may include "[l]eague standing and attendance as an indication of public acceptance."[74] In recent years, many have debated the utility in spending time to use and explain advanced metrics to the panel of arbitrators as one of many factors to promote the player or team's position. Such statistical analysis and the explanation of same can eat up considerable time in an arbitration hearing, but at a minimum, it is worth preparing for in case the opposition decides to use that type of material in its own case, especially because nonstandardized statistics (e.g., wins above replacement player) continue to become accepted within many baseball circles.

---

72. 2012 Basic Agreement, art. VI(E)(10)(a).
73. *Id.*
74. *Id.*

The CBA also specifies the items expressly prohibited from being examined by the arbitrators. Those items are (1) "[t]he financial position of the Player and the Club"; (2) media commentary concerning the player under examination (however, there is an exclusion for "recognized annual Player awards for playing excellence"); (3) prior offers made by the player and/or team in an effort to settle outside of the arbitration hearing; (4) costs of representation; and (5) "[s]alaries in other sports or occupations."[75]

It is believed that the purpose of maintaining a final offer type of arbitration system is to encourage settlements in advance of hearings.[76] Settlements allow the parties to avoid the extreme costs of preparing for and arguing in front of arbitrators in addition to the sometimes large psychological cost for the player who chooses to attend a hearing and learn the reasons his employer (the team) asserts that he is not as valuable a player as he may have believed. MLB catcher Jeff Mathis believes that the salary arbitration process is "not something that any player wants to go through or deal with. It's a rough process, especially if you go all the way to the hearing like I did. There's stuff that goes on in that room that I wouldn't suggest anybody experience or be a part of . . . . You don't want to be a part of anything like that."[77] Mathis won his 2010 hearing and was awarded $1.3 million as opposed to the $700,000 offer filed by the Los Angeles Angels of Anaheim. While Mathis's agent stated that there were no hard feelings on either side, Mathis reflected on the hearing by saying, "When you first sign up to play this game you don't ever think of that part of professional baseball . . . It stinks. It's not something that you want to do or hear or hear from anybody else."[78] MLB right-handed pitcher Kyle Lohse described the process as follows: "I've never been in a court case but it feels like that. They talk about how bad you are and why you deserve their number and

---

75. *Id.* art. VI(E)(10)(b).

76. *See* Darren Heitner, *A Deep Look into Baseball's Salary Arbitration System*, Sports Agent Blog, Apr. 8, 2010, *at* http://www.sportsagentblog.com/2010/04/08/a-deep-look-into-baseballs-salary-arbitration-system/.

77. *See* B. J. Rains, *Players Reflect on Arbitration Hearings: Jeff Mathis*, MLBTradeRumors .com, Feb. 25, 2013, *at* http://www.mlbtraderumors.com/2013/02/jeff-mathis-arbitration-case .html.

78. *Id.*

everything that's wrong with you and then your team has equal amount of time to pump you up and say everything good about you. You're sitting there, 'Man I stink,' and then, 'I'm the greatest ever.'"[79] If a case goes to hearing, both sides are provided one hour to present their respective case and an additional one-half hour to rebut the other party's contentions.[80] A decision is typically offered to the parties within 24 hours of the completion of the hearing.[81] The panel does not provide the parties with a written opinion, however.[82] Rather, the award is in the form of a single number that represents the value of one year's worth of compensation for the player and excludes any bonuses and incentives.[83]

Baseball's final-offer salary arbitration system is also credited for significantly increasing the salaries of MLB players. It is very rare for a player to conclude the arbitration process with a future salary below his prior compensation.[84] Further, players are typically not only aided in preparation and at the actual hearing by their agents, but commonly also seek the assistance of outside counsel; sometimes, the MLBPA makes a determination to get involved as well. In fact, the MLBPA is happy to help with a player's case and will often reach out to the player and his representative to offer assistance.[85] After all, the result of the hearing has a major effect on the remaining players who are represented as a unit by the MLBPA. A positive result could lead to inflated salaries for other players, whereas a negative result may serve as a major detriment to others considering entering the final-offer salary arbitration system.

---

79. *See* B. J. Rains, *Players Reflect on Arbitration Hearings: Kyle Lohse*, MLBTRADERUMORS
.COM, Feb. 19, 2013, *at* http://www.mlbtraderumors.com/2013/02/arbitration-rewind-kyle-l
ohse-beats-minnesota-in-2005-and-2006.html.

80. 2012 Basic Agreement, art. VI(E)(7).

81. *Id.* art. VI(E)(13).

82. *Id.*

83. Ethan Lock & Allan DeSerpa, *Salary Increases under Major League Baseball's System of Final Offer Salary Arbitration*, 2 LAB. LAW. 801, 804 (1986); Jeffrey D. Schneider, *Unsportsmanlike Conduct: The Lack of Free Agency in the NFL*, 64 S. CAL. L. REV. 797, 836 (1991).

84. John L. Fizel, *Play Ball: Baseball Arbitration after 20 Years*, 49 DISP. RESOL. J. 42, 45 (1994).

85. *See* Darren Heitner, *Baseball Agent Jamie Murphy Opened Up to Buster Olney about His Practice*, SPORTS AGENT BLOG, Apr. 24, 2013, *at* http://www.sportsagentblog.com/2013
/04/24/baseball-agent-jamie-murphy-opened-up-to-buster-olney-about-his-practice/.

Certain teams refuse to negotiate with arbitration-hearing-bound players after there is a formal exchange of salary figures. These teams employ a so-called file-and-go or file-and-trial strategy and will not, under any circumstances, come to a settlement with a player unless it occurs prior to the deadline to exchange numbers.[86] The most well-known file-and-go teams are the Miami Marlins, the Tampa Bay Rays, and the Chicago White Sox. Second baseman Dan Uggla recognized the difference of negotiating in advance of a salary arbitration hearing with a file-and-trial team when he said: "My case was a little bit different because with the Marlins, once you submit your number, there's no more negotiations. Usually in arbitration you can submit your numbers and still come to an agreement but with the Marlins, if you don't come to an agreement before that then you're going into the room and going to the hearing, so mine was different."[87] Their belief is that using such a strategy will actually induce players to settle earlier in the process and save the clubs money in preparation for arbitration hearings, which typically settle prior to hearing even for teams that do not subscribe to such a strategy.

Sports Lawyers who are determined to be involved in professional baseball's salary arbitration system must have a solid understanding of the types of data points that are acceptable to use in a hearing, the allotted time for each party to present its case, and which teams employ a file-and-trial strategy. A select few Sports Lawyers—including but not limited to Jay Reisinger of Farrell & Reisinger, LLC; Carter DeLorme of Jones Day; and Jeff Fannell of Jeff Fannell & Associates, LLC—have been able to create a considerable business of representing players and teams in salary arbitration cases.

---

86. See Edmonds, *supra* note 61, at 28–29. Committing to a hearing at that point may serve as an attempt to avoid potential wasted resources in preparing for a hearing only to settle just beforehand. *Id.* at 28–29.

87. *See* B. J. Rains, *Players Reflect on Arbitration Hearings: Dan Uggla*, MLBTRADERUMORS.COM, Mar. 13, 2013, *at* http://www.mlbtraderumors.com/2013/03/players-reflect-on-arbitration-hearings-dan-uggla.html.

Chapter 2

Amateurism

During the second-to-last weekend of September 2013, a combined total of 28 National Collegiate Athletic Association (NCAA) football players from Georgia Tech, Northwestern University, and the University of Georgia wore the letters "APU" on their wrist tape.[1] "APU" stands for "All Players United," a phrase concocted by Ramogi Huma, who serves as president of an organization called the National College Players Association (NCPA).[2] That organization and the APU movement desire to reduce full-contact practices for student-athletes, gain access to independent concussion experts during game play, receive a piece of the college football playoff revenues, and more.[3] After feeling as if their voices were being muted, they took to their wrist tape and then to social media, where the hashtags "#APU" and "#AllPlayersUnited" proliferated Twitter.

The unity surrounding APU was not an overnight occurrence; rather, it was something that took months for the National College Players Association to organize behind closed doors and keep quiet until that important weekend in September. Its most ambitious goal is to "Stand behind individual players being 'harmed by NCAA rules.'"[4] Those rules are a by-product of

---

1. *See* Dennis Dodd, *'APU' Campaign Gaining Steam, Has Precedent in Fighting NCAA*, CBSSPORTS.COM, Sept. 23, 2013, *at* http://www.cbssports.com/collegefootball/writer/dennis-dodd/23805205/apu-campaign-gaining-steam-and-has-some-precedent-in-fighting-ncaa.
2. *Id.*
3. *Id.*
4. *See* Tom Farrey, *Players Mark Gear in Protest*, ESPN.COM, Sept. 21, 2013, *at* http://espn.go.com/espn/otl/story/_/id/9702040/football-players-multiple-schools-mark-gear-protest-ncaa.

a concept called amateurism, and it seems as if the NCAA will go to any length to at least provide some modicum of justification that the amateur concept still exists and remains relevant. That concept will be discussed in the following section. The "#AllPlayersUnited Campaign" also intends to show support for those who have in some way assisted players in the large *O'Bannon v. NCAA, EA Sports and Collegiate Licensing Company* lawsuit (in addition to other lawsuits pending across the United States) related to the use of athletes' likenesses without compensating them for same. Likeness issues involving amateurism will also be fleshed out later this chapter. Additional matters that may be taken up by the APU campaign include whether student-athletes (as currently defined) should be deemed to be employees for the purposes of receiving certain mandatory benefits, if student-athletes deserve to be paid in addition to receiving compensation for widespread use of their likenesses, and how the NCAA's rules regarding sports agents should be modified to reflect the needs of the athletes. With regard to the NCAA's rules governing agents, even Southeastern Conference commissioner Mike Slive says that said rules are part of the problem, not part of the solution.[5]

The NCAA's Concept

"Amateurism provides no benefit to the athlete, neither enhancing his education nor making him a better person. The Olympics began taking amateurism out of its charter in the 1970s, yet the N.C.A.A. holds onto it as a cherished ideal."[6]

—Jay Bilas, commentator, writer and studio analyst for ESPN

---

5. See *Slive: Agent Rules Part of Problem*, Associated Press, Sept. 20, 2013, *at* http://espn.go.com/college-football/story/_/id/9695377/sec-commissioner-mike-slive-says -ncaa-rules-agents-part-problem.

6. *See* Jay Bilas, *College Athletes Should Be Compensated—Room for Debate*, N.Y. Times, Mar. 14, 2012, *at* http://www.nytimes.com/roomfordebate/2012/03/13/ncaa-and-the -interests-of-student-athletes/college-athletes-should-be-compensated (the author contends that student-athletes should not be restricted from earning compensation from their talents if the NCAA is able to do same).

More than 1,200 colleges from more than 175 athletic conferences make up the NCAA.[7] The United States Supreme Court has found the NCAA to be "the guardian of an important American tradition:" amateurism in intercollegiate athletics.[8] The Association's Principle of Amateurism reads:

> Student-athletes shall be amateurs in an intercollegiate sport, and their participation should be motivated primarily by education and by the physical, mental and social benefits to be derived. Student participation in intercollegiate athletics is an avocation, and student-athletes should be protected from exploitation by professional and commercial enterprises.[9]

That stated principle has been disputed by many, including some prominent journalists and academics who believe that it is nothing more than a "veil of amateurism" that keeps the massive revenue associated with college sports "in the hands of a select few administrators, athletic directors, and coaches."[10] Member schools in the NCAA have the potential to make a significant profit off their athletic programs,[11] yet student-athletes (a term that has received general acceptance as a description of the athletes who participate for the respective institutions where they take classes and perform their athletic talents) receive no salary. Their compensation sometimes

---

7. *See* Worldwide Basketball & Sport Tours, Inc. v. National Collegiate Athletic Association, 388 F.3d 955, 957 (6th Cir. 2004); http://en.wikipedia.org/wiki/List_of_NCAA _conferences; NCAA v. Board of Regents, 468 U.S. 85, 99 (1984).

8. Bloom v. NCAA, 93 P.3d 621, 626 (Colo. Ct. App. 2004) (quoting NCAA v. Bd. of Regents, 468 U.S. 85, 101, 104 S. Ct. 2948, 2960, 82 L. Ed. 2d 70 (1984)); *see also* NCAA Manual art. 1.2(c) (one of the stated purposes of the NCAA is "[t]o encourage its members to adopt eligibility rules to comply with satisfactory standards of scholarship, sportsmanship and amateurism").

9. NCAA Manual art. 2.9.

10. Amy Christian McCormick and Robert A. McCormick, *The Emperor's New Clothes: Lifting the NCAA's Veil of Amateurism*, 45 SAN DIEGO L. REV. 495 (2008); Marc Edelman, note, *Reevaluating Amateurism Standards in Men's College Basketball*, 35 U. MICH. J.L. REFORM 861, 864 (2002).

11. *See, e.g.*, Paula Lavigne, *Kansas State Most Profitable Athletic Department in 2010–11*, ESPN.COM, May 4, 2012, *at* http://espn.go.com/espn/otl/blog/_/name/assael_shaun/id/7889475 /kansas-state-most-profitable-athletic-department-2010-11-file. (In only one fiscal year, Kansas State made a profit of about $23 million. Other schools, such as Texas, LSU, Alabama, Florida, Michigan, and Arkansas, also made over $10 million in profits.)

comes in the form of full or partial scholarships, which are typically year-to-year and are renewed at the option of the institution of higher education. These scholarships have been scrutinized for not even covering the full cost of attendance for the student-athletes, who often arrive on campus after spending their prior years in depressed socioeconomic territories and are subjected to put their bodies on the line with the hope that someday they will be able to profit off of their chiseled physiques.

Case Study

Johnny Manziel

Johnny Manziel, 2012 Heisman Trophy winner and Texas A&M quarterback, was suspended for the first half of his team's first 2013 regular-season game against Rice University. The suspension was essentially a settlement between the NCAA and Texas A&M, brokered by the parties after the NCAA began an investigation to determine whether the Heisman Trophy winner had signed autographs in exchange for compensation and/or allowed a third party to receive compensation by selling his autographed memorabilia. If either of the aforesaid scenarios would have been proved, it could have been deemed a violation of NCAA Bylaw 15.2.2.2, which reads in part, "If a student-athlete's name or picture appears on commercial items ... or is used to promote a commercial product sold by an individual or agency without the student-athlete's knowledge or permission, the student-athlete ... is required to take steps to stop such an activity in order to retain his or her eligibility for intercollegiate athletics."[12] Instead, Manziel accepted a half-game suspension, and the NCAA called Manziel's act an "inadvertent violation."[13] Meanwhile, college

---

12. *See Title: 12.5.2.2—Use of a Student-Athlete's Name or Picture without Knowledge or Permission*, NCAA.ORG, May 12, 2005, *at* https://web1.ncaa.org/LSDBi/exec/bylawSearch ?bylawSearchSubmit=viewHtml&division=1&textTerms=&titleTerms=&keyValue=269 &reportType=NotMain&adopted=0.

13. *See* Dan Wolken, *Analysis: Manziel Case Shows Challenge of NCAA Enforcement*, USA TODAY, Aug. 28, 2013, *at* http://www.usatoday.com/story/sports/ncaaf/sec/2013/08/28 /johnny-manziel-texas-am-autographs-suspension-analysis/2724605/.

basketball analyst and lawyer Jay Bilas noted, through his popular Twitter account, that the NCAA continued to sell Johnny Manziel jerseys on its official e-commerce website, making a handsome profit off of such sales and reverting none of that revenue to the athlete.[14] "Amateurism" often works in mysterious ways.

An athlete must have a core grade point average of at least 2.3 to be cleared to earn student-athlete status at a university.[15] The NCAA Eligibility Center has other academic eligibility requirements along with amateurism eligibility requirements. Athletes are thoroughly reviewed by the NCAA Eligibility Center prior to receiving certification to participate in NCAA Division I or II athletics. Among the items that may be reviewed are whether the athletes have ever (1) contracted with a professional team; (2) received a salary for participating in athletics; (3) received prize money; (4) participated with professional athletes; (5) engaged in a tryout, practice, or competition with a professional team; (6) received benefits from an agent or prospective agent; (7) agreed (orally or in writing) to be represented by a sports agent; or (8) benefited from any financial assistance based on their athletics skills or participation.[16] A finding that an athlete engaged in any of these activities could cause that athlete to lose his or her amateurism status or receive some other form of penalty.

Games inherently have rules, and for games to be fair and equitable, those rules are meant to be followed. The NCAA has taken a beating in the public for its inequitable rules and its inconsistency in enforcing same. Its practices in enforcing such rules have also been scrutinized.

One instance in which the NCAA took a public beating was in the matter concerning former United States Marine Steven Rhodes, who desired

---

14. *See* Terrence Payne, *Jay Bilas Blasts NCAA on Twitter in Wake of Johnny Manziel Scandal, Ed O'Bannon Case*, NBC SPORTS, Aug. 6, 2013, *at* http://collegebasketballtalk .nbcsports.com/2013/08/06/jay-bilas-blasts-ncaa-on-twitter-in-wake-of-johnny-manziel -scandal-ed-obannon-case-photos/.

15. *See 2013–14 Guide for the College-Bound Student-Athlete*, NCAA.ORG, *at* http://www .ncaapublications.com/productdownloads/CBSA.pdf.

16. *Id.*

to play football for Middle Tennessee State University (MTSU) after serving five years of active service in the Marine Corps. That dream of playing for MTSU was quickly derailed when the NCAA informed Rhodes that his amateurism eligibility was threatened due to his participation in a military-only recreational football league.[17] Even though Rhodes was not paid to participate in the recreational league and the league was highly unorganized, the 24-year-old Rhodes was told that he would have to sit out the season.[18] Under NCAA Bylaw 14.2.3.2.1, a student-athlete who does not enroll in college as a full-time student in a regular academic term within one year after his high school graduation date, or the graduation date of his class (whichever occurs earlier), is subject to being charged with a season of student-athlete eligibility for each year after the one-year time period. If that athlete is engaged in competition after the time period, he must fulfill an academic year in residence before being able to participate for the college team.[19] Those recreational league games were deemed to be competition under the referenced bylaw, and Rhodes was told that he would be forced to sit out a season and forfeit a couple of years of eligibility. The two years of eligibility were returned to Rhodes after a partially successful appeal filed by MTSU.[20] Days later, the NCAA determined that Rhodes would receive no penalty, would maintain his four years of student-athlete eligibility, and would be permitted to play immediately.[21]

NCAA Bylaw 12.3.1 prohibits student-athletes from agreeing to be represented (orally or in writing) by an agent "for the purpose of marketing his or her athletic ability or reputation in that sport."[22] NCAA Bylaw 12.3.3

---

17. *See* Adam Sparks, *Red(shirt), White & Blue: Marine Fighting for Eligibility to Play for MTSU This Season*, Daily News J., Aug. 18, 2013, *at* https://www.coshoctontribune.com/article/D4/20130818/SPORTS/308180046/Red-shirt-White-Blue-Marine-fighting-eligibility-play-MTSU-season.

18. *Id.*

19. *See* Matthew Futterman, *Recruiting Regulations—Seasons of Competition*, CBS Sports, *at* http://grfx.cstv.com/photos/schools/gewa/genrel/auto_pdf/Seasonsofcompetition.pdf.

20. *See supra* note 17.

21. *See MTSU's Rhodes to Compete Immediately*, NCAA.org, Aug. 2013, *at* http://www.ncaa.org/wps/wcm/connect/public/NCAA/Resources/Latest+News/2013/August/MTSUs+Rhodes+to+compete+immediately/.

22. *See NCAA Addresses Cam Newton's Eligibility*, NCAA.org, Dec. 1, 2010, *at* http://www.ncaa.org/wps/wcm/connect/public/NCAA/Resources/Latest+News/2010+news+stories/December/NCAA+addresses+eligibility+of+Cam+Newton.

says that if an individual represents a student-athlete for compensation in exchange for placing the athlete in a collegiate institution, that individual is labeled as an agent, which then threatens the student-athlete eligibility of the player.[23] Thus, when it was alleged that former Auburn University quarterback and Heisman Trophy winner Cam Newton was part of a pay-for-play scenario wherein his father and the owner of a scouting service were shopping Newton around to various collegiate institutions in exchange for possible compensation, the quarterback's eligibility to compete in intercollegiate athletics became a worldwide concern.[24] The NCAA initially concluded that Newton violated the NCAA's amateurism rules, which caused Auburn to declare Newton ineligible.[25] In a statement concerning Newton's eventual reinstatement, Kevin Lennon, NCAA vice president for academic and membership affairs, stated, "Based on the information available to the reinstatement staff at this time, we do not have sufficient evidence that Cam Newton or anyone from Auburn was aware of this activity, which led to his reinstatement."[26] University of Southern California athletic director Pat Haden wondered how the NCAA could make such a finding regarding Cam Newton, yet ruthlessly punished former USC running back Reggie Bush.[27] It is often difficult to hypothesize how the NCAA will act and understand the justifications it proffers.

I experienced the games that the NCAA is willing to play in my representation of University of Miami Hurricanes defensive lineman Dyron Dye. He was rated the number six weakside defensive end prospect in the United States, coming out of Seminole High School in Sanford, Florida, and helped lead his high school team to a Class 6A state championship. Needless to say, he was a highly touted prospect and a promising recruit who most coaches would have loved to have on their football teams. The eventual winner of the recruiting battle for Dye was the University of Miami, but the methods by

---

23. *Id.*
24. *Id.*
25. *Id.*
26. *Id.*
27. *See* Gary Klein, *USC Football: Pat Haden Surprised by NCAA Decision Regarding Cam Newton*, L.A. TIMES, Dec. 1, 2010, *at* http://latimesblogs.latimes.com/sports_blog/2010/12/usc-football-cam-newton-reggie-bush-pat-haden-usc-ncaa-lane-kiffin.html.

which the school recruited Dye and the NCAA's actions thereafter became a subject that received national attention and made many question just how far the NCAA would go to do what it believed was necessary to maintain the sanctity of amateurism.

The NCAA's recruiting regulations define a prospective student-athlete as someone who has at least begun taking ninth-grade classes or an individual who receives financial assistance or other benefits from a college that are not standard benefits received to the general student population.[28] Prospective student-athletes will often make official visits and unofficial visits to universities that express interest in offering scholarships in exchange for a commitment to perform. The college is permitted to pay for some of or all a prospective student-athlete's transportation expenses, room and meals, and reasonable entertainment expenses during an official visit.[29] On an unofficial visit, the prospective student-athlete must cover his or her own costs, except that the school may provide the athlete with three complimentary admissions to a home athletics contest.[30]

On August 16, 2011, Yahoo! Sports expert investigator Charles Robinson published a massive exposé on the NCAA's investigation into the relationship between the University of Miami (UM) and former school booster Nevin Shapiro, who was incarcerated for orchestrating a $930 million Ponzi scheme and allegedly providing thousands of impermissible benefits to many UM athletes over the span of almost a decade.[31] The listed impermissible benefits included cash, prostitutes, high-end dinners, and purchases at nightclubs.[32] One of the players implicated as being the recipient of impermissible benefits was my client, Dyron Dye. Nevin Shapiro pointed the finger at Dye at some point within the 100 hours of jailhouse interviews conducted by Robinson and his team. Specifically, Shapiro stated that he provided

---

28. *See 2013–14 Guide for the College-Bound Student-Athlete*, NCAA.ORG, *at* http://www
.ncaapublications.com/productdownloads/CBSA.pdf.

29. *Id.*

30. *Id.*

31. *See* Charles Robinson, *Renegade Miami Football Booster Spells Out Illicit Benefits to Players*, YAHOO! SPORTS, Aug. 16, 2011, *at* http://sports.yahoo.com/investigations/news
?slug=cr-renegade_miami_booster_details_illicit_benefits_081611.

32. *Id.*

transportation to Dye (in his $200,000 Mercedes-Benz); spent thousands of dollars to show Dye and other players a good time at nightclubs and a strip club; paid for Dye's food, drinks, and entertainment; and implicated recruiting coordinator Clint Hurtt and wide receivers coach Aubrey Hill as being around the players when the impermissible benefits were arranged.[33]

It was later determined that Dye received a total of approximately $738 in impermissible benefits, which included the receipt of housing, transportation, meals, and entertainment from institutional staff.[34] This determination was made after Dye was interviewed by the NCAA twice on the same day regarding the types of benefits he received and who provided those benefits to him. The testimony provided by Dye in the course of the first interview was changed when the second interview, on the same day, was conducted. Dye was suspended for a total of four games during the 2011 football season and was required to repay the $738 determined to reflect the amount of money in impermissible benefits received.[35]

Two years later, Dyron Dye executed an affidavit on behalf of former wide receivers coach Aubrey Hill, which stated in part that in the second interview he "felt compelled to testify in a manner that would be consistent with the manner in which Mr. Johanningmeier was directing" him so as to keep his eligibility.[36] Former UM quarterback Jacory Harris executed a very similar affidavit.[37] Rich Johanningmeier was the NCAA investigator in charge on the day of Dye's first two interviews. Former Hurricanes quarterback Jacory Harris echoed Dye's statements, also signing an affidavit that said that Johanningmeier threatened the sanctity of his scholarship and remaining eligibility

33. *See* Charles Robinson, *Allegations: Dyron Dye*, YAHOO! SPORTS, Aug. 16, 2011, *at* http://sports.yahoo.com/investigations/news?slug=ys-dyron_dye_allegations.

34. *See Eight Miami Players Suspended*, NCAA.COM, Aug. 30, 2011, *at* http://www.ncaa.com/news/football/2011-08-30/eight-miami-players-suspended/.

35. *Id.*

36. *See* Tim Reynolds, *AP Source: NCAA Looking to Talk to Dye Again*, AP.ORG, May 24, 2013, *at* http://bigstory.ap.org/article/ap-source-ncaa-looking-talk-dye-again.

37. *See* Susan Miller Degnan, *Miami's Dyron Dye Preps for Third Interview with NCAA in Nevin Shapiro Case*, MIAMI HERALD, May 25, 2013, *at* http://www.miamiherald.com/2013/05/25/3415389/miamis-dyron-dye-preps-for-third.html.

to get him to testify in a way that would assist the NCAA in its investigation concerning Miami.[38]

The NCAA wanted a chance to interview Dye for a third time based on his new claim that the Association's former lead investigator had coerced him into providing untruthful testimony. The justification for a third interview was that the NCAA was interested in learning whether Dye violated NCAA Bylaw 10.1, "Unethical Conduct." Bylaw 10.1(d) states that it is unethical for a student-athlete to knowingly furnish the NCAA or the individual's institution false or misleading information concerning the individual's involvement in or knowledge of matters relevant to a possible violation of an NCAA regulation.[39] Despite Dye's insistence that he was forced to doctor his testimony based on the threat of losing out on his ability to perform, the NCAA pushed forward with the third interview. Dye affirmed the statements made in his affidavit and healed from an injury to his Achilles tendon— an injury that typically sidelines players for much longer periods and oftentimes proves to be a major setback. The university confirmed that it did not matter whether Dye was medically cleared to play in his redshirt senior season; that the NCAA made it seem that Dye violated Bylaw 10.1 was enough of a justification for the university to keep him out of play. Miami's in-house legal counsel said that because there were still unresolved eligibility issues and there was too much at risk, the institution decided that it would no longer play Dye on the field. Later, UM informed me that Dye was no longer a member of the Hurricanes football team. An official statement disseminated by the university stated, "Given the totality of the circumstances and unresolved issues regarding the NCAA investigation, the University has decided to move ahead."[40] All that was for amateurism.

---

38. *Id.*

39. *See NCAA Division I Manual*, 10.1 Unethical Conduct, *at* https://admin.xosn.com /fls/600/academics/PDFs/NCAAAcceptance.pdf?DB_OEM_ID=600.

40. *See* Michael Casagrande, *Dyron Dye Booted from Miami Football Team*, South Florida Sun Sentinel, Aug. 19, 2013, *at* http://www.sun-sentinel.com/sports/um-hurricanes/sfl-dyron -dye-booted-from-miami-football-team-20130819,0,2016040.story.

Employer–Employee Relationship

Despite the "veil of amateurism," it is possible that the relationship between the NCAA and its student-athletes constitutes a valid employer–employee relationship even though student-athletes are unpaid, at least according to a precedent set within the workers' compensation system. A "contract of hire" may be formed between an employer and employee "even though not every formality attending commercial contractual arrangements is observed, as long as the fundamental elements of contract formation are present."[41] Thus, despite the absence of "commercial contractual arrangements," the employment relationship between student-athletes and the NCAA may be adequately formed under the "Student-Athlete Statement"[42] that must be signed by student-athletes prior to participating in intercollegiate sports.[43]

Case Study

Waldrep v. Texas Employers Insurance Association

Perhaps the most prominent case to deal with the issue of whether student-athletes are considered employees under the workers' compensation system is *Waldrep v. Texas Employers Ins. Ass'n*.[44] The case involved former Texas Christian University (TCU) tailback Kent Waldrep. During a 1974 game against the University of Alabama, Waldrep suffered a severe spinal cord injury that left him paralyzed from the neck down.[45] In 2000, almost 20 years after the injury took place, Waldrep filed a workers' compensation claim against TCU's

---

41. *See* Aspen Highlands Skiing Corp. v. Apostolou, 866 P.2d 1384, 1387 (Colo. 1994).

42. Attached hereto in Appendix B, Student-Athlete Statement, NCAA Division I.

43. *See* NCAA Form 08-3a.

44. *See* Waldrep v. Texas Employers Ins. Ass'n, 21 S.W.3d 692, 697 (Tex. App. 2000). (The issue to be determined by the court is whether "evidence is legally sufficient to support the jury's refusal to find that Waldrep was an employee of TCU" at the time of injury.)

45. *See* Ivan Maisel, *Legal Issues Could Arise from Paying Student-Athletes*, ESPN.COM, July 15, 2011, *at* http://espn.go.com/college-sports/story/_/id/6768571/legal-issues-arise-pay ing-student-athletes (stating that Ken Waldrep, a TCU running back, became paralyzed in a 1974 game against Alabama).

insurer, Texas Employers Insurance Association (TEIA).[46] The commission initially ruled in Waldrep's favor, finding the relationship between Waldrep and the NCAA to be a valid employer–employee relationship, but TEIA ultimately overturned the decision on appeal. However, the most notable part of the *Waldrep* decision was the language in the opinion explicitly acknowledging that college athletes have "changed dramatically over the years since Waldrep's injury."[47] Thus, if a student-athlete were to file a workers' compensation claim in today's world, where college sports are a "big business,"[48] a ruling in favor of the student-athlete would be a possibility.

The member institutions that grant authority to the nonprofit NCAA technically do not pay student-athletes for the athletic services they provide (unless scholarships are deemed to be payment) and thus largely escape being required to pay social security taxes, Medicare, federal and state unemployment tax, and worker's compensation insurance.[49] Such a regime may not be plausible should any of the various proposals to allow schools to pay student-athletes for the playing of sports become reality. It could also lead to those athletic departments that pay players to lose their coveted tax-exempt status with the Internal Revenue Service as the concept of amateurism appears to rest on student-athletes being distinguished from professionals, which are granted professional status because they are compensated for their play.

NCAA president Mark Emmert has clearly indicated that there are no plans to turn student-athletes into full-time employees. He has been quoted

---

46. *See generally* Waldrep v. Texas Employers Ins. Ass'n, 21 S.W.3d 692 (Tex. App. 2000).

47. *Id.* (stating that the ruling was based on the facts and circumstances as they existed at the time of Waldrep's injury, rather than at the time the case was decided).

48. *See* Joe Nocera, *Let's Start Paying College Athletes*, NYTimes.com, Dec. 30, 2011, *at* http://www.nytimes.com/2012/01/01/magazine/lets-start-paying-college-athletes.html. (The author states that "the hypocrisy that permeates big-money college sports takes your breath away.")

49. *See* Kristi Dosh, *Why College Athletes Will Never Be Paid*, Business of College Sports, Aug. 10, 2011, *at* http://businessofcollegesports.com/2011/08/10/why-college-athletes-will-never-be-paid/.

as saying, "One thing that sets the fundamental tone is there's very few members and, virtually no university president, that thinks it's a good idea to convert student-athletes into paid employees. Literally into professionals. Then you have something very different from collegiate athletics. One of the guiding principles [of the NCAA] has been that this is about students who play sports."[50]

Stipends for Players and the Pay-for-Play Scenario

"If we move toward a pay-for-play model—if we were to convert our student athletes to employees of the university—that would be the death of college athletics. Then they are subcontractors. Why would you even want them to be students? Why would you care about their graduation rates? Why would you care about their behavior?"[51]
—Mark Emmert, president of the NCAA

For the fiscal year ending in 2008, college athletic departments generated roughly $11 billion in revenues. Although said athletic departments are able to earn as much money as feasibly possible, the student-athletes who indirectly generate a significant portion of the departments' revenues are restricted from receiving any pay based on their status as athletes. Some have alleged that such "no pay" rules equate to an illegal group boycott by the universities that, without the prohibition being in place, would gladly compensate athletes (thus gaining a competitive advantage over their peers) according to the players' market value.[52] A total of 13,877 Division I college football players earned a sum salary of $0.00 in exchange for the

---

50. *See* Chip Patterson, *Emmert: No One Wants to Convert Student-Athletes into Employees*, CBSSPORTS.COM, Sept. 17, 2013, *at* http://www.cbssports.com/collegefootball /eye-on-college-football/23697765/emmert-no-one-wants-to-convert-studentathle tes-into-employees.

51. *See* Joe Nocera, *Let's Start Paying College Athletes*, N.Y. TIMES, Dec. 30, 2011, *at* http://www.nytimes.com/2012/01/01/magazine/lets-start-paying-college-athletes.html ?pagewanted=all&_r=0.

52. *See* Marc Edelman, note, *Reevaluating Amateurism Standards in Men's College Basketball*, 35 U. MICH. J. L. REFORM 861, 871 (2002).

services they provided their respective universities, athletic departments, and coaches in 2011.[53] Meanwhile the top-paid coaches who benefitted from the non-salaried student-athletes' on-field performances earned a total of $53.4 million that same year, which included a one-year salary of $5.1 million to University of Texas head football coach Mack Brown.[54] As The New York Times' op-ed columnist Joe Nocera so eloquently put it, "The hypocrisy that permeates big-money college sports takes your breath away."[55]

A great, albeit sad, example of how the college pay rules work against players is the story of Jonathan Benjamin, who was a basketball player at the University of Richmond until he was told by the school's director of compliance that he was no longer eligible to participate in intercollegiate sports.[56] Benjamin was ruled ineligible for something that the rest of the world respected and admired: his sense of entrepreneurialism. The basketball player started his own company to design and sell T-shirts bearing his unique designs. Because some of the clothing he created contained Benjamin's name and/or image, it was deemed that he violated NCAA Bylaw 12.4.4, which reads, "A student-athlete may establish his or her own business, provided the student-athlete's name, photograph, appearance or athletics reputation are not used to promote the business."[57] It was one more instance of a student-athlete being denied an opportunity to receive financial compensation above and beyond his or her scholarship, which may not even meet the true cost of attending his or her university.

The NCAA board of directors once approved a proposal for the NCAA to permit the payment of an additional $2,000 stipend to college athletes on scholarship,[58] yet that proposal (which received momentary acceptance) was overridden by the 161 schools with authority to determine which measures get pushed through the NCAA and become the rule of the land.[59] That

---

53. *See* Nocera, *supra* note 51.
54. *Id.*
55. *Id.*
56. *See* Patrick Hruby, *How Amateurism Is the Real Problem with College Sports*, Sportsonearth.com, Aug. 21, 2013, *at* http://www.sportsonearth.com/article/57680744/.
57. *Id.*
58. *Id.*
59. *Id.*

was in December 2011. The $2,000 stipend, which once seemed like a nice gesture to bridge the gap between scholarship amounts awarded and the actual cost of attendance, has so far failed to come to fruition. A major point of contention is that the less wealthy Division I schools may not be able to afford the increase in accordance with the payment of the $2,000 stipends or may find themselves at a distinct disadvantage as compared to the larger schools that will easily be able to shoulder the new costs.

Likeness Issues

"The U.S. Supreme Court and numerous lower courts have determined that the NCAA's amateurism rules are fully consistent with the nation's antitrust laws."[60]
—Donald Remy, NCAA executive vice president and general counsel

EA Sports is one of the more recognizable labels within the Electronic Arts, Inc. (EA) umbrella of video games. The video game manufacturer's long-time slogan has been, "It's in the game." Lately, the actual material contained within EA Sports games has become the subject of a considerable amount of controversy regarding the use of images that strongly reflect the personas of players participating in college football and basketball.

On May 5, 2009, former Arizona State University and University of Nebraska quarterback Sam Keller filed a lawsuit on behalf of himself and all others similarly situated against EA, the NCAA, and the Collegiate Licensing Company (CLC). The complaint alleged that the NCAA and the CLC sanctioned EA's blatant and unlawful use of NCAA student-athlete likenesses in EA videogames. Key claims made by Keller were that EA never had permission to use player names and likenesses in its video games and that neither the NCAA nor the CLC had the right or ability to approve EA's use of same.

---

60. *See* Donald Remy, *NCAA Seeks to Respond in Likeness Case*, NCAA.ORG, July 30, 2013, *at* http://www.ncaa.org/about/resources/media-center/press-releases/ncaa-seeks-resp ond-likeness-case.

In July 2013, the NCAA said that it would no longer license its name and logo to EA Sports for the purpose of including same within EA Sports' *NCAA Football* video game.[61] In its press release announcing the decision, the NCAA cited the "current business climate" and "costs of litigation" as reasons behind its determination that continuing to serve as licensor was not in its best interests. Soon thereafter, major conferences including the Southeastern Conference, Big Ten, and Pac-12 followed suit and informed EA Sports that it no longer held licenses to use those respective conference names and logos in future college football video games.[62] In an effort to distance itself from the pending litigation and define its nominal involvement in past video games, the Southeastern Conference noted, "Neither the SEC, its member universities, nor the NCAA have ever licensed the right to use the name or likeness of any student to EA Sports."[63]

Case Study

Hart v. Electronic Arts, Inc.

One of the most popular titles among EA's line of video games is its *NCAA Football* product. More than 700,000 copies of *NCAA Football 12* were sold to consumers within two weeks of the game's release in July 2012.[64] Although the franchise has undoubtedly found success with this particular line of video games, it has not avoided legal scrutiny. One case concerns former Rutgers University quarterback Ryan Hart, who sued EA based on a claim that the company violated his publicity rights by including a replica of him in the *NCAA Football* video game without his consent and by failing to compensate him for

---

61. *See NCAA Will Not Renew EA Sports Contract*, NCAA.ORG, July, 2013, *at* http://www.ncaa.org/wps/wcm/connect/public/NCAA/Resources/Latest+News/2013/July/NCAA+will+not+renew+EA+Sports+contract.

62. *See* Kristi Dosh, *SEC Won't License Trademarks in EA NCAA Football Game*, ESPN.COM, Aug. 14, 2013, *at* http://espn.go.com/college-football/story/_/id/9566556/sec-license-trademarks-ea-ncaa-football-game.

63. *Id.*

64. *See* Stephany Nunneley, *EA Sports: NCAA Football 12 Moves 700,000 Copies in Two Weeks*, VG 24/7, July 26, 2011, *at* http://www.vg247.com/2011/07/26/ea-sports-ncaa-football-12-moves-700000-copies-in-two-weeks/.

such commercial use. It would have been highly improbable for EA to take the position that it had not generated the characters in its game from the actual college football competitors who took the field during the year in which each game was based. *NCAA Football* characters wore jerseys with the same numbers as the players they were meant to depict and largely mimicked the height, weight, and biographical information as their real-life counterparts. However, EA's position was that its line of *NCAA Football* video games was protected against Hart's right to publicity claim based on First Amendment grounds. EA filed a motion to dismiss Hart's complaint, which was granted, only to later be reversed and remanded by the United States Court of Appeals for the Third Circuit. That court acknowledged that the First Amendment of the U.S. Constitution protects expressive speech, including the contents of video games; however, it noted that when right of publicity issues arise, the court must use a balancing test to manage the tension between the First Amendment and the right of publicity. The court analyzed three types of tests, eventually selecting the "transformative use" test, which focused on whether EA provided the requisite amount and type of creative contributions to render the ultimate product to be transformed enough from its original form. Judge Greenaway, for the court, wrote in his opinion: "The digital Ryan Hart does what the actual Ryan Hart did while at Rutgers: he plays college football, in digital recreations of college football stadiums, filled with all the trappings of a college football game. This is not transformative; the various digitized sights and sounds in the video game do not alter or transform [Hart's] identity in a significant way."[65]

In late 2013, six then-current student-athletes were added as plaintiffs in the litigation against the NCAA, the CLC, and EA.[66] The litigation, which

---

65. *Available at* http://www2.ca3.uscourts.gov/opinarch/113750p.pdf, page 53.
66. *See* Terrance Harris, *Ed O'Bannon Antitrust Lawsuit Has Serious Implications for Student-Athletes*, NCAA, NOLA.COM, Aug. 30, 2013, *at* http://www.nola.com/tulane/index.ssf/2013/08/ed_obannon_antitrust_lawsuit_h.html.

was once based on compensating former student-athletes for the use of their image and likeness without permission and payment, expanded to include current student-athletes and the request for additional compensation via a claim that athletes should be entitled to a percentage of the enormous television revenue received by the NCAA and its member schools.[67] Although the NCAA has not shown signs of willingness to cave in to the former and current student-athletes' demands, it disassociated itself from EA and decided to cease selling player jerseys and memorabilia on its official website, two steps that led many to believe that the NCAA at least secretly admitted some guilt.[68]

The Ryan Hart case was purportedly settled when the plaintiffs' attorneys came to a proposed agreement with EA and the CLC that called for the latter parties to pay the plaintiffs $40 million and left the NCAA as the only remaining defendant.[69] However, in a twist somewhat similar to that discussed concerning the pending concussion settlement between former football players and the NFL, the plaintiff players in the publicity rights litigation had their own issues with their attorneys. In fact, lead plaintiff Ryan Hart said he was completely uninformed about a proposed settlement, hired new counsel and found out that an effort was underway to remove him as a named plaintiff.[70] This is a glimpse of the battle lawyers face not only in the courtroom and in their offices against opposing counsel, but also the wars sometimes fought against their own clients when a plethora of money is on the line.

The NCAA's Jurisdiction over Agents

"The dirty secret behind student athletes is that they toil for long hours pursuing their dreams but are often living in poverty. They are very

---

67. *Id.*

68. *Id.*

69. *See* Steve Berkowitz, *Ryan Hart Says He Was Not Informed About EA Settlement,* USAToDAY.COM, Oct. 21, 2013, *at* http://www.usatoday.com/story/sports/ncaaf/2013/10 /21/ea-lawsuit-settlement-ryan-hart-ed-obannon-sam-keller/3147405/.

70. *Id.*

*vulnerable to unscrupulous agents preying on them in the hopes of a
future reward."[71]*
—Senator Kevin de León, chairman of the California Senate Select
Committee on Sports and Entertainment

It is tough to discuss any facet of Sports Law without somehow tying in the
sports agent profession. Although not having any true jurisdictional control
over sports agents and their actions, the NCAA has taken an active role
in at least attempting to regulate their involvement with student-athletes.
Often, such regulation is indirectly effectuated through the discipline of
those whom the NCAA can control (to an extent): student-athletes and
the institutions they attend.

NCAA Bylaw 12.3 specifically puts student-athletes on notice that they
will be ruled ineligible to participate in intercollegiate athletic competition
if they agree (either verbally or in writing) to be represented by a sports
agent for the purpose of marketing his or her ability or reputation.[72] Student-
athletes are also prohibited from receiving anything of value from a sports
agent, including but not limited to a ride in a sports agent's car.[73] However,
there is no NCAA prohibition against a sports agent communicating with
a student-athlete as long as there is no commitment made that the agent
will represent the student-athlete.[74] Various schools have implemented more
stringent regulations intended to curb communication between their student-
athletes and sports agents interested in eventually representing said players.

---

71. *See RELEASE: De Leon Bill Protecting Student Athletes from Unscrupulous Sports Agents Signed by the Governor,* SD22.SENATE.CA.GOV, Aug. 2, 2011, *at*
http://sd22.senate.ca.gov/news/2011-08-02-release-de-leon-bill-protecting-student-athletes
-unscrupulous-sports-agents-signed-g.
72. *See* NCAA bylaws, *Overview of NCAA Bylaws Governing Athlete Agents,* NCAA.ORG,
July 29, 2010, *at* http://www.ncaa.org/wps/wcm/connect/public/NCAA/Resources/Latest+News
/2010+news+stories/July+latest+news/Overview+of+NCAA+bylaws+governing+athlete+agents.
73. *Id.*
74. *Id.*

Case Study

Teague Egan

One of the many NCAA rules that has been ridiculed based on its absurdity prohibits student-athletes from receiving a "free ride" from a sports agent. The rule is based on a theory that the ride is a benefit to the student-athlete that a "normal student" (non-student-athlete) would not traditionally receive. Thus, it is impermissible because it is something of value received by the student-athlete based on his or her athletic ability. Receipt of such a benefit is punishable, but the rule is rarely enforced. When University of Southern California (USC) tailback Dillon Baxter received a ride on a golf cart owned by a sports agent, however, he was ruled ineligible by his school.[75] The golf cart belonged to football agent Teague Egan, who was 22 years old at the time of the incident.[76] In response to USC ruling Baxter ineligible, Egan reportedly stated: "To me, a golf cart ride wasn't an extra benefit, since I give 15–20 rides a day to all my friends to and from class. The question is would they consider riding on the handle bars of a bicycle against the rules? Say we all wanted to go to the movies together, would we have to take separate cars, and the player ride by himself? . . . I wouldn't even buy a player's ticket to that movie. But a ride?"[77]

In May 2012, the University of Miami (UM) instituted a new football agent policy intended to restrict communications between its football players and "covered individuals," a term meant to include agents, runners, financial planners, sports marketing representatives, sports public relations firms, brand managers, and employees of any of those described.[78] The policy

---

75. *See* Pedro Moura, *USC Trojans: Student/Agent Warned before Dillon Baxter Ride,* ESPN LA, Nov. 22, 2010, *at* http://sports.espn.go.com/los-angeles/ncf/news/story?id=5836913.
76. *Id.*
77. *Id.*
78. *See* Darren Heitner, *University of Miami Unveils Football Agent Policy Aimed at "Limiting Distractions,"* Forbes, May 14, 2012, *at* http://www.forbes.com/sites/sportsmoney/2012/05/14/university-of-miami-unveils-football-agent-policy-aimed-at-limiting-distractions/.

sought to completely restrict communication between UM football players and covered individuals until said players exhausted their student-athlete eligibility.[79] UM's cut-and-dry policy is an example of an extreme effort to limit the influence of sports agents on campus. A less restrictive agent policy was announced by the University of Washington (UW) a couple of months after UM put its policy into effect. UW's policy also restricted communication between agents and players, but it included specific carve-outs wherein certain types of contact would be permissible.[80] Contact would only be allowed between seniors and redshirt senior football players and agents from April through December, with no in-person contact permitted from August until the end of the year.[81] Additionally, UW offered its football players an "agent day" on its campus, whereas UM provided no such opportunity for student-athletes to become familiar with their potential future representatives.[82]

The NCAA has a broad definition of the term "agent." Such an individual includes runners (intermediaries between the agent and student-athlete for purposes of recruiting the player to the agent) and financial advisors.[83] In January 2012, the NCAA expanded the definition of agents to include family members who market student-athletes' athletic abilities or reputations for personal financial gain, financial advisors, marketing representatives, brand managers, and anyone employed by or associated with said individuals.[84]

A concern surrounding various universities' overt attempts to restrict many types of communication between agents and student-athletes is the perceived enhanced influence that coaches of those student-athletes may gain as a consequence. While coaches are believed to operate with the best interests of their athletes in mind, it is possible that they could persuade

---

79. *Id.*
80. *See* Darren Heitner, *University of Washington Announces Agent Day and Restrictive Agent Policy*, SPORTS AGENT BLOG, July 5, 2012, *at* http://www.sportsagentblog.com/2012/07/05/university-washington-announces-agent-day-restrictive-agent-policy/.
81. *Id.*
82. *Id.*
83. *Id.*
84. *See* NCAA News, *Council Broadens 'Agent' Definition, Several Other Proposals Tabled in Light of Ongoing Discussions*, NCAA.COM, Jan. 12, 2012, *at* http://www.ncaa.com/news/ncaa/article/2012-01-12/council-broadens-'agent'-definition

their players to pick specific agencies for their future representation. Whether or not a coach benefits from the referral, it is a concern that should be addressed. The federal government is considering a revision to the Uniform Athlete Agents Act (UAAA) that would include head coaches and assistant coaches who encourage student-athletes to sign with specific agents in a revised "agent" definition.[85]

85. *See* Jon Solomon, *Sports Agent Laws Reboot: Uniform Athlete Agents Act Tries Again 13 Years Later*, AL.com, Sept. 26, 2013, *at* http://www.al.com/sports/index.ssf/2013/09/whats _the_best_way_to_control.html.

Chapter 3

Athlete Agents

Drew Rosenhaus, Leigh Steinberg, and Scott Boras are among the most well-known sports agents in the world. For decades, the aforementioned individuals have represented some of the best and most handsomely rewarded athletes in their contractual negotiations with the teams that wished to retain them for their on-field services. Agents take a small commission on said contracts; however, many individuals, including those referenced above, have been able to create successful careers negotiating deals on behalf of professional players. It has led to outsiders believing that they too can easily enter the world of athlete representation and create a thriving practice from scratch. The two largest sports agent-related stories in 2013 were the announcements that hip-hop artist and entrepreneur Jay Z established a sports agency named Roc Nation Sports and entertainment agency William Morris Endeavor put forth the winning bid (over $2 billion) to purchase sports, fashion, and media conglomerate IMG Worldwide. The former story hit the Internet in early April when the official Roc Nation, LLC (the entertainment company founded by Jay Z) website formally declared the formation of Roc Nation Sports, a partnership with Creative Artists Agency (CAA), and the signing of second baseman Robinson Cano, who was formerly represented by baseball agent Scott Boras. Jay Z has since become certified by the players' unions for the NBA and MLB, assisted in the negotiation of a 10-year, $240 million contract between Cano and the Seattle Mariners, and signed New York Jets quarterback Geno Smith, Oklahoma City Thunder forward Kevin Durant and New York Giants wide receiver Victor Cruz to representation agreements. Jay Z's immediate success as a sports agent has caused other entertainment-related professionals to consider entering the world of representation. On October 25, 2013, Cash Money Records, Inc., a label founded by brothers Bryan "Birdman" Williams and Ronald "Slim" Williams that also features Drake, Lil Wayne and Nicki Minaj, filed a trademark application with the U.S. Patent and Trademark Office for the mark "Visionaire Sports Group," with the description of use being, in part, "sports agency services."[1] Sources also indicate that those in connection with Cash Money Records may be reaching out to at least one existing agency to partner with as opposed to entering the world of sports agency from scratch.[2]

Perhaps even bigger than Jay Z becoming a sports agent was the purchase of IMG Worldwide by William Morris Endeavor. While IMG Worldwide had phased out a large section of its athlete representation division prior to the sale, it remains the marketing agency of record for Joe Mauer, Peyton Manning, Matthew Stafford, Maria Sharapova, and others.[3] Additionally, the purchase includes the very valuable IMG Academy based in Bradenton, Florida, an athletic training facility used to develop young athletes into future talented professionals in their respective sports and a premier destination for football players preparing for their Pro Days and the NFL Combine. It is a facility commonly used by CAA to place its clients for pre-Draft preparations; however, it may no longer serve such a purpose as William Morris Endeavor will be not only a competitor for CAA in the world of entertainment, but also sport.

1. *See* Darren Heitner, *Jay Z May Soon Compete with Drake, Lil Wayne and Birdman Over Blue-Chip Athletes*, FORBES.COM, Dec. 23, 2013, *at* http://www.forbes.com/sites/darrenheitner/2013/12/23/jay-z-may-soon-compete-with-drake-lil-wayne-and-birdman-over-blue-chip-athletes/.

2. *Id.*

3. *See* Darren Heitner, *William Morris Endeavor's Purchase of IMG Worldwide Will Have Electrifying Effect on Sports Business*, Forbes.com, Dec. 18, 2013, *at* http://www.forbes.com/sites/darrenheitner/2013/12/18/william-morris-endeavors-purchase-of-img-worldwide-will-have-electrifying-effect-on-sports-business/.

Fiduciary Duties

"I am on the phone with Dallas Cowboys defensive end Marcus Spears. I'm trying to persuade him to switch agents, and I'm telling him to come to L.A. I sense hesitation, so I put the phone out the window. 'Do you hear that, Marcus? Do you hear it?' I yell. 'You know what that is? That's Hollywood, baby. Hollywood's calling. You gonna answer the call?' A week later, Marcus was in my office signing a representation agreement."
—Josh Luchs, former NFLPA contract advisor

The sports agent/athlete relationship is, at its core, an agent/principal relationship. As such, sports agents are obligated by law to serve in a fiduciary capacity on behalf of their athlete clients. Certain fiduciary duties are part and parcel of that relationship. The Restatement (Third) of Agency states, "An agent has a fiduciary duty to act loyally for the principal's benefit in all matters connected with the agency relationship."[4] This particular duty to act loyally has been referenced as the most fundamental fiduciary obligation imposed on a sports agent in his or her representation of professional athletes.[5]

Agents do not have a duty to disclose to their clients all affairs that touch or concern their lives. However, an agent does have a duty to discover and disclose any material information that is not clearly obvious and apparent and is reasonably obtainable.[6] A failure to disclose such information could be deemed to constitute negligence.

---

4. Restatement (Third) of Agency § 8.01 (2012).
5. *See* Rand Getlin, *Prominent NFL Agent Drew Rosenhaus Scrutinized for Relationship with Former Financial Adviser*, YAHOO! SPORTS, Sept. 4, 2012, *at* http://sports.yahoo.com/news/nfl--prominent-nfl-agent-drew-rosenhaus-scrutinized-for-relationship-with-former-financial-adviser-.html.
6. Douglas v. Steele, 816 P.2d 586, 590 (Okla. Civ. App. 1991).

Case Study

Roman Colon v. J. D. Smart and Hendricks Sports Management, LP

On October 29, 2012, professional baseball player Roman Colon filed suit against his former baseball agent John David (J. D.) Smart and Hendricks Sports Management, LP (the agency that Smart worked for while representing Colon). Colon, a right-handed pitcher, listed as his first claim for relief a stated breach of fiduciary duty against Hendricks and Smart. The complaint alleged that Hendricks and Smart acted out of self-interest by mismanaging and failing to disclose a qualifying offer submitted to Colon from a Korean baseball team that had previously signed the pitcher. Colon claimed that he would have immediately signed with the Korean team had his agents informed him of the qualifying offer. Instead, Colon returned to the United States and signed a contract with the Los Angeles Dodgers for a monthly stipend of $12,500. The final paragraph of the breach of fiduciary duty claim for relief reads, "Hendricks and Smart breached their fiduciary responsibilities, obligations, and duties imposed on them by engaging in dishonest, disloyal, and immoral conduct."[7] On February 12, 2013, the court dismissed the complaint without prejudice because the agency contract that Colon signed with Hendricks included an arbitration provision, which required that the parties resolve the dispute through the final and binding arbitration procedures set forth in Section 7(a) of the Regulations Governing Player Agents of the Major League Baseball Players Association (MLBPA).

Team contract offers are among the most important items that sports agents should disclose to their clients because teams will largely respect the athlete/agent relationship and not go behind an agent's back in an effort to present

---

7. *Available at* http://sportsagentblog.com/2012/11/01/baseball-pitcher-roman-wants-1-million-from-sports-agent-for-failing-to-disclose-a-teams-offer/

an offer directly to the player. Additionally, agents should notify their clients of what substances are permitted and banned by players' associations and sport governing bodies. An agency should never be involved in assisting its client's illicit use of nonapproved performance-enhancing drugs.[8]

Unless given specific permission by his or her client, a sports agent must not use his or her position or an athlete's property for personal benefit or to benefit a third party. Veteran sports marketer and athlete marketing agent Bill Henkel secured a memorability deal for former National Football League (NFL) running back LaDanian Tomlinson while employed at global sports, fashion, and media company IMG Worldwide.[9] Without Tomlinson's knowledge or consent, Henkel structured a deal with the company that signed Tomlinson that contemplated the payment of a $25,000 kickback to Henkel for joining the parties in contract.[10] It could be argued that Henkel's withholding of said information from his client constituted a violation of his fiduciary duties to Tomlinson. The athlete marketing agent faced felony charges for commercial bribery and theft based on his actions.[11]

Agents should also always take caution when asked to or voluntarily offer to provide services outside of their core competency. Former football agent Tank Black found himself in prison when he ventured off the path of providing contract negotiation services for high-profile athletes, including running back Fred Taylor and wide receivers Ike Hilliard and Rae Carruth, and began to manage his clients' money. In 2000, Black was sued for money laundering, conspiracy, and criminal forfeiture and was accused of

---

8. *See* Darren Heitner, *How the Melky Cabrera Chaos Is Affecting ACES Baseball Agency*, SPORTS AGENT BLOG, Oct. 17, 2012, *at* http://www.sportsagentblog.com/2012/10/17/how-the -melky-cabrera-chaos-is-affecting-aces-baseball-agency/. (In 2012, ACES Baseball Agency was alleged to have had a professional relationship with an individual who attempted to cover up Major League Baseball player Melky Cabrera's use of performance-enhancing drugs. ACES and its founders were investigated to better determine the role the agents had (if any at all) in the cover-up. Multiple clients terminated their agency contracts with ACES soon after it was reported that ACES was being investigated).

9. *See* Darren Heitner, *Bill Henkel Is Looking for Some Positive Endorsements*, SPORTS AGENT BLOG, Apr. 24, 2007, *at* http://www.sportsagentblog.com/2007/04/24/bill-henkel-is -looking-for-some-positive-endorsements/.

10. *Id.*

11. *Id.*

mismanaging roughly $15 million of his clients' money.[12] He spent eight years in jail as a result of his actions.[13]

More recently, football agent Drew Rosenhaus was investigated by the National Football League Players Association (NFLPA) regarding his relationship with a financial planner who influenced athletes to invest in an Alabama bingo casino that cost said players somewhere in the range of $43 million.[14] The NFLPA was reportedly looking into whether Rosenhaus had a duty to more fully look into the financial planner's background and advise his clients to stay away from him.[15] In August 2013, former National Football League (NFL) wide receiver and Rosenhaus client Terrell Owens sued Rosenhaus on the basis that he breached his fiduciary duty to Owens, among other causes of action.[16] Owens's attorney went on the record saying: "It is completely ridiculous that Rosenhaus would refer a five-time Pro Bowler to a financial advisor who has been accused of stealing from his clients in the past, whose college degree was in Exercise Science, and who was inexperienced. Rosenhaus should have steered Terrell away from Rubin, not toward him."[17]

Finally, an athlete should never feel forced to apologize for the actions of his advisor. Oakland Raiders quarterback Terrelle Pryor did just that after his agent Jerome Stanley demonized head coach Dennis Allen, saying that the coach was setting up his young quarterback client to fail.[18] Pryor took

---

12. *See* L. Jon Wertheim, *Smooth-Talking Agent Tank Black Allegedly Ensnared Nearly Two Dozen NFL and NBA Players, Including Vince Carter, in a Mind-Boggling Series of Scams and Defrauded Them of Some $15 Million,* SI VAULT, May 29, 2000, *at* http://sportsillustrated.cnn.com/vault/article/magazine/MAG1019341/.

13. *See* Michael O'Keeffe, *Tank Black Is Out of Jail and Out to Prove in New Book That He Didn't Defraud Sports Stars, Defraud Sports Stars,* N.Y. DAILY NEWS, Sept. 12, 2009, *at* http://www.nydailynews.com/sports/football/tank-black-jail-prove-new-book-didn-defraud-sports-stars-article-1.407165.

14. See Getlin, *supra* note 5.

15. *Id.*

16. *See* Rand Getlin, *Terrell Owens Suing Former Agent Drew Rosenhaus,* YAHOO! SPORTS, Aug. 22, 2013, *at* http://sports.yahoo.com/news/nfl—terrell-owens-suing-former-agent-213336186.html.

17. *Id.*

18. *See* Scott Bair, *Pryor's Agent Believes Allen Wants Terrelle to Fail vs. Denver,* CSNBAYAREA.COM, Dec. 23, 2013, *at* http://www.csnbayarea.com/raiders/pryors-agent-believes-allen-wants-terrelle-fail-vs-denver.

it upon himself to Tweet an apology for his agent's comments, thanked the Raiders organization for giving him an opportunity to perform and distanced himself from his agent's words.[19] Taking action without a client's consent which has the consequence of tarnishing a client's reputation is a huge gaffe, especially in an industry as competitive as sports agency and considering how common it is for players to change representation.

Registration and Certification

"[Don't] ever represent any player that is a resident or goes to school in the state of Alabama. I am not an agent anymore, but I wouldn't do it."[20]
—Mike Trope, author of *Necessary Roughness* and former NFLPA contract advisor

In 2000, the Uniform Athlete Agents Act (UAAA) was passed by the federal legislature in an effort to create a uniform system of rules governing the sports agent profession, with a specific focus on the legal recruitment of student-athletes to agency contracts.[21] By November 2011, the UAAA had been adopted by 42 states, Washington D.C., and the U.S. Virgin Islands.[22] Since then, however, many states have determined that the UAAA as originally written is in need of a change to more appropriately govern a sports agency landscape that had been altered over time.[23] In February 2012, the

---

19. *See* Ryan Wilson, *Pryor Apologizes for Agent Blasting Raiders' Decision to Start Him*, CBSSPORTS.COM, Dec. 24, 2013, *at* http://www.cbssports.com/nfl/eye-on-football/24386813 /terrelle-pryor-apologizes-for-agent-blasting-raiders-decision-to-start-him.

20. *See* Darren Heitner, *Don't Represent Alabama Athletes?* SPORTS AGENT BLOG, Nov. 10, 2008, *at* http://www.sportsagentblog.com/2008/11/10/dont-represent-alabama-athletes /.

21. *See* National Collegiate Athletic Association, *FAQ on Uniform Athlete Agents Act*, July 29, 2010, http://www.ncaa.org/wps/wcm/connect/public/NCAA/Resources/Latest+News /2010+news+stories/July+latest+news/FAQ+on+Uniform+Athlete+Agents+Act.

22. *See* Latest News, *UAAA Summit Reinvigorates Agent Oversight*, NCAA.ORG, Nov. 22, 2011, *at* http://www.ncaa.org/wps/wcm/connect/public/NCAA/Resources/Latest+News /2011/November/UAAA+Summit+reinvigorates+agent+oversight.

23. *See New ULC Drafting and Study Committees to Be Appointed*, UNIFORM LAW COMMISSION, Feb. 3, 2012, *at* http://www.uniformlaws.org/NewsDetail.aspx?title=New%20ULC %20Drafting%20and%20Study%20Committees%20to%20be%20Appointed.

executive committee of the Uniform Law Commission (ULC) therefore authorized a new study committee called the Study Committee on Amending the Uniform Athlete Agents Act, that will make recommendations regarding any need and/or ability to make meaningful changes to the UAAA on a national level.[24] Thus far, there has not yet been a meaningful alteration to the UAAA, even though many states have altered their agent regulations over recent years to adapt to changing times.

Individuals who wish to recruit student-athletes to sign agency contracts in states that have passed athlete agent laws (whether or not they mimic the UAAA) must become licensed in those particular states. Each state has its own system of licensing and regulating athlete agents. For instance, in Florida, the licensing and regulation of athlete agents is controlled by the Athlete Agents Unit within the Department of Business and Professional Regulation. There are specific requirements that one must meet to have his or her application to become an athlete agent approved. The applicant must be at least 18 years old, be found to have good moral character, complete an application form, remit the appropriate fees, and submit electronic fingerprints as a part of a required criminal records check. The application fee in Florida is $750, and the criminal history records check fee varies by vendor. If approved as an athlete agent in Florida, there is a separate licensure fee of $750. For athlete agents to renew their Florida licenses, further payment of $445 is due on May 31 of every even-numbered year.

According to the Florida Department of Business and Professional Regulation, an athlete agent license is required for any individual who directly or indirectly recruits or solicits a student-athlete to enter into an agent contract or for any type of financial gain. Student-athletes are defined as any student who resides in Florida and participates or plans to participate in college sports or does not reside in Florida but plans to participate in a Florida school's college sports program.

Operating as an athlete agent in Florida without a license or assisting a third party in his or her efforts to provide agent services to an athlete without proper certification is considered a felony of the third degree.

---

24. *Id.*

The state also provides colleges and universities with a statutory right to sue an unlicensed agent if his or her acts cause the institution to be penalized, disqualified, or suspended from participation in intercollegiate athletics.

Certain states enforce their athlete agent laws more than others. One such state is Texas, which contacted a sports agent client of mine who was alleged to have violated the Texas Athlete Agent Act when he signed a basketball player who formerly performed at a university within the state. My client did not hold a certification to conduct business as an athlete agent in the state of Texas when he signed the player to a representation agreement. However, the agency contract was not executed by said agent and player until after the player had departed from the university. Additionally, the agreement was consummated beyond the borders of Texas—player and agent had not communicated at all during the player's collegiate career; their first face-to-face meeting was outside of Texas and the agency contract was signed in another state. I closed my file on the matter after delivering initial correspondence to the appropriate party in Texas and not receiving any response.

The process of becoming certified as an athlete agent in a state is not extremely complicated, but can take some time to accomplish. I vividly recall the excitement I experienced when I first received information that my Florida athlete agent application was processed and I was thereafter permitted to recruit student-athletes in the state. It took slightly less than ten months for the state to grant me clearance to hold myself out as a certified athlete agent. After paying the application and licensure fees and renewing my certification, I had a feeling this particular game was not for me. Perhaps the war stories found in the following case studies may lead the reader to the same conclusion.

Case Study

Barry Rona v. MLBPA

Barry Rona is a former executive director and general counsel of the MLB Player Relations Committee, the counterpart to the MLB Players Association (MLBPA) on the other side of the collective bargaining table.[25] During the time Rona served his term as executive director, he was involved in a collusion scandal against free agent players.[26] In 1985, team owners essentially destroyed the market for free agents by failing to make offers to *any* of the 62 available players.[27] When the issue was challenged in MLB's arbitration system, arbitrator Tom Roberts ruled for the players and demanded the league pay them remedies.[28] Barry Rona publicly stated, on behalf of the Player Relations Committee, that he disagreed with the ruling in the players' favor.[29] After Rona's employment with the MLB Player Relations Committee, Rona submitted an application to the MLBPA for certification as an MLB player agent.[30] As a result of his involvement with the collusion scandal, Rona's application was rejected.[31] The MLBPA found that Roma's conduct in association with the attempt to deprive free agents of the market rendered him unfit and ineligible to become certified to represent the players.[32] The attempt to deny Rona certification was done under MLBPA rules and regulations that stated that the association may bar any agent whose conduct "may adversely affect his credibility [or] integrity ... to serve in a representative and/ or fiduciary capacity on behalf of the players."[33]

---

25. *See* John Powers, *Baseball Owners Found to Have Had Conspiracy*, SUN SENTINEL, Sept. 22, 1987, *at* http://articles.sun-sentinel.com/1987-09-22/sports/8703180075_1_free -agents-roberts-decision-players-representatives.

26. *Id.* (The article describes the scandal as one in which "MLB owners set out to 'destroy' the market for free agents in 1985 by not bidding for available players, an arbitrator ruled Monday in a landmark decision.")

27. *Id.*

28. *Id.*

29. *Id.* The article quotes Rona saying: "With all due respect to the arbitrator, we disagree with his conclusion concerning club conduct in 1985. We will, however, comply with his decision and are prepared to deal with the remedy portion of the case."

30. *See* Murray Chass, *BASEBALL; Union Sues to Bar Rona as Agent*, SUN SENTINEL, Dec. 21, 1993, *at* http://www.nytimes.com/1993/12/21/sports/baseball-union-sues-to-bar -rona-as-agent.html.

31. *Id.* (The article states that Rona was denied certification because he "lacked credibility and integrity because he created and administered a fraudulent scheme" that deprived players of their rights.)

32. *Id.*

33. *See* Glenn M. Wong, *Essentials of Sports Law*, p. 585, http://www.amazon.com/ Essentials-Sports-Law-Glenn-Wong/dp/0313356750.

In response to the rejection of his application, Rona appealed to MLB's arbitration system.[34] The independent arbitrator, Collins, ruled that the MLBPA's attempt to deny Rona certification as a player agent was arbitrary and capricious and ordered that Rona be rightfully certified so as to work as a player agent.[35] The MLBPA then filed suit in New York Supreme Court seeking to overturn the arbitrator's decision, contending that Collins incorrectly considered state law requiring that, as a lawyer, Rona had a responsibility to represent his clients vigorously.[36]

Separate from the state licensure, to represent clients in contractual negotiations with professional organizations, sports agents must be granted permission from the various players' associations. The National Hockey League Players Association (NHLPA) requires applicants to complete an agent certification program prior to earning certification to represent hockey players in contract talks with National Hockey League teams.[37] Interested applicants must first write to the NHLPA to receive a thorough questionnaire called the Application for Certification as an NHLPA Player Agent and submit the completed questionnaire by fax or mail to the union for review.[38]

To represent National Basketball Association players, interested individuals must file a verified application for certification and have received a degree from an accredited four-year college or university.[39] The National Basketball Players Association (NBPA) Committee on Agent Regulation has the power to grant certification to certain individuals who may have not received such

---

34. *See* Chass, *supra* note 29.

35. *Id.*

36. *Id.* ("Instead of measuring Rona's conduct against the standards set forth in the Regulations," the suit reads, "the Arbitrator stated that Rona's actions were to be judged solely in terms of external law—the New York Code of Professional Responsibility.")

37. *See Certified Player Agents*, NHLPA.COM, *at* http://www.nhlpa.com/inside-nhlpa/certified-player-agents (accessed on December 25, 2013).

38. *Id.*

39. *See* National Basketball Players Association, *NBPA Regulations Governing Player Agents*, NBPA.ORG, as amended June, 1991, *at* http://www.nbpa.org/sites/default/files/users/sean.brandveen/Agent%20Regulations%20PDF.pdf.

a degree but who are able to exhibit relevant negotiating experience as a substitute.[40] A nonrefundable $100 application fee is required, along with the payment of initial annual dues of $1,500.[41] However, applicants who apply between January 1 and July 1 are only required to make a half payment (of $750) in addition to the nonrefundable application fee.[42]

The most expensive application fee is courtesy of the NFLPA, which requires payment of $2,500, also nonrefundable.[43] The NFLPA stipulates that applicants must have an undergraduate and a postgraduate degree (master's or law degree).[44] Similar to the NBPA, the NFLPA includes a provision that enables the association to certify an applicant if he or she has sufficient negotiating experience. The NFLPA requires at least seven years of sufficient negotiating experience to meet the exception; however, it provides little to no guidance as to what constitutes "sufficient negotiating experience" or the criteria necessary to qualify under the carve-out.[45] Another distinguishing attribute to the NFLPA's certification regimen is that all applicants must sit for a written proctored examination in Washington, D.C., based on the then-current NFL collective bargaining agreement.[46] Finally, individuals may only file applications for certification during a one-month span. In 2013, that period was limited to January 11 through February 11.[47]

The NFLPA, along with other players' unions, also has the right to deny an applicant's request to be certified as a Contract Advisor and represent players with regards to their team contract negotiations. In 2013, I had the opportunity to represent one such individual who was informed that his application for certification as an NFLPA Contract Advisor had been denied

---

40. *Id.*
41. http://www.nbpa.org/sites/default/files/users/sean.brandveen/NBPA%20Agent%20Application.pdf (accessed on December 25, 2013).
42. *Id.*
43. *See* NFL Players Association, *Agent Regulations*, NFLPlayers.com, *at* https://www.nflplayers.com/About-us/Rules—Regulations/Agent-Regulations/ (accessed on Dec. 25, 2013).
44. *Id.*
45. *See* NFL Players Association (NFLPA), *Regulations Governing Contract Advisors*, NFLPlayers.com, as amended through June 2012, *at* http://images.nflplayers.com/mediaResources/files/PDFs/SCAA/2012_NFLPA_Regulations_Contract_Advisors.pdf.
46. *See* NFL Players Association, *Agent Regulations*, NFLPlayers.com, *at* https://www.nflplayers.com/About-us/Rules—Regulations/Agent-Regulations/.
47. *Id.*

because he had "engaged in conduct that significantly impacts adversely on your credibility, integrity and competence to serve in a fiduciary capacity on behalf of players." An arbitration hearing was held to determine whether the NFLPA had justification to deny my client's application. The arbitrator was informed of my client's prior conviction of theft stemming from incidents in 2006, but it was also demonstrated that my client had worked relentlessly and successfully to take his life in a positive, law-abiding direction since the incidents. The arbitrator ruled that the NFLPA failed to meet its burden to prove that it had a "reasonable basis in the circumstances of the case under review" to deny my client's application. My favorite line of the arbitrator's opinion was the sentence, "The evidence made clear that the [individual] of seven (7) to ten (10) years ago is not the [individual] of today." It was a win for my client and me, and an eye-opener as to how difficult players' associations can be at times.

The Canadian Football League Players Association (CFLPA) has its own regulations governing the approval of contract advisors, one of which also requires applicants to successfully complete an examination administered by the CFLPA. The vast consequences of registration and licensure of CFLPA contract advisors was put to test when Chris Williams, a wide receiver from New Mexico State, came to terms with the CFL's Hamilton Tiger-Cats but then asked to be released from the contract because his agent, who negotiated the deal, was unlicensed at the time that it was executed.[48] An arbitrator heard that case upon the filing of a grievance and made a determination that the contract was legal and binding even though the Tiger-Cats breached the CFL's collective bargaining agreement by negotiating a player's contract with an unlicensed agent.[49] The CFLPA applied for judicial review of the arbitration decision, and the Ontario Superior Court of Justice quashed and set aside the arbitrator's ruling based on the understanding that contracts between contract advisors and players that are not in the prescribed form

---

48. *See* Darren Heitner, *Canadian Football League Contract Negotiated by Unlicensed Agent Has the Player Association Up in Arms*, FORBES, Aug. 3, 2013, *at* http://www.forbes.com/sites/darrenheitner/2013/08/03/canadian-football-league-contract-negotiated-by-unlicensed-agent-has-the-players-association-up-in-arms/.

49. *Id.*

are unenforceable.[50] On review, the court found evidence that 50 percent of CFL players use unregistered contract advisors to negotiate on their behalf and "while the arbitrator could have declared that Williams was no longer obligated to perform the contract, the arbitrator's decision to hold him to its terms falls within the range of possible reasonable outcomes."[51] The court, however, still quashed and set aside the arbitrator's ruling on the grounds that the Tiger-Cats failed to properly execute its team option over the player because instead of using clear language to communicate its intention to exercise the option, the club instead provided the player an "offer," which implied that the player's consent was required.[52]

The MLBPA also contains a unique condition that individuals must meet to be granted general certification. The MLBPA will not certify an agent unless he or she is first designated by an MLB player as his representative.[53] Thus, unless an individual has a client on a team's 40-man roster, he or she will be denied general certification. However, limited certification is available for those who recruit or provide services for or on behalf of an agent negotiating contracts between MLB players and MLB organizations.[54] The MLBPA's application fee is a nonrefundable payment of $500.[55] The MLBPA makes a presumption that any applicant who has never been certified by the association and does not at least have a bachelor's degree is not eligible to be granted general certification as a player agent, but also gives the applicant an opportunity to demonstrate sufficient knowledge and relevant professional or employment experience.[56]

---

50. *See Decision of Ontario Court of Justice Re CFLPA Application for Judicial Review of Williams' Arbitration*, NFLPLAYERS.COM, Aug. 29, 2013, *at* http://www.scribd.com/doc/164848664/Decision-of-Ontario-Court-of-Justice-Re-CFLPA-Application-for-Judicial-Review-of-Williams-Arbitration.

51. *Id.*

52. *Id.*

53. *See* MLBPA Info, *MLBPA Regulations Governing Player Agents*, MLBPLAYERS.COM, *at* http://mlbplayers.mlb.com/pa/info/agent_regulations.jsp.

54. *Id.*

55. *Id.*

56. *See* MLBPA, *Agent Regulations Section 4(A)*, MLBPAAGENT.ORG, *at* http://reg.mlbpaagent.org/Documents/AgentForms/Agent%20Regulations.pdf.

Noncompete Provisions with Agencies

"There are plenty of other agents out here that are trying to get the same thing you are after. And many of them have more experience, more money etc."[57]
—Greg Linton, NFLPA contract advisor

A constant in the athlete representation industry is the movement of individuals from one agency to another. This pattern typically takes the form of athletes terminating their contractual relationships with what become their former agents in favor of new representation, and the process occasionally occurs multiple times throughout the life of an athlete's professional career. However, change is not simply reserved for athletes; agents are also often moving from one agency to another, always in search of a better platform for them to recruit and represent players. As a result of this constant change, agencies have purposefully inserted restrictive covenants known more colloquially as "noncompete provisions" within the employment agreements they draft and provide to agents in order for them to join their companies. However, agencies should be careful to draft such provisions in a way that will increase the likelihood of them being enforceable because if deemed void, they have little to no use at all.

Until the passage of the MLBPA Regulations Governing Player Agents (as amended effective October 1, 2010), the MLBPA opposed honoring noncompete provisions in agency contracts based on the belief that they could be used to possibly restrict players from being represented by their preferred agents.[58] Consider, for example, the experienced baseball agent Dan Lozano, who decided to end his employment by baseball agency Beverly Hills Sports Council (BHSC) in favor of starting up his own competing agency.[59] The MLBPA, prior to the implementation of the 2010 regulations,

---

57. *See* Darren Heitner, *Interview with the Agent: Greg Linton*, Sports Agent Blog, June 28, 2012, *at* http://www.sportsagentblog.com/2012/06/28/interview-with-the-agent-g reg-linton/.

58. Darren A. Heitner and Jason B. Wolf, "In Baseball's Best Interest? A Discussion of the October 2010 MLBPA Regulations Governing Player Agents," 10 Va. Sports & Ent. L.J. 249.

59. *See* Darren Heitner, *Albert Pujols Agent Leaves Beverly Hills Sports Council*, Sports Agent Blog, May 26, 2010, *at* http://www.sportsagentblog.com/2010/05/26/albert-pujols

would have been concerned that a noncompete within Lozano's employment agreement with BHSC may have prevented his clients, including first baseman Albert Pujols, from choosing to remain with Lozano and would force him to stay with BHSC or find another agent. However, under the rules currently in effect, noncompete provisions are permissible as long as they meet certain criteria[60] and are reasonable.[61] That said, the noncompete signed by Lozano has become the subject of a heated dispute between agent and former employer. Over two years have passed since Lozano's departure from BHSC and an arbitration decision remains pending between the parties, wherein BHSC claims roughly $40 million in damages based on Lozano leaving the firm.[62]

For a noncompetition agreement to be deemed valid by the MLBPA, it has to be in writing, supported by consideration, and executed by the employee agent and the employer agency.[63] Additionally, the agreement must be disclosed to the MLBPA,[64] drafted with terminology set forth in the 2010 Regulations,[65] unaccompanied by any breach of the underlying employment agreement, and be void of bad faith.[66] The noncompete will meet the "reasonableness" requirement if its (1) geographical scope is limited to an area that is not larger than what is reasonably necessary,[67] (2) duration is reasonable,[68] (3) restriction is limited to include only the agent's players who have a relationship with the agency so as to justify the restriction,[69] and (4) language does not require the departing agent to share compensation

---

-agent-leaves-beverly-hills-sports-council/. (The hypothetical is based on reality. In May 2010, Lozano left BHSC to form his own company, and the first player to leave with him was his highest profile client, Albert Pujols.)

60. *MLBPA Regulations Governing Player Agents* (2010) at §§ 4(L)(2)(a)–4(L)(2)d.

61. *See Id.* at pp. 13–15; § (4)(L)(2)(e).

62. *See* Darren Heitner, *Albert Pujols' Agent Begins Arbitration Against Former Baseball Agency*, Forbes.com, Oct. 28, 2013, *at* http://www.forbes.com/sites/darrenheitner/2013/10/28/albert-pujols-agent-begins-arbitration-against-former-baseball-agency/.

63. *Id.* at § 4(L)(2)(a).

64. *Id.* at § 4(L)(2)(b).

65. *Id.* at § 4(L)(2)(c).

66. *Id.* at § 4(L)(2)(d).

67. *Id.* at § 4(L)(2)(e)(i).

68. *Id.* at § 4(L)(2)(e)(ii).

69. *Id.* at § 4(L)(2)(e)(iii).

or forfeit benefits for breaching the provision more than what would be deemed to be a reasonable amount.[70]

Case Study

Aaron Mintz v. Mark Bartelstein and Associates, Inc., d/b/a Priority Sports & Entertainment

A Complaint for Declaratory Relief was filed by athlete agent Aaron Mintz against Mark Bartelstein & Associates, Inc., d/b/a Priority Sports & Entertainment, on March 23, 2012.[71] The complaint specifically focused on California Business and Professions Code Section 16600, which states, in part, that "every contract by which anyone is restrained from engaging in a lawful profession, trade, or business of any kind is to that extent void."[72] Mintz, a citizen of the California (residing in Los Angeles), claimed that the noncompete provision within his employment agreement with Priority Sports & Entertainment was unenforceable as a matter of law.[73] The provision specifically stated that Mintz could not compete against Priority Sports & Entertainment for a period of two years after the termination of the employment contract, and Mintz alleged that because the injunction required enforcement in California, a jurisdiction that voids any such provision, the clause was void and unenforceable.[74] It read:

> For two (2) years following the termination of the Employee's employment, regardless of the reason therefore, the Employee agrees that the Employee will not, directly or indirectly, on behalf of himself or others either as an employee, consultant, owner, independent contractor or in any other capacity whatsoever: 1. Solicit Company Clients; 2. Recruit Company employees

---

70. *Id.* at § 4(L)(2)(e)(iv).
71. *See* Aaron Mintz v. Priority Sports, *at* http://www.scribd.com/doc/88017207/Aaron-Mintz-v-Priority-Sports.
72. *Id.*
73. *Id.*
74. *Id.*

for or on behalf of Company Competitors; 3. Disclose Confidential Business Information to persons not affiliated with the Company, including, without limitation, Company Competitors, without the Company's prior written consent; or 4. Provide or assist in providing, either directly or through a Company Competitor, services that are, or are similar to the services, provided by the Company to a Company Client.[75]

Mintz, who had been employed by Priority Sports & Entertainment for 11 years prior to his departure in 2012, had resided and worked in Los Angeles, where he maintained an office that focused on the recruitment and representation of professional basketball players.[76] The agent was concerned that the noncompetition clause would prohibit him from engaging in the business of representing basketball players and would restrict Mintz's new employer from having Mintz represent said athletes.[77] However, a dispute resolution section of the employment agreement stipulated that any disputes arising under the agreement will be governed by the laws of Illinois and that the parties consent to the jurisdiction of the state courts of Cook County, Illinois, "and further agree to waive any objection that they may have to the jurisdiction of venue of such courts to adjudicate any dispute arising under this Agreement."[78] That could have complicated matters for Mintz because Illinois does not have a law banning covenants to not compete.[79] Instead of providing an opinion that addressed jurisdiction and/or the enforceability of a noncompetition clause such as the one found in Mintz's employment agreement, the court found that no proof was provided to demonstrate that Priority Sports & Entertainment

---

75. *Id.*

76. *Id.*

77. *Id.*

78. *See* Darren Heitner, *Basketball Agent Aaron Mintz Sues Former Employer Priority Sports & Entertainment*, Sports Agent Blog, Apr. 5, 2012, *at* http://www.sportsagentblog.com /2012/04/05/basketball-agent-aaron-mintz-sues-former-employer-priority-sports-entertainment/.

79. *See* Darren Heitner, *Tackling the Choice of Law Issue in Aaron Mintz v. Priority Sports*, Sports Agent Blog, Apr. 24, 2012, *at* http://www.sportsagentblog.com/2012/04/24 /tackling-the-choice-of-law-issue-in-aaron-mintz-v-priority-sports/.

attempted to enforce the clause and thus there was no actual controversy with "sufficient immediacy and reality to warrant the issuance
of a declaratory judgment."[80]

The enforceability of a noncompete provision is not only up to the players'
association governing the relationships between athletes and agents, but
also the states in which agents choose to conduct business. A restrictive covenant's enforceability could rest entirely on the laws of the jurisdiction that
adjudicates a dispute based on the clause's applicability.[81] Noncompetition
clauses tend to be heavily scrutinized by courts of law and disfavored unless
narrowly drawn and "reasonable in view of the totality of the circumstances,
including the scope of geographical, temporal, and competitive activity
restrictions."[82] They are also only upheld if they protect the employer's
legitimate proprietary interest, which can be tough to prove in the scope of
the sports agent industry, where few secrets remain hidden from the public
and questionable "trade secret" labels are often attached to information that
hardly qualifies as such. Trade secrets, along with confidential information,
customer lists (including contact information), and goodwill, are often considered by courts in states that choose to enforce (at times) noncompetes;[83]
however, with players' associations often providing agencies' client lists,
along with the public availability of player contact information,[84] it may be

---

80. *See* Robert Milligan, *NBA Sports Agent Slams Non-Compete and Trade Secret Claims and Scores 85K Jury Verdict against Former Agency for Privacy Violation*, LEXOLOGY, Dec. 8, 2012, *at* http://www.lexology.com/library/detail.aspx?g=6b702834-0184-4022-87 b1-ec230b337aec.
81. See E. H. Schopler, *Conflict of Laws as to Validity, Enforceability, and Effect of Ancil- lary Restrictive Covenant Not to Compete, in Contract of Employment or for Sale of Business,* 70 A.L.R.2d 1292 (1960).
82. Stephen L. Sheinfeld and Jennifer M. Chow, *Protecting Employer Secrets and the "Doctrine of Inevitable Disclosure,"* 600 PRAC. L. INST./LITIG. 367, 392 (1999).
83. *See* William Lynch Schaller, *Jumping Ship: Legal Issues Relating to Employee Mobil- ity in High Technology Industries,* 17 LAB. LAW. 25, 37 (2001).
84. A subscription-based website, InsideTheLeague (www.insidetheleague.com), provides a feature that highlights NFL draft prospects at each NCAA Division I university along with information including the players' family members' names, addresses, phone numbers, e-mail addresses, Facebook URLs, Twitter URLs, etc.

difficult to prove any type of true propriety interest in an effort to defend restrictive covenants in the world of sports agency.

California has taken an even more drastic approach, effectively prohibiting noncompetition agreements throughout the state. Its public policy is "to ensure that every citizen shall retain the right to pursue any lawful employment and enterprise of their choice";[85] thus, its courts will void noncompetes as a matter of law. There are only limited statutory exceptions to that rule, and they are rarely invoked.

Agency/Player Disputes

Disputes between sports agents and athletes typically revolve around the nonpayment of fees. All the major U.S. players' associations provide standard representation agreements to certified player agents, which include a provision for the percentage of the represented player's salary that the player is obligated to distribute to his representative throughout the life of the executed team contract. The NFLPA caps that percentage at 3 percent.[86] However, many football agents choose to lower the fee charged to clients to remain competitive. A recent finding by the NFLPA states that the average fee charged by agents is 2.9 percent.[87] The agent fee cap instituted by the NBPA is 4 percent, which may be recouped if the player agent negotiates a contract above the minimum applicable compensation for league players.[88] If a National Basketball Association (NBA) player signs a contract at the established minimum salary threshold, the agent may only receive a maximum of 2 percent commission on the contract.[89] The MLBPA takes a more protective approach for minimum-salary players and prohibits player

---

85. KGB, Inc. v. Giannoulas, 164 Cal. Rptr. 571 (Cal. Ct. App. 1980).

86. *See* Darren Heitner, *Rumor: NFL Rookie Deal Agent Fees to Be Capped at 2%*, SPORTS AGENT BLOG, July 22, 2011, *at* http://www.sportsagentblog.com/2011/07/22/rumor-nfl-rookie-deal-agent-fees-to-be-capped-at-2/.

87. *Id.*

88. NBPA Regulations Governing Player Agents (as amended June, 1991), http://www.nbpa.org/sites/default/files/users/sean.brandveen/Agent%20Regulations%20PDF.pdf.

89. *Id.*

agents from earning a fee based on a client's contract that compensates him the minimum salary.[90] Also, unlike the NBPA and the NFLPA, the MLBPA does not impose a cap on the percentage of a player's contract that an agent can demand as his fee.[91] The standard agent commission in the representation of professional baseball players is 5 percent.[92] The NHLPA follows the MLBPA's model, which allows for the free market to determine a reasonable agent fee for the player to pay his representative for the services provided with regards to team contract negotiations.[93]

The main problem arises when professional athletes who approve, in writing, to pay said fees to their agents of record then fail to distribute the commissions when due, resulting in a great amount of grievances being filed by agents against players who often are already or will become former clients. For instance, the NBPA requires that any dispute between a player and his agent concerning the payment of agent fees for contracts negotiated by the agent (on behalf of the player) with an NBA team be arbitrated and initiated through the filing of a written grievance.[94] The outside "impartial" arbitrator who makes a decision as to the amount of fees, if any, that are due is selected by the NBPA.[95] These proceedings are commonly heard more expediently than they would be if filed in a court of law, and they often protect the parties from having their disputes become a public matter for consumption by outsiders. Many fee disputes that I have been involved in were resolved without a hearing. Often, the player has no defense for the nonpayment of agent fees and will settle the case prior to an actual hearing. Sometimes, the most difficult part of the process is collecting on the arbitration award or the out-of-arbitration settlement. Chasing around

---

90. *See* Darren Heitner, *Insight into Being a Baseball Agent*, SPORTS AGENT BLOG, Feb. 10, 2009, *at* http://www.sportsagentblog.com/2009/02/10/insight-into-being-a-baseball-agent/.

91. *Id.*

92. *Id.*

93. Diane Sudia & Rob Remis, *Ethical and Statutory Limitations on Athlete Agent Income: Fees, Referrals, and Ownership Interests*, 27 FLA. ST. U.L. REV. 787, 808 (2000).

94. *See* NBPA, *Regulations Governing Player Agents*, NBPA.ORG, as amended June 1991, *at* http://www.nbpa.org/sites/default/files/users/sean.brandveen/Agent%20Regulations%20PDF.pdf.

95. *Id.*

players for nonpaid fees is hardly a glorious job, but it is often part of the job description for a sports attorney.

The various players' associations' rules and regulations are not so expansive as to bring all disputes within the bounds of their mandatory arbitration proceedings. Sometimes, cases fall outside of arbitration and the grievance procedure, and the public gains access to the heart of the matters.

Case Study

Miami Sports Consulting, LLC v. Yasiel Balaguer

Miami Sports Consulting, LLC, managed by baseball agent Carlos Perez, was a visible representative of Cuban baseball players who have defected to the United States and wish to play professional baseball.[96] To woo clients to his agency, Perez would provide players thousands of dollars in loans.[97] In the case of young prospect Yasiel Balaguer, who signed a $400,000 contract with the Chicago Cubs organization, Miami Sports Consulting coughed up roughly $200,000 throughout their professional relationship.[98] The money was used to pay for Balaguer's housing, transportation, and many other "necessities" so that Balaguer could live comfortably and train his body in hopes that an MLB team would take interest in his talents. Balaguer terminated his agreement with Miami Sports Consulting and signed with baseball agent Jaime Torres prior to executing a deal with the Cubs.[99] The baseball player then failed to reimburse Miami Sports Consulting for the money lent and refused to pay the company any commission based on the contract he signed with the Cubs. The representation agreement stipulated that Miami Sports Consulting was entitled to 5 percent of Balaguer's professional baseball contract. Miami Sports Consulting filed a lawsuit against Balaguer in Miami-Dade County,

---

96. *See* Gus Garcia-Roberts, *Cuban Baseball Agents: Risks and Lies*, MIAMI NEW TIMES, Apr. 18, 2012, *at* http://www.miaminewtimes.com/2012-04-19/news/cuban-baseball-agent -carlos-perez-miami-sports-consulting-risks-and-lies/.

97. *Id.*

98. *Id.*

99. *Id.*

seeking compensation based on money lent, unjust enrichment, and breach of the representation agreement. Balaguer attempted to have the court dismiss the case based on a lack of jurisdiction. His claim was that the October 1, 2010, MLBPA Regulations Governing Player Agents require that Miami Sports Consulting's claim be brought in final and binding arbitration as opposed to the Circuit Court of Miami-Dade County. However, the court disagreed. It found that Miami Sports Consulting is not a "Player Agent" pursuant to the MLBPA Regulations Governing Player Agents because Perez is not certified by the MLBPA. According to the Regulations, "The capitalized term 'Player Agent' means *an individual who is certified by the MLBPA* and authorized thereby to engage in certain conduct, as more fully described in Sections 3(A) or 3(B)" (emphasis added).[100] The parties settled the lawsuit for an undisclosed amount of money shortly after the court denied Balaguer's motion to dismiss.

Agent/Agent Disputes

"What I've learned through my time in the business is that you can't worry about external factors. You just have to focus on being the best you can be."[101]
—Scott Boras, MLBPA player agent

Sports agents are not only constantly worried and preparing for potential disputes with their clientele; they are also concerned with their competition resorting to unethical and/or illegal means to compete in what is a cutthroat environment with low margins. Players' associations in the major

---

100. MLBPA Regulations Regarding Player Agents, http://reg.mlbpaagent.org/Documents /AgentForms/Agent%20Regulations.pdf.

101. *See Jay-Z Takes Shot at Veteran MLB Agent Scott Boras on New Album*, ESPN NEW YORK, July 4, 2013, *at* http://espn.go.com/new-york/mlb/story/_/id/9449111/jay-z-takes -shot-veteran-mlb-agent-scott-boras-new-album.

professional team sports in the United States have observed the often high-stakes, ultra dramatic tensions that arise between agents and have instituted mechanisms, including mandatory grievance procedures, to shift actual disputes out of the public sphere and into closed-door arbitration procedures. Disputes arising from the breach of noncompete provisions within agent employment contracts have already been addressed. This section will focus primarily on the contentious concern of client stealing.

An agent who loses a client to a rival should first consider whether an action against the beneficiary agent is worth the former agent's time and money. If the beneficiary agent earns the right to represent a Minor League Baseball player who fails to show up on any "top prospect" lists and poses a greater risk (in terms of cost to maintain as a client through equipment provisions) than reward (with regards to potential commissions on MLB contracts above the league's minimum salary requirement), an action against the beneficiary agent may not be economically worthwhile for the former agent. However, even if the departing player is set to negotiate a multimillion dollar contract, an action against the beneficiary agent may not be in the former agent's best interests because showing that the former client broke his agency contract to sign with the beneficiary agent will not amount to the required proof for a successful action within the economic tort known as tortious interference with contractual relations.

Case Study

Keith Glass v. Andy Miller

The dispute between basketball agents Keith Glass and Andy Miller arose through Miller's recruitment of former Rutgers Scarlet Knights basketball player Quincy Douby. Douby was the 19th overall selection in the 2006 NBA draft, selected by the Sacramento Kings. After performing under his rookie contract with the Kings, Douby had a short stint with an NBA Development League team and the Toronto Raptors. Thereafter, he played for a variety of teams overseas. Douby began his professional career as a client of Keith Glass. After his first season with the Kings, Douby terminated his representation agreement with Glass and signed with rival agent Andy Miller of ASM Sports.

Glass filed a grievance against Miller for purportedly tortiously interfering with the contractual relationship between Glass and Douby.
On July 24, 2010, arbitrator George Nicolau awarded Glass damages
in the amount of $40,000 for said interference. The arbitrator was
provided telephone records between Miller and a man whom Douby
described as someone who was like his "other father" while Douby
was still under contract with Glass.[102] Additionally, documentation
showed that one of Miller's employees had made a call to Douby
only nine minutes prior to Douby terminating his relationship with
his former agent.[103] The $40,000 awarded to Glass by the arbitrator
was described as damages based on what Glass could have anticipated to have earned from managing Douby's money in the final two
years of his contract.[104]

The business of sports agency is inherently competitive. Although rival
agents are constantly scouting players already under representation agreements with their competitors, players themselves are constantly shopping
around for new representation. Standard representation agreements provided by players' associations to licensed agents are valid, enforceable
contracts, but are also terminable at will.

When I was an agent and represented baseball players as chief executive
officer of Dynasty Athlete Representation, LLC, I was also writing articles
covering the business of sports agency at Sports Agent Blog.[105] As a watch-
dog of the industry, Sports Agent Blog not only highlighted the positives
but also sometimes the negatives concerning sports agents. One particular
article, "Howard Kusnick Charged with Conspiracy to Commit Wire Fraud,"
led to the subject's son hiring counsel to send me a "libel letter/take-down
notice," demanding that the article be removed and a retraction statement

102. *See* Howard Beck, *Tampering Leads to Rare Penalty against N.B.A. Agent*, N.Y.
TIMES, Sept. 17, 2010, *at* http://www.nytimes.com/2010/09/18/sports/basketball/18agent.html
?pagewanted=2&_r=4&hpw.
103. *Id.*
104. *Id.*
105. Found at http://www.sportsagentblog.com.

be posted. Upon my refusal to comply with his request, a lawsuit was filed against me with stated claims of libel, tortious interference, and an effort to enjoin any potential future defamatory speech I may utter or write. The plaintiff was Double Diamond Sports Management, Inc., which specifically alleged that I engaged in a conspiracy with my wholly owned Sports Agent Blog and Dynasty Athlete Representation to publish false and otherwise libelous remarks regarding Howard Kusnick's ties to Double Diamond Sports Management, Inc. Double Diamond also alleged that I intentionally interfered with its business relationships with clients by, among other unjustified actions, providing false and defamatory information to such clients via the Internet, encouraging said clients not to continue their relationships with Double Diamond, and inciting others to inappropriately approach and steal clients from Double Diamond. This example shows that it does not pay to file a tortious interference claim without justification for the underlying action. The court granted my motion to dismiss the complaint, and I filed a separate lawsuit against Double Diamond, its principal, and the company's legal counsel for abuse of process, malicious prosecution, and intentional infliction of emotional distress. That case settled with a payment to me that cannot be disclosed pursuant to the nondisclosure portion of the settlement agreement.

In the case of *Speakers of Sport, Inc. v. ProServ, Inc.*, 178 F.3d 862 (7th Cir. 1999), the plaintiff argued that rival agency ProServ was guilty of tortiously interfering with the plaintiff's contractual relations with MLB catcher Ivan Rodriguez. Specifically, the plaintiff alleged that ProServ invited Rodriguez to the agency's office and promised Rodriguez a threshold amount in endorsement money if he would switch agencies. ProServ was granted summary judgment, which was affirmed on appeal. The appellate court held that even though a contract may be terminable at will, inducing a player to terminate his contract with his former agency was still actionable under the tort law of Illinois. However, the court went on to say:

> Competition is not a tort, but on the contrary provides a defense (the "competitor's privilege") to the tort of improper interference. It does not privilege inducing a breach of contract, but it does privilege inducing the lawful termination of a contract that is terminable

at will. Sellers (including agents, who are sellers of services) do not "own" their customers, at least not without a contract with them that is not terminable at will.

The cause of action known as tortious interference with contractual relations is difficult to prove because there is a natural deference by arbitrators and courts of law to permit competition within all industries. However, it is not an impossible cause of action for agents to rely on, in collecting damages, when a rival *intentionally* interferes with an agency contract to the detriment of the former agent. Although there also exists a cause of action concerning the interference with an expectancy or an advantageous business relationship (in the absence of a contractual relationship between the parties), a true cause of action for tortious interference with contractual relations requires the existence of a valid contract. Two keys to the cause of action are that the beneficiary agent has actual knowledge of the former agent's rights under the former agency contract with the player and that the beneficiary intentionally interfered with those rights. Negligent interference does not constitute the tort of wrongful interference. The beneficiary agent may have an applicable defense if the former agent cannot prove that the beneficiary agent had knowledge of the former agent's agency contract with the player. Further, the former agent must prove that there was a lack of justification for the beneficiary agent's acts. Finally, without any proof of damages, the claim is suspect and not worth the time or energy of the former agent.

There is also a lingering question as to whether such claims may be properly filed in a court of law as opposed to through players' associations' respective mandatory grievance procedures, which typically require that all such agency vs. agency claims be presented to an arbitrator as opposed to a judge and/or jury. In 2009, prior to the later updated MLBPA Regulations Governing Player Agents (as amended effective October 1, 2010)[106] (which contains a provision that says the impartial, final, and binding arbitration

---

106. *See* MLBPA, *Agent Regulations*, MLBPAAGENT.ORG, *at* http://reg.mlbpaagent.org /Documents/AgentForms/Agent%20Regulations.pdf.

process provided shall be the exclusive method for resolving disputes between or among player agents and other player agents that relate to the representation of players), baseball agency Athletes Premier International, Inc. filed a lawsuit against rival agency Hendricks Sports Management, LP and included a count for tortious interference with contractual relations. The claim stated that Hendricks Sports Management knowingly and willfully induced Cincinnati Reds pitcher and Cuba defector Aroldis Chapman to terminate and breach the contract between Athletes Premier and Chapman. Athletes Premier alleged that Hendricks Sports made false and disparaging statements to Chapman about Athletes Premier and provided improper inducements to persuade Chapman to depart from Athletes Premier and sign with Hendricks Sports. The lawsuit, filed in a Massachusetts Superior Court, was settled out of court.

Although the Chapman case was adjudicated outside of baseball's arbitration system, a similar case may not withstand a motion to dismiss on jurisdictional grounds post-October 1, 2010, when the MLBPA Regulations Governing Player Agents were updated. However, said regulations do not include clear prohibitions or references to actions concerning tortious interference of contractual relations. This issue may come up in the future with new entrants into the sports agency industry who appear to have little care for torts grounded in improper efforts to compete. For instance, rapper Jay Z, who is now a certified agent with the MLBPA, was able to recruit New York Yankees second baseman Robinson Cano away from veteran agent Scott Boras in 2013. He later included Boras in song lyrics that read: "Scott Boras, you over baby. Robinson Cano, you coming with me."[107] Such blatant disregard for existing contractual relations may become a major issue that the MLBPA will have to confront in the future.

---

107. *See supra* note 99.

Chapter 4

Intellectual Property Matters

Does an athlete have an absolute right to own his or her domain name (i.e., should Miami Heat star LeBron James be able to require a third party to transfer www.LeBronJames.com no matter what type of use is made by the third party)? Can an athlete who wants to create her own clothing line use whatever images she wants on the T-shirts her newly formed company manufactures, markets, sells, and distributes? Regarding the name of the company the athlete created, does it matter whether it is confusingly similar to another brand of T-shirts already existing in commerce? And can a corporate entity use an athlete's image to advertise and promote its products and/or services without that athlete's consent and without compensating the athlete the fair market value for such use? The first question deals with trademark consideration, the second is the use of an athlete's publicity rights, or a right of publicity issue, the third is based in copyright, and the last concern is cybersquatting. Each type of intellectual property matter will be discussed at length within this chapter, starting with a section on trademarks.

Trademarks

"It's smart to reserve your trademark rights, even if you're not positive yet all the different uses that you're going to make [of them]. There aren't any ground rules, per se. It's usually organic. Once something does kind of stick,

then and there I kind of recommend that an athlete move forward as soon as possible with trademarking that name or logo."[1]
—Intellectual property lawyer Joseph Mandour

Trademark protection is a legal right designed to designate ownership over specific marks and prevent consumer confusion. Federal registration of trademarks is ensured and governed by the Lanham Act.[2] Trademark acquisition, protection, and enforcement tends to be a tricky section of the law, but highly relevant in the Sports Law context; thus, to protect clients from any issues that may come up as a result of third parties infringing on their marks or clients' use of marks that may infringe on those owned by others, it is important to have at least a general understanding of the subject. Although there is the potential for a trademark owner to receive what is known as common-law trademark protection (without the need of acquiring official federal registration of a mark), it is wise to encourage clients to formally apply to register any protectable mark through the U.S. Patent and Trademark Office[3] and conduct due diligence to compare the cost with potential added value of protecting marks in overseas markets where the goods and/or services are being sold.

There are four classifications of types of marks with which sports agents and attorneys should be familiar: (1) generic marks, (2) descriptive marks, (3) suggestive marks, and (4) arbitrary and fanciful marks.[4] Arbitrary and fanciful marks and suggestive marks are inherently distinctive and generally

---

1. *See* Doug Williams, *Athletes Trademarking the Phrase That Pays*, ESPN.com, July 13, 2012, *at* http://espn.go.com/blog/playbook/fandom/post/_/id/6108/athlete-trademarks -becoming-commonplace.

2. § 43(a) of the Trademark Act of 1946 (Lanham Act).

3. *See generally* Thrifty Rent-A-Car System v. Thrift Cars, Inc., 831 F.2d 1177 (case where an issue arose with a similar mark being used after Thrift failed to register and put Thrifty on notice.); *see also* Park 'N Fly, Inc. v. Dollar Park & Fly, Inc., 469 US 189 (1985) (another benefit to registering a mark is to eventually gain "incontestable status" on a descriptive mark, an option not possible absent a formal registration with the U.S. Patent and Trademark Office); *see also* Eastman Kodak Co. v. Bell & Howell Doc. Mgt. Products Co., 994 F.2d 1569 (1993) (another benefit to filing a mark is the option to make a showing of an "intent to use," which puts potential infringers on notice of the mark in advance).

4. *See* Abercrombie & Fitch Co. v. Hunting World, Inc., 537 F.2d 4 (1976).

have no relation to the business or product they provide.[5] An example is the trademark "Apple" being used by a company involved with computers and technology. A descriptive mark does exactly as the term implies and describes the mark; these types of marks are only protectable upon a showing that they have acquired a secondary meaning.[6] Otherwise, they are deemed to simply describe a feature, characteristic, or purpose of function of the applicant's goods and/or services and thus the mark's registration will be refused. "A mark may be merely descriptive even if it does not describe the 'full scope and extent' of the applicant's goods or services."[7] Generic marks are not protectable at all.[8]

To succeed in an action for trademark infringement (once it has been established that the mark is protectable), a plaintiff must establish that there is a likelihood of consumer confusion as a result of the defendant's use of the mark.[9] To do so, most courts have adopted a balancing test that was largely spawned by the *Polaroid* case.[10] This test incorporates eight factors for the court to analyze so as to determine whether or not there is a likelihood of confusion: (1) strength of the plaintiff's mark, (2) similarity of uses, (3) proximity of the products or services, (4) likelihood that the prior owner will expand into the domain of the other, (5) actual confusion, (6) the defendant's good or bad faith in using the plaintiff's mark (intent), (7) the quality of the junior user's product or services, and (8) the sophistication of

---

5. *See, i.e.,* Eastman Kodak Co. v. Weil, 137 Misc. 506, 243 N.Y.S. 319 (1930) (the term *Kodak* is properly classified as an arbitrary and fanciful term for photographic supplies); *see also* Abercrombie & Fitch Co. v. Hunting World, Inc., 537 F.2d 4, 9 (1976) (to define an arbitrary and fanciful mark, the court used the term *ivory* as an example as it is applied to soap).

6. *See* International Kennel Club of Chicago, Inc. v. Mighty Star, Inc., 846 F.2d 1079 1987 (describing the steps to determine whether a secondary meaning has been developed: survey data to show whether the public has come to identify the term with a particular product or service, amount of money spent on advertising, etc.).

7. *In re Oppedahl & Larson LLP,* 373 F.3d 1171, 1173, 71 USPQ2d 1370, 1371 (Fed. Cir. 2004) (citing *In re Dial-A-Mattress Operating Corp.,* 240 F.3d 1341, 1346, 57 USPQ2d 1807, 1812 (Fed. Cir. 2001)); TMEP §1209.01(b).

8. *See* King-Seeley Thermos Co. v. Aladdin Industries, Inc., 321 F.2d 577 (1963) (finding that the term *thermos* had become a generic term of a vacuum-insulated container after the public at large had begun to use the term to describe all items of that sort, rather than strictly the item sold by Thermos. "Thermos" was thereafter removed from the trademark registry.).

9. *See* Universal City Studios, Inc. v. Nintendo Co., Ltd., 746 F.2d 112 (1985).

10. *See* Polaroid Corp. v. Polara Electronics Corp., 287 F.2d 492 (2nd Cir. 1961).

the relevant consumers. In the context of sports, trademark cases have come up regarding the use of team logos,[11] team colors,[12] and even team names.[13]

Case Study

Indianapolis Colts, Inc. v. Metro. Baltimore Football

In 1953, the Dallas Texans, a National Football League (NFL) team, went bankrupt and moved to Baltimore, where the team was renamed the Baltimore Colts.[14] More than 30 years later, the team once again moved, this time to Indianapolis, where the team was renamed the Indianapolis Colts.[15] The citizens of Baltimore were outraged by the move, which took place in the dead of night and was accomplished in a very discreet manner.[16] The city of Baltimore went as far as to try to bring suit against the NFL so as to prevent the move, but the effort was unsuccessful.[17] Nine years later, the Canadian Football League (CFL) came calling. The CFL established a team in Baltimore and attempted to name the club the Baltimore Colts.[18] Once

---

11. *See* Board of Supervisors of Louisiana State University v. Smack Apparel Company (2006) (a group of NCAA schools brought a trademark infringement suit against an apparel company that was creating T-shirts that featured the schools' team logos and team colors).

12. *Id.*

13. *See* Pro-Football, Inc. v. Harjo, 284 F. Supp. 2d 96 (2003). (In September 1992, Harjo and six other Native Americans brought suit against the NFL to cancel six trademarks associated with the Washington Redskins. Plaintiffs argued the use of the term *Redskins* is scandalous and offensive to Native Americans, in violation of § 2(a) of the Lanham Trademark Act of 1946.)

14. *See* http://www.colts.com/team/history.html. ("On January 23, 1953, under the principal ownership of Carroll Rosenbloom, the NFL's Dallas Texans franchise was moved to Baltimore where, keeping the "Colts" nickname, the Texans team colors of blue and white were inherited.")

15. *See* Candus Thomson, *Colts Leave Town: Getting the Story Straight*, BALTIMORE SUN, Mar. 29, 2009, *at* http://www.baltimoresun.com/sports/ravens/bal-sp.coltsmyths29mar29,0,3257615.story. (The author explains, in detail, the controversial move where the Colts fled from Baltimore and headed to Indianapolis in the middle of a "snowy December night.")

16. *Id.*

17. *Id.* ("A legal battle ensued, which ultimately reached the U.S. Supreme Court, and bills were filed in both the U.S. House and Senate seeking to block the move.")

18. *See* Ken Murray, *NFL Throws Legal Block at CFL Colts*, BALTIMORE SUN, Apr. 30, 1994, *at* http://articles.baltimoresun.com/1994-04-30/news/1994120077_1_colts-speros-cfl. (The article quotes NFL spokesman Greg Aiello saying the CFL is "obviously trading on the

the NFL heard of the name, it threatened the CFL with a lawsuit.[19] As a result, the CFL renamed the team the Baltimore CFL Colts.[20] The NFL demanded that the name be changed altogether, and when the CFL did not comply with the NFL's request, the league filed suit against the CFL, alleging trademark infringement under the Lanham Act.[21] The NFL conducted a study and used consumer surveys as evidence to prove that consumer confusion was present as a result of the CFL's similar team name. The court ruled for the NFL, and an injunction was issued by the court, which prevented the CFL from continuing to use the team name Baltimore CFL Colts.

The trademarking process can also serve as an important tool for individual athletes who wish to protect certain trademarks that have inherently become associated with them or their public personas. For instance, when Washington Redskins quarterback Robert Griffin III won the coveted Heisman Trophy as a member of the Baylor football team, Griffin said that the moment was "unbelievably believable." That phrase became associated with Griffin, and the quarterback, under his limited liability company, Thr3escompany, decided to file for a federal trademark registration of the phrase for the specific use in "promoting the goods and services of others, sponsorship of sports and athletic events and activities."[22] Griffin's limited liability company also filed applications to protect the terms *RGIII*, *RG3*, *Robert Griffin III*, *Know Your Why*, *Light You Up*, *Go Catch Your Dream*, *No Pressure No Diamonds*, and many other phrases for a wide range of

---

name built up by the NFL team. They're using the goodwill built up by the Colts, what is now the Indianapolis Colts.")

19. *See* Indianapolis Colts, Inc. v. Metro. Baltimore Football, 34 F.3d 410 (1994).
20. *Id.*
21. *See generally* Indianapolis Colts, Inc. v. Metro. Baltimore Football, 34 F.3d 410 (1994).
22. *See* Brent Jones, *RGIII Trademarks Name, 'Unbelievably Believable,'* USA Today, May 9, 2012, *at* http://content.usatoday.com/communities/thehuddle/post/2012/05/report-redskins-robert-griffin-iii-trademarking-name-phrase-unbelievably-believable/1?csp=34sports&utm_source=twitterfeed&utm_medium=twitter&utm_campaign=USA&utm_content=NFL+NEWS&utm_term=NFL+NEWS#.UhzNELxrUwx.

apparel, including shirts, sweatshirts, jackets, pants, shorts, and footwear.[23] So far, none of the 14 trademark applications filed by Thr3escompany has received a registration number from the U.S. Patent and Trademark Office.

Although Griffin was more concerned with securing trademark protection for his name, nicknames, and catchphrases, former number one overall National Basketball Association (NBA) Draft selection Anthony Davis thought that it would be a good idea to earn protection for an item on his face, specifically his very noticeable unibrow. Instead of taking the steps necessary to remove the unibrow, which is a feature many people abhor, Davis thought that he should make some money from its overt presence. He filed federal trademark applications for the terms *Fear the Brow* and *Raise the Brow* to cover many different international classes, including those that cover apparel, charitable services, entertainment services, appliances, accessories, and hygienic products.[24]

Then there is the ever-popular "Johnny Football" nickname that became closely affiliated with Texas A&M quarterback and Heisman Trophy winner Johnny Manziel. Manziel's family and Texas A&M actively sought to trademark the nickname after an unrelated third party attempted to apply for federal registration of the Johnny Football trademark.[25] Similar to Griffin, Manziel set up a limited liability company to hold his intellectual property and filed for protection of the nickname in the apparel, educational, and entertainment services categories. His holding company even filed a lawsuit against a claimed infringer soon after filing for trademark protection.[26] The alleged infringing use was by a third-party company selling T-shirts containing the phrase, "Keep Calm and Johnny Football."[27] Yet, for all the efforts undertaken by Manziel and his advisors to protect the

---

23. *Id.*

24. *See* Darren Rovell, *Anthony Davis Trademarks His Brow*, CNBC, June 25, 2012, *at* http://www.cnbc.com/id/47951613.

25. *See* Darren Rovell, *Johnny Manziel Family to Trademark 'Johnny Football,'* ESPN .COM, Nov. 11, 2012, *at* http://espn.go.com/college-football/story/_/id/8619087/johnny-manziel-family-trademark-johnny-football.

26. *See* Paul Myerberg, *Manziel's Corporation Files Lawsuit to Protect 'Johnny Football,'* USA TODAY, Feb. 25, 2013, *at* http://www.usatoday.com/story/gameon/2013/02/25/johnny-manziel-files-lawsuit-johnny-football-phrase/1946701/.

27. *Id.*

Johnny Football trademark via the USPTO's trademark application filing system, as of September 2013, Manziel's limited liability company had not received registration for the mark.[28] Meanwhile, that same month an individual not affiliated with or related to Manziel earned the registration for "Juanito Fútbol" to be used in commerce in connection with hats, jerseys, sweatshirts and, t-shirts.[29]

Right of Publicity

"Players should profit from such business transactions once their eligibility has ended. When did it become the right of the NCAA to sell me into perpetuity?"[30]
—Sonny Vaccaro, former Reebok senior director of Grassroots Basketball

The right of publicity is an intellectual property right that has emerged from state law, with the goal of protecting the commercial interests of public figures.[31] To bring a valid right of publicity claim against an offender, a plaintiff must show that (1) the defendant used the plaintiff's identity, (2) the use was for the purpose of commercial gain, (3) it was without consent, and (4) the plaintiff suffered monetary harm as a result.[32]

Prior to 1953, there was no such thing as a right of publicity. However, over time, it has made its way into a number of sports-related cases. The first known Sports Law case to recognize such a right was *Haelan Laboratories, Inc. v. Topps Chewing Gum, Inc.*[33] Haelan made chewing gum

---

28. *See* Darren Heitner, *Johnny Manziel's Trademark Battle: Johnny Football Vs. Juanito Futbol*, FORBES.COM, Sept. 14, 2013, *at* http://www.forbes.com/sites/darrenheitner/2013/09/14/johnny-manziels-trademark-battle-johnny-football-vs-juanito-futbol/.
29. *Id.*
30. *See Basketball Guru Vaccaro Lashes Out against NBA, NCAA*, SPORTSBUSINESS DAILY, Sept. 20, 2007, *at* http://www.sportsbusinessdaily.com/Daily/Issues/2007/09/Issue-7/Sports-Industrialists/Basketball-Guru-Vaccaro-Lashes-Out-Against-NBA-NCAA.aspx.
31. *See* Zacchini v. Scripps-Howard Broadcasting Co., 433 U.S. 562, 573 (1977) (the court defined the right of publicity as one that protects "the proprietary interest of the individual in his act in part to encourage such entertainment").
32. *See* Hilton v. Hallmark Cards, 599 F.3d 894, 909 (2010).
33. Haelan Laboratories v. Topps Chewing Gum, 202 F.2d 866, 868 (2d. Cir. 1953).

and entered into a contract with sports figures for the exclusive rights to use their images on baseball cards to be included with the gum.[34] However, despite the expected exclusivity, Topps began using the same types of baseball cards with its own gum.[35] In response, Haelan brought suit against Topps to enjoin the company from infringing on what Haelan believed to be a valid, exclusive license.[36] The court, in an attempt to rule in favor of Haelan once the realization occurred that a tortious interference claim would not stand, came up with the idea of the common-law right of publicity.[37] The court recognized the need for a right of publicity with regard to professional athletes, being that the inability of these athletes to protect their publicity rights (which include their names, images, voices, and likenesses) could have a chilling effect and that athletes would no longer have the same interest in being viewed in the public sphere.

On the other end of the spectrum, Tiger Woods was defeated in a right of publicity suit he filed against an artist who included Woods's image in one of his paintings without permission from the professional golfer.[38] In *ETW Corp. v. Jireh Publishing*, the court ruled against Woods, explaining that because the artwork in question contained paintings of other golfers in conjunction with his image, it met the "transformative element" requirement and was protected by the first amendment to the U.S. Constitution.[39] The artwork depicted Woods with other golf legends as being "part of their world."[40] In addition to a ruling for the artist, the court used language that seemed to indicate that because Woods was handsomely compensated for playing the game of golf and did not depend on his right of publicity earnings as a source of his livelihood, the balance of equity should be shifted in favor of the artist.[41]

---

34. *Id.*
35. *Id.*
36. *Id.*
37. *Id.*
38. ETW Corp. v. Jireh Pub., Inc., 332 F.3d 915, 928 (6th Cir. 2003).
39. *Id.*
40. *Id.*
41. *Id.*

Another relevant Sports Law case involving right of publicity was *C.B.C. Distribution & Marketing, Inc. v. MLB Advanced Media.*[42] This case involved the company C.B.C. Distribution (CBC), which operated a fantasy sports website.[43] When MLB Advanced Media (MLBAM) denied CBC the license to use the publicity rights of Major League Baseball players in its fantasy games, CBC filed suit, arguing that the player names, statistics, and images needed to participate in the game did not require a license.[44] The court ruled in favor of CBC, reasoning that (1) the economic interests of the players would not be completely harmed by CBC's use of their likenesses because they were still making a generous amount of money playing baseball, (2) the information used was in the public domain, and (3) the public would not be confused into believing that the players were actually endorsing the fantasy game operated by CBC.[45]

Case Study

Mike Spinner v. Bell Sports, Inc. and Easton-Bell Sports, Inc.

In December 2012, my client and bicycle motocross (BMX) athlete Mike Spinner filed suit against Bell Sports, Inc. and Easton-Bell Sports, Inc. alleging that the companies violated his right to publicity. Specifically, Spinner stated that the defendants continued to use his name and likeness in connection with the advertisement, promotion, and marketing of their products on a widespread basis after the conclusion of an endorsement agreement that had given the defendants' rights to do same (as long as they received prior approval of the particular usage of Spinner's publicity rights that were granted). The lawsuit, which was examined by the U.S. District Court for the Southern District of Florida, detailed the defendants' use of Spinner's

---

42. C.B.C. Distribution & Marketing, Inc. v. Major League Baseball Advanced Media, 505 F.3d 818, 822 (8th Cir. 2007).
43. *Id.*
44. *Id.*
45. *Id.*

name and likeness, which included usage on their website and in-store advertisements. In particular, Spinner documented a Sports Authority in-store advertisement for a "Bell Faction Multi-Sport Helmet." Spinner's single-count complaint was based on a violation of Florida's plaintiff-friendly right of publicity statute, Florida Statute Section 540.08, which entitles a prevailing plaintiff to a reasonable royalty, plus the potential recovery of exemplary damages and/or punitive damages. Spinner asked for a total of $800,000. The matter settled prior to trial for an undisclosed sum of money.

Copyright

"Only one thing is impossible for God: to find any sense in any copyright law on the planet . . . . Whenever a copyright law is to be made or altered, then the idiots assemble."[46]
—Mark Twain, American author and humorist

Copyright is an area of law embodied within the U.S. Constitution.[47] Article I, Section 8 of the Constitution gives Congress the power "[t]o promote the Progress of Science and useful Arts, by securing for limited Times to Authors and Inventors the exclusive Right to their respective Writings and Discoveries."[48] The Copyright Act of 1976, in a general sense, protects "original works of authorship fixed in any tangible medium of expression."[49] Under the Copyright Act, to establish a copyright infringement claim, a plaintiff must show the existence of two elements: (1) ownership of a valid

---

46. *See The Law: Righting Copyright,* TIME MAGAZINE, Nov. 1, 1976, *at* http://www.time.com/time/magazine/article/0,9171,914652,00.html.
47. *See* U.S. Const. Art. I, § 8.
48. U.S. Const. Art. I, § 8, cl. 8.
49. 17 U.S.C. § 102(a) (1988).

copyright[50] and (2) actionable copying by the defendant of constituent elements of the work that are original.[51]

Once a plaintiff has sufficiently demonstrated the existence of both elements, the court must then consider any affirmative defenses presented by the defendant. The most popular defense used by defendants in Sports Law copyright cases is the fair use defense.[52] The fair use doctrine permits use of copyrighted material (in certain circumstances) that would ordinarily be considered copyright infringement but for the existence of certain factors.[53] Three different types of works are protected by the fair use doctrine under 17 U.S.C § 107: (1) comment or criticism, (2) education, and (3) news reporting.[54] The majority of Sports Law cases involve the third element, news reporting.[55] In fact, in the realm of sports, a large number of copyright cases have involved the legality of broadcasting rights with respect to televised games.[56]

---

50. *See* Norma Ribbon & Trimming, Inc. v. Little, 51 F.3d 45, 47 (5th Cir. 1995). (The first element, ownership of a valid copyright, is established by (1) proving the originality and copyright-ability of the material and (2) compliance with the statutory formalities.)

51. *See* Bridgmon v. Array Systems, 325 F.3d 572, 576 (5th Cir. 2003). (The second element, proof of actionable copying, is established by proving that (1) the defendant factually copied the protected material and (2) there is a "substantial similarity" between the two works.)

52. *See* 17 U.S.C. § 107.

53. *See, e.g.,* Campbell v. Acruff-Rose Music, Inc. 510 U.S. 569, 575 (1994) (discussing that the defendant's song "Oh, Pretty Woman" would be an infringement of the plaintiff's rights under the Copyright Act, "but for a finding of fair use through parody").

54. 17 U.S.C. § 107.

55. *See, e.g.,* National Basketball Ass'n v. Motorola, Inc., 105 F.3d 841 (1997). (Motorola and STATS, Inc. developed a pager device that provided real-time event scores to those users of the product. The NBA brought suit under copyright infringement and misappropriation, but the court made clear that sporting events themselves are not copyrightable and that the statistics and other real-time information being delivered to the public fall within the news-worthy exception.)

56. *See, e.g.,* Nat. Football League v. McBee & Bruno's, Inc., 792 F.2d 726 (1986). (The NFL and the St. Louis (football) Cardinals brought a copyright suit against the owners of "several St. Louis restaurants." The plaintiffs alleged that the owners violated federal copyright by showing "Cardinals' home games which had been 'blacked out'" in their restaurants by picking up signals using satellite antennae.). *See also* Baltimore Orioles v. Major League Baseball Players, 805 F.2d 663 (1986). (The case involved a dispute between MLB team owners and the MLPA "regarding the ownership of the broadcast rights of the players' performances during major league baseball games." The players alleged that the MLB and various cable companies should not be able to show telecasts of games without the players' consent.)

Because the majority of copyright cases in Sports Law involve the ownership of broadcasting rights and information within the public domain (e.g., game footage and statistics), it is important to understand the landmark case that sets much of the precedent in this area: *Associated Press v. International News*. It is the first U.S. Supreme Court case that addressed the newsworthy exception of the fair use defense.[57] In *Associated Press*, the plaintiff Associated Press (AP) was putting in the work to gather and report the news.[58] After the news was reported on the East Coast, the defendant, International News, was taking that same news, summarizing it in its own words, and reprinting it by the time that AP's reporting of such news made its way to the West Coast.[59]

The court ruled that even though news itself is not copyrightable because it is the "history of the day," AP held a quasi-property right over the news that it reports.[60] Based on the economic value of the news, the company that does the initial reporting has a limited proprietary interest in the content and may protect against a competitor that tries to take an unfair advantage of the information.[61] The public policy line of thinking is that although there

---

57. *See* Internat'l News Serv. v. Assoc. Press, 248 US 215 (1918). (The court stated that the question of "whether one who has gathered general information or news at pains and expense [...] has such an interest in its publication" has been raised "many times, although never, perhaps, in the precise form" as it was in this case.)

58. *Id.* at 229. (The court, in describing AP, stated it "gathers in all parts of the world, by means of various instrumentalities of its own, by exchange with its members, and by other appropriate means, news and intelligence of current and recent events of interest to newspaper readers and distributes it daily to its members for publication in their newspapers.")

59. *Id.* at 231. (AP brought suit against International News because they were "copying news from bulletin boards and from early editions" of AP's newspapers and "selling this, either bodily or after rewriting it" to their own customers.)

60. *Id.* at 234. ("But the news element—the information respecting current events contained in the literary production—is not the creation of the writer, but is a report of matters that ordinarily are *publici juris*; it is the *history of the day*. It is not to be supposed that the framers of the Constitution, when they empowered Congress 'to promote the progress of science and useful arts, by securing for limited times to authors and inventors the exclusive right to their respective writings and discoveries,' intended to confer upon one who might happen to be the first to report a historic event the exclusive right for any period to spread the knowledge of it.") (Emphasis added.)

61. *Id.* at 245. (The court found that AP had a right to restrain International News from "any taking or gainfully using" of AP's news, "either bodily or in substance, from bulletins issued by the complainant or any of its members, or from editions of their newspapers," until the "commercial value" of the hot topics and breaking news has "passed away.")

is a justifiable interest to want the public to be informed of news and current events, there is a more significant benefit in rewarding those who put in the time, effort, and energy to deliver such information in an expedient manner. Granting news outlets the unfettered right to use the work of competitors without providing just compensation for said use would create a slippery slope and have a chilling effect that could potentially lead to less time, effort, and energy being put in to collect the news, thus depriving the public of valuable, timely information.

Compare *Associated Press* with the more recent case of *New Boston Television v. ESPN*. All sports fans should be familiar with ESPN's flagship *Sportscenter* television program and its highlights of sporting event broadcasts, which are collected and compiled from other television stations across the country, both local and national.[62] At the time that the *New Boston Television* case went to trial, New Boston Television (NBT) had the exclusive right to broadcast Boston Red Sox and Boston Bruins games. ESPN would rebroadcast NBT's recordings of the games and feature the highlight segments created by NBT. NBT was not pleased and filed suit against ESPN, alleging copyright infringement.[63]

ESPN attempted to use the newsworthy exception under the fair use doctrine in an effort to avoid copyright infringement liability.[64] The court ruled that although the public has a right to be informed of the news and current events, ESPN does not have the right to use the plaintiff's *expression*.[65] In other words, although it is permissible to use the footage of the

---

62. *See New Boston Television, Inc., v. Entertainment Sports Programming Network, Inc.*, 215 U.S.P.Q. (BNA) 755 (Mass. 1981). (The court describes Sportscenter as a television program "composed of highlights of current sporting events." In the pleadings, ESPN admitted that the highlights used on Sportscenter "are obtained by taping sports broadcasts of regular television stations from the public airwaves.")

63. *Id.* (New Boston Television brought a copyright infringement suit against ESPN claiming that ESPN's conduct in "videotaping, excerpting, and distributing portions of their copyrighted films, and the cable system defendants' conduct in broadcasting these excerpts constitute an infringement of their exclusive copyright under federal law.")

64. *Id.* (ESPN asserted that because its use in showing New Boston Television's footage was "primarily for news purposes" it should be "protected by the fair use doctrine in order to assure the public's right of access to newsworthy information.")

65. *Id.* (The court stated that "while protection of the public right of access to such information is a primary justification for the fair use defense, this right is sufficiently protected merely by enabling defendants to report the underlying facts which the plaintiff's videotapes record.")

games, ESPN (or any other network) cannot simply show the compilation of the highlights created by a third party.[66]

Another recently filed case dealt with claims made by seven photographers who claimed that the NFL, Replay Photos, Getty Images, and the Associated Press used the photographers' photos in violation of their copyrights and in conjunction with the NFL's advertisements, news, promotions, and products.[67] The plaintiffs alleged that Getty Images and the Associated Press encouraged the NFL to commercially use the copyrighted photos without seeking the consent of the photographers and sought statutory damages for what they alleged to be willful infringement.[68]

In addition to the traditional copyright issues relating to broadcasting, footage, and photography of sporting events, a more recent controversy has come up regarding the tattoos athletes bear and the issue of who owns the rights to them.

Case Study

Athlete Tattoos

NFL's San Francisco 49ers quarterback Colin Kaepernick, whose tattoos (along with his strong arm and accuracy) have aided his immense rise in popularity among sports fans, was featured in a Yahoo! Fantasy Sports advertisement that prominently showcased his body ink.[69] In the commercial, Kaepernick is situated in a tattoo artist's chair while holding a tablet featuring the Yahoo! Fantasy Football app.[70] Although it may concern some branding experts that Kaepernick's tattoos will detract from his brand, there may be a more pressing legal issue regarding the tattoos on his body, which are

---

66. *Id.* (The court stated that even though ESPN does have a right to report the news found within the footage of the games in question, it cannot "appropriate the plaintiff's expression of that information by copying the plaintiff's films themselves.")

67. *See* Darren Heitner, *Is The NFL Committing Copyright Infringement by Using Photos Without Consent?*, FORBES.COM, Oct. 23, 2013, *at* http://www.forbes.com/sites/darrenheitner /2013/10/23/is-the-nfl-committing-copyright-infringement-by-using-photos-without-consent/.

68. *Id.*

69. *See* http://www.youtube.com/watch?v=UQse_JHkb_4.

70. *Id.*

featured throughout the presentation.[71] The ink issue presents the question of who owns the copyrights to the images depicted by the tattoos on NFL athletes' bodies? Although the issue is only beginning to garner attention in the world of sports, copyright ownership of body ink was the subject of a lawsuit between S. Victor Whitmill and Warner Brothers after the movie *Hangover 2* featured a tattoo on actor Ed Helm's face that mirrored the tattoo that Whitmill had designed for Mike Tyson.[72] The case between Whitmill and Warner Brothers wound up settling out of court,[73] which leaves unresolved the question of who owns the copyrights to tattoos: the artist or the recipient? Absent a signed work-for-hire agreement between the two, it is likely that a court would rule that the copyright actually remains with the artist or the artist's employer.[74] That conclusion may be altered if the image itself is created by the athlete and then given to the artist to copy onto the body of the athlete. Although it is possible that the fair use defense would be valid, Electronic Arts and other companies using athletes' likenesses in commerce would be prudent to shield themselves as best as possible from potential liability. In addition, agents should advise any clients interested in getting a tattoo to bring a release with them and have the artist sign the release before entering any ink.

---

71. *See* Darren Heitner, *Questions Concerning Copyright of Athlete Tattoos Has Companies Scrambling*, FORBES.COM, Aug.14, 2013, *at* http://www.forbes.com/sites/darrenheitner /2013/08/14/questions-concerning-copyright-of-athlete-tattoos-has-companies-scrambling.

72. *See* Josh Grossberg, *Did Hangover II Rip Off Tyson Tattoo?* EONLINE, Apr. 29, 2011, *at* http://www.eonline.com/news/239366/did-hangover-ii-rip-off-tyson-tattoo. ("The ink mastermind who came up with Mike Tyson's famous facial tattoo has filed suit against Warner Bros., accusing the studio of ripping him off via a very similar-looking design on Ed Helms' mug in the upcoming *The Hangover Part II*.")

73. *See* Claudia Rosenbaum, *"Hangover 2" Tattoo Lawsuit Settled*, TODAY.COM, June 20, 2011, *at* http://www.today.com/id/43472637/ns/today-today_entertainment/t /hangover-tattoo-lawsuit-settled/#.UhVCXrxrUwy.

74. *See* Heitner, *supra* note 71.

Cybersquatting

"Some people collect jewelry, I like domain names."[75]
—J. Taikwok Yung, purchaser of domain names that feature Donald Trump's name

In 1999, the Anticybersquatting Consumer Protection Act became a federal law that armed the proprietors of domain names with a cause of action against those squatting on the trademark owned by another and/or another's personal name. It not only empowered victims with the ability to sue violators so that they must transfer the domain name to the rightful owner, it also provided the potential of monetary relief for those harmed. The monetary damages available include either actual damages or those imposed by the statute, and they also allow a plaintiff to attempt to recover his or her fees and costs involved with litigating the cybersquatting matter.

Wronged individuals and entities have the option of using an alternative to the U.S. judicial system in an effort to rectify any wrong committed by a cybersquatter. The Uniform Domain Name Dispute Resolution Policy does not allow a trademark owner to receive monetary relief from a cybersquatter infringing on the mark; however, it presents the option of an expedited administrative proceeding to cancel or transfer a domain name to its rightful owner. This proceeding, which is governed by the Internet Corporation for Assigned Names and Numbers, is often more cost-effective for cybersquatting victims.

Case Study

Manchester United Falls Victim to Cybersquatting
In 2000, a "self-confessed internet gold-digger" registered several soccer domain names, one of which happened to be

---

75. *See* Richard Schapiro, *Donald Trump Sues Brooklyn Man for $400,000 over Disparaging Websites*, N.Y. Daily News, Mar. 29, 2013, *at* http://www.nydailynews.com/new-york/trump-sues-b-klyn-man-400k-websites-article-1.1303096.

manchesterunitedfc.com.[76] It just so happens that the culprit, 31-year-old Paul Averkiou, was a fan of rival team Arsenal and admitted that there was a "certain amount of revenge" involved in his decision to purchase the URL.[77] Manchester United threatened legal action against Averkiou for what it believed was a domain address that rightfully belonged to the soccer club.[78] However, no such action was ever actually taken.[79] The Manchester United marketing manager said that the team had "no intention" of buying the URL, but it would "take whatever action is necessary to protect interests against people trying to pass themselves off" as its organization moving forward.[80]

Celebrities and athletes are easy targets for individuals who believe that they have the right to snatch up any domain name without consequence. The most well-known instance of an athlete standing up for the right to own his or her own name in URL form is the case of *Chris Bosh v. Luis Zavala and Hoopology.com.*[81] In July 2008, Bosh filed an action for cybersquatting against the defendants for their registration and use of the ChrisBosh.com domain name and within the complaint highlighted Zavala's extensive history of abusive domain name registrations. Bosh included an exhibit listing off almost 800 domain names registered by the defendants in an effort to demonstrate to the court that the scheme was far-reaching. URLs owned by the defendants included other basketball player names, such as Steve Nash, Shawn Marion,

76. *See* Faisal Alani, *Cybersquatting Cases: Number 3—Manchester United*, COMPUTERWEEKLY.COM, Mar. 17, 2009, *at* http://www.computerweekly.com/photostory/2240107814/Photos-Top-ten-cybersquatter-cases/8/Cybersquatting-cases-Number-3-Manchester-United#contentCompress.
77. *See Man Utd 'for sale' on internet*, BBC NEWS, Feb. 22, 2000, *at* http://news.bbc.co.uk/2/hi/uk_news/652062.stm.
78. *See* Faisal Alani, *Cybersquatting Cases: Number 3—Manchester United*, COMPUTERWEEKLY.COM, Mar. 17, 2009, *at* http://www.computerweekly.com/photostory/2240107814/Photos-Top-ten-cybersquatter-cases/8/Cybersquatting-cases-Number-3-Manchester-United#contentCompress.
79. *Id.*
80. *Id.*
81. Bosh v. Zavala, No. 08-04851 (C.D. Cal. Sept. 24, 2009).

Sam Cassell, Ray Allen, and Kirk Hinrich.[82] Importantly, Bosh was able to prove that the defendants not only were squatting on the players' domain names, but were also profiting from the ownership of the URLs through paid advertisements contained on the websites. Such profiting was an indicator of bad faith, which is an important element in cybersquatting litigation. Bosh was awarded $120,000 in damages, but instead asked the court to transfer the roughly 800 domain names illegally owned by the defendants so that he could distribute them to their rightful owners.[83]

Athletes should be careful before jumping to the conclusion that any third party that owns their name as a URL is immediately guilty of cybersquatting. Domain names that are similar or the same to trademarked names and phrases are not illegal per se. Bad faith is a key element that must be proven by the plaintiff. I once represented the owner of BrittneyGriner.com. My client had the intention of using the domain name to create a fan page for the former Baylor national champion and current starter for the Women's National Basketball Association's Phoenix Mercury. However, my client also saw an opportunity to avoid spending the countless hours to build and constantly update the fan site and instead offered the domain to Brittney Griner in exchange for a payment. After good faith discussions, we came to an agreement on price, and the domain name was transferred to Griner, who currently uses the URL for her official website. This situation shows how a Sports Lawyer can avoid unnecessary legal confrontation if or she is willing to explore opportunities for amicable resolution.

Although I had success negotiating a transfer of domain name for an athlete client, there was to be no amicable resolution between the NBA's Brooklyn Nets and Cyber Mesa Computer Systems, which is the owner of Nets.com. The valuable domain name was purchased by Cyber Mesa prior to NBA Media Ventures, LLC (the owner of all NBA team domain names) attempting to become its registrant. The Nets expressed interest in

---

82. *See List of Domain Names Awarded to Chris Bosh in Cybersquatting Case, at* http://www.winston.com/images/content/1/6/v2/1604/2335-ATTACH.pdf.

83. *See* Chris Herring, *NBA's Chris Bosh Gets Legal Slam Dunk, Then Plays Team Ball,* Wall Street J., Oct. 14, 2009, *at* http://blogs.wsj.com/law/2009/10/14/nbas-chris-bosh-gets-legal-slam-dunk-then-plays-team-ball/.

acquiring the domain only to receive a demand of $5 million in exchange for the transfer of the URL.[84] Nets management said that the demand was so exorbitant that it would not be taken into consideration.[85] While the Nets may not have had any interest in spending millions of dollars to acquire a domain name, other professional sports organizations and/or leagues may be able to justify such a high price tag for a valuable URL. For instance, in the beginning of 2013, MLB purchased the domain name Rockies.com for an initially reported amount of $1.2 million, which was later retracted after MLB Advanced Media stated that the price tag was inaccurate; however, it is believed to be at or near the amount of money actually paid for the transfer of the domain.[86] The URL was formerly owned by the Canadian tourism portal Tourism Canadian Rockies, an entity that was legitimately using the domain to further its advertising and promotional efforts, in a good-faith manner. Thus, a cybersquatting claim was not a concern. Instead, MLB had to pony up the requisite cash in order to consummate a transfer of Rockies.com.

---

84. *See* Darren Heitner, *The Brooklyn Nets Are Not Found at Nets.com, but They Should Be!* FORBES, Oct. 14, 2012, *at* http://www.forbes.com/sites/darrenheitner/2012/10/14/the-brooklyn-nets-are-not-found-at-nets-com-but-they-should-be/.

85. *Id.*

86. *See* Darren Heitner, *Did MLB Overpay in Its Purchase of Rockies.com?*, FORBES, Jan. 9, 2013, *at* http://www.forbes.com/sites/darrenheitner/2013/01/09/did-mlb-overpay-by-spending-1-2-million-for-rockies-com/.

Chapter 5

Gambling and Gaming

In 2012, New Jersey passed a sports wagering law that would have instituted a system of licensing certain establishments to allow for betting on college and professional sports matches. Since then, the overwhelming focus of gambling-related litigation has been on the state's unilateral action taken clearly in contradiction to the federal Professional and Amateur Sports Protection Act (PASPA), which only provides a (limited) gambling carve-out for four states (New Jersey not included). PASPA will be discussed in-depth early in this chapter. Litigation arising from efforts to strike PASPA is considered in a following section.

PASPA is not the sole focus of this chapter. It is important to remember that not all types of competition are considered to be forms of gambling, and even some types of games that may look like gambling have received preferential treatment by the federal government. Particularly, fantasy sports, a quickly growing industry, has been protected (to an extent) from scrutiny concerning whether or not it is a form of gambling (when money is exchanged between participants). Individual states, however, have crafted their own laws, sometimes restricting the element of consideration from said games and making it illegal for individuals to make wagers based on the success of their manufactured teams.

PASPA

"Whether the voters approve of or reject legalized sports betting in New Jersey, the decision should be up to them—not a federal ban which gives four states

a monopoly on sports wagering. This is about empowering New Jersey voters to decide for themselves whether they want sports betting in our State."[1]
—Stephen Sweeney, New Jersey Senate president

PASPA is a federal prohibition that became law in 1992 with the purpose of curbing sports betting throughout the United States. It was at least partially a response to a mounting concern that multiple states were in the process of generating support to pass legislation that would enable state-sponsored sports betting within their borders.[2] Specifically, PASPA deems that it shall be unlawful for

(1) a governmental entity to sponsor, operate, advertise, promote, license, or authorize by law or compact, or (2) a person to sponsor, operate, advertise, or promote, pursuant to the law or compact of a governmental entity, a lottery, sweepstakes, or other betting, gambling, or wagering scheme based, directly or indirectly (through the use of geographical references or otherwise), on one or more competitive games in which amateur or professional athletes participate, or are intended to participate, or on one or more performances of such athletes in such games.[3]

However, certain states were grandfathered into an exclusion that allows them to continue offering games that were in place prior to the enactment of PASPA. The unlawful sports gambling provision does not apply to those states where there was "a lottery, sweepstakes, or other betting, gambling, or wagering scheme in operation . . . at any time during the period beginning January 1, 1976, and ending August 31, 1990."[4] The only states to benefit from this exclusionary section are Delaware, Oregon, Montana, and

---

1. *See* Jason Butkowski, *Lesniak-Sweeney Disappointed Governor Christie Hasn't Joined Sports Betting Lawsuit*, POLITICKER NJ, July 12, 2010, *at* http://www.politickernj.com /lesniak-sweeney-disappointed-governor-christie-hasn-t-joined-sports-betting-lawsuit.
2. Senator Bill Bradley, *The Professional and Amateur Sports Protection Act-Policy Concerns Behind Senate Bill 474*, 2 SETON HALL J. SPORT L. 5, 8 (1992).
3. 28 U.S.C. § 3702.
4. 28 U.S.C. § 3704.

Nevada, with Nevada reaping the rewards of having the most expansive gambling scheme in operation prior to PASPA's passage.

Case Study

Pete Rose's Lifetime Ban from Major League Baseball due to Gambling

Pete Rose, also known as "Charlie Hustle," is a former MLB player and manager of the Cincinnati Reds.[5] Rose was a switch hitter, and he holds the MLB record for the most hits and the most games played.[6] During his time as a player, Rose won the Most Valuable Player award,[7] Rookie of the Year award,[8] and three World Series rings.[9] After he retired in 1986, he managed the Reds until 1989. Unfortunately for Rose, on February 20, 1989, he was summoned to meet with baseball commissioner Peter Ueberroth in New York City.[10] Rumors began circulating in regard to the topic of the meeting, and one month later, an official statement was released by the commissioner's office confirming that there were "serious gambling allegations" pending against Rose.[11] An investigation was conducted, with the ultimate finding that Rose had gambled on baseball during

---

5. *See* Bob Carter, *Hustle Made Rose Respected, Infamous*, ESPN CLASSIC, *at* http://espn .go.com/classic/biography/s/rosepete000824.html (Rose's nickname was "Charlie Hustle" because he was known to play every game as if it was "the seventh game of the World Series," according to Joe Morgan, a former teammate); *see also* Dan Tylicki, *14 Questions We'd Love to Ask Pete Rose*, BLEACHER REPORT, July 10, 2012, *at* http://bleacherreport.com/articles /1251820-14-questions-wed-love-to-ask-pete-rose/page/3.

6. *See Games Played Records*, BASEBALL ALMANAC, *at* http://www.baseball-almanac.com /recbooks/rb_gam1.shtml

7. *See Pete Rose Biography*, ESPN.COM, *at* http://espn.go.com/mlb/player/bio/_/id/397 /pete-rose. (After finishing in the top 10 for voting of the MVP award, Rose finally won it in 1973, with a .338 batting average and 230 hits.)

8. *See Pete Rose Career Biography and Statistics*, SPORTHAVEN.COM, *at* http://www .sporthaven.com/players/pete-rose/.

9. *See* Kenneth Shouler, *Lord of the Rings*, CIGAR AFICIONADO, July/Aug. 2011, *at* http://www.cigaraficionado.com/webfeatures/show/id/16042/p/3. (Rose won World Series rings in 1975 and 1976 with the Cincinnati Reds and in 1980 with the Phillies.).

10. *See* Rick Weinberg, *Pete Rose Banned from Baseball*, ESPN.COM, July/Aug. 2011, *at* http://sports.espn.go.com/espn/espn25/story?page=moments/5.

11. *Id.*

the time that he was managing the Reds.[12] On August 24, 1989, the commissioner stated that "one of the game's greatest players" had engaged in "a variety of acts that stained" the game of base-ball.[13] The commissioner announced the league's decision to ban Rose for life.[14] Almost 20 years later, Rose admitted to betting on his team "every night," saying that he did so because he "loved his team" and believed in his players.[15] Rose also stated that following the bets he made on each game, he "did everything" in his power to win.[16] Because of the lifetime ban, Rose is not eligible for induction into the Reds' or the MLB's Hall of Fame, nor is he allowed to be involved "in most on-field activities, which has prevented the Reds from retiring his uniform No. 14."[17]

Proponents of PASPA's adoption made reference to the public image of professional and amateur sports and expressed a general fear that expanded access and availability of sports betting schemes would jeopardize the character and integrity of team sports.[18] A relevant section of a statement made by PASPA author Senator Dennis DeConcini concerning his stance on the bill reads: "Is sports gambling a good thing? I think most people would agree that it is not. The spread of legalized sports gambling . . . [t]hreatens the very foundation of professional and amateur sports events."[19] *Integrity* is a word that is widely trumpeted by supporters of PASPA's preservation today. National Hockey League (NHL) commissioner Gary Bettman claims that the NHL "works tirelessly to earn and protect its reputation

---

12. *Id.*
13. *Id.*
14. *Id.*
15. *See Rose Admits to Betting on Reds "Every Night,"* ESPN.com, Mar. 16, 2007, *at* http://sports.espn.go.com/mlb/news/story?id=2798498.
16. *Id.*
17. *Id.*
18. See S. Rep. No. 102-248, at 4.
19. *Prohibiting State-Sanctioned Sports: Hearing on S. 473 and S. 474 Before the Subcomm. on Patents, Copyrights and Trademarks of the S. Comm. on the Judiciary,* 102d Cong. 1 (1991) [hereinafter S. 473 and S. 474 Hearing] (statement of Sen. Dennis DeConcini).

for integrity of competition, without which the league will no longer be viewed as quality family entertainment," and relies on such language to justify his position in opposition of allowing any additional states (other than the four grandfathered in by PASPA) to offer any kind of sports betting scheme.[20] Similarly, the National Collegiate Athletic Association (NCAA) has explained its opposition to state-sponsored betting schemes by maintaining that "the spread of legalized sports wagering is a threat to the integrity of athletic competition and student-athlete well-being."[21]

Litigation Arising from Sports Betting Prohibitions

"We have been in this business for decades and haven't had any problems with . . . any of our universities. The game-fixing scandals have happened in other states where gambling is illegal. What we have here is a regulatory process specifically to monitor what happens on both sides of the counter. This is all we do, and we're good at it."[22]
—A. G. Burnett, chairman of the Nevada Gaming Control Board

In one month in 2012, Nevada sports books (where gamblers may wager on various sports competitions) received almost $289 million in bets on college and professional basketball games.[23] That amount only accounted for the incoming money on bets placed in the month of March. Other states, not as fortunate to have received an exemption from being affected by PASPA's widespread prohibition against state-sponsored gambling schemes, have looked to Nevada with ire and feel prejudiced by their predicament. They have budgets in desperate need of an infusion of capital and search

---

20. *See* Sara Hoffman, *Setting the Stakes*, THE JEFFREY S. MOORAD CENTER FOR THE STUDY OF SPORTS LAW, Jan. 17, 2013, *at* http://lawweb2009.law.villanova.edu/sportslaw/?p=1461.

21. *See* Joe Drape, *More States Look to Sports Betting as Leagues Line Up against It*, N.Y. TIMES, Mar. 27, 2013, *at* http://www.nytimes.com/2013/03/28/sports/more-states-look-to -get-in-the-sports-betting-game.html?hp&_r=0.

22. *Id.*

23. *See* David Purdum, *How Much Money Is Bet Worldwide on NCAA Tournament?* SPORTINGNEWS, Mar. 19, 2013, *at* http://linemakers.sportingnews.com/ncaa-basketball /2013-03-19/rj-bell-ncaa-tournament-betting-worldwide-estimate-las-vegas-nevada-offhshore.

aimlessly for new sources of revenue. State-sponsored gambling appears to be a partial cure, but one that is not currently a possibility. The result is heavily contested litigation with no apparent end in sight.

New Jersey and its outspoken governor, Chris Christie, have recognized the shortcomings of the state's budget and realized that state-sponsored sports betting would help alleviate some of its problems. Since the potential (or at least perceived potential) of a state-sponsored sports betting scheme became a reality, Christie has supported such efforts and has been a vocal leader in the effort to shape public opinion in his favor.[24] In the November 2011 elections, an option to vote for or against state-sponsored sports betting via the amending of the New Jersey constitution was placed on the ballot.[25] The referendum garnered the requisite votes needed to amend New Jersey's constitution, and plans were developed to allow for legalized sports betting in Atlantic City and four other racetracks in the state.[26] Those plans failed to come to fruition, however, as the four major professional sports leagues and the NCAA rushed to the court to seek an injunction based on the claim that New Jersey's hurried attempt to amend its constitution was "in clear and flagrant violation of [PASPA]."[27]

The State of New Jersey's first line of defense against the professional leagues and the NCAA was to allege that they failed to have legal standing to ask the court for an injunction.[28] They were required to make a showing that they were "under threat of suffering 'injury in fact' that is concrete and particularized; the threat must be actual and imminent, not conjectural and hypothetical; it must be fairly traceable to the challenged action of the defendant; and it must be likely that a favorable judicial decision will

---

24. *The Case for Legal Sports Betting*, New Jersey L. J. (Nov. 25, 2012, 5:38 p.m.), *at* http://www.law.com/jsp/nj/PubArticleNJ.jsp?id=1202575706899&The_Case_for__Legal _Sports_Betting.

25. *Id.*

26. *Id.*

27. 7 Mary Pat Gallagher, *No Quick Resolution in Sight for Suit Challenging N.J. Sports-Betting Law*, New Jersey L. J. (Aug. 28, 2012).

28. Reply Br. in Supp. of Def.'s Mot. to Dismiss, Pursuant to Fed. Rule of Civil Procedure 12(b)(1), NCAA v. Christie, No. 3:12-cv-04947 (MAS) (LHG) (D.N.J. Sept. 7, 2012) (2012 WL 5231455 (D.N.J.)).

prevent or redress the injury."[29] The first inquiry concerning threat of suffering "injury in fact" brings back the discussion about the leagues' interest in maintaining the integrity of their games. Without attacking the justification provided by the leagues, it is important to recognize that this argument is theoretical; there was no tangible proof that the leagues could rely on to persuade the court that the lack of an injunction would necessarily tarnish the sports fan's perception of the game played. Instead, the leagues relied on a congressional committee's belief that "widespread legalization of sports gambling would inevitably promote suspicion about controversial plays and lead fans to think 'the fix was in' whenever their team failed to beat the point-spread."[30] The leagues also took the position that based on a prior ruling by the U.S. Supreme Court, the "actual or threatened injury required by Art. III [of the U.S. Constitution] may exist solely by virtue of statutes creating legal rights, the invasion of which creates standing."[31] New Jersey countered that PASPA is not a type of statute intended to create legal rights; instead, it simply served to prevent states from instituting sponsored sports betting schemes.

Case Study

Katz's Delicatessen, Inc. v. O'Connell

Some states take a stricter stance on the illegality of poker than others. For example, *Katz's Delicatessen, Inc. v. O'Connell* illustrates New York's position through a case involving a game of poker that was played on the premises of the well-known Katz's Deli.[32] The gambling in question "was not of the variety condemned by the criminal statutes"; rather, it was a friendly game of poker played in the basement of the

---

29. *Id.*

30. Br. in Supp. of Pl.'s Mot. of Summ. J and, if Necessary, to Preserve the Status Quo, NCAA v. Christie, No. 3:12—cv-04947 (MAS) (LHG) (D.N.J. Aug. 10, 2012) (2012 WL 3964728 (D.N.J.) (citing S. Rep. No. 102-248, at 5 (1991)).

31. Pl.'s Mem. of Law in Opp'n Def.'s Mot. to Dismiss the Compl., *supra* note 23 (citing Havens Realty Corp. v. Coleman, 455 U.S. 363, 373 (1982); (quoting Warth v. Seldin, 422 U.S. 490, 500 (1975)).

32. *See generally* Katz's Delicatessen, Inc. v. O'Connell, 302 N.Y. 286, 97 N.E.2d 906 (1951).

deli between officers of the corporation and five other men.[33] The stakes involved in the game "were nominal."[34] As a result of the execution of the game; however, Katz's retail beer license was suspended for five days by the State Liquor Authority after a finding that the informal game of poker was forbidden under New York's Alcoholic Beverage Control law.[35] Katz's Deli challenged the suspension to the Court of Appeals of New York, alleging that the decision regarding the suspension was arbitrary and capricious.[36] The court affirmed the suspension, stating that "the phrase 'any gambling' as used in the statute is susceptible of only one interpretation: it is all inclusive and may be read to embrace both casual and professional betting."[37] The court went on to say that the prohibition of "any" gambling under the statute is not unreasonable and can apply to social gambling.[38]

On June 26, 2013, the U.S. Court of Appeals for the Third Circuit heard oral arguments from representatives for the State of New Jersey and those representing the professional sports leagues and the NCAA in the contentious PASPA litigation.[39] The State of New Jersey reiterated its position that the federal PASPA is unconstitutional and that the leagues and NCAA lacked standing.[40] On September 17, 2013, the federal appeals court sided with the professional sports leagues and the NCAA by affirming the lower court's ruling. The Third Circuit published

---

33. *Id.*
34. *Id.*
35. *See* subdivision 6 of Section 106 of the Alcoholic Beverage Control Law, Consol.Laws, c. 3-B, which provides: "6. No person licensed to sell alcoholic beverages shall suffer or permit any gambling on the licensed premises, or suffer or permit such premises to become disorderly."
36. See Katz's Delicatessen, Inc. v. O'Connell, 302 N.Y. 286, 288, 97 N.E.2d 906 (1951) (In February 2014, a thirty-five page petition for writ of certiorari was filed with the U.S. Supreme Court.).
37. *Id.*
38. *Id.*
39. *See* Griffin Finan, *Appeals Court Hears Argument on N.J. Sports Betting Law, with Uncertain Outcome,* Crime in the Suites, June 26, 2013, *at* http://crimeinthesuites.com /appeals-court-hears-argument-on-n-j-sports-betting-law-with-uncertain-outcome/.
40. *Id.*

a 128-page opinion that included a partial yet powerful dissent wherein U.S. Circuit Judge Thomas I. Vanaskie said that the federal government has used PASPA to step on state governments' right to regulate what occurs within their borders. The State of New Jersey sought a rehearing en banc, which was denied.[41] Now the state must determine whether it wishes to file for a writ of certiorari to the U.S. Supreme Court, which it was obligated to do by February 2014.

Litigation concerning sports betting prohibitions is not only centered on PASPA. Is poker considered a sport? If so, it is also subject to hefty debate concerning its legality across the United States. In 2011, Lawrence DiCristina was arrested, charged, and convicted of running a poker game in violation of the Illegal Gambling Business Act (IGBA). When the court determined that poker is not covered by the IGBA, the federal government stepped in and appealed the decision. On appeal, the U.S. Court of Appeals for the Second Circuit reversed the lower court's ruling, stating that "the plain language of the IGBA covers DiCristina's poker business, we reverse the judgment of acquittal and remand to the District Court with instructions to reinstate the jury verdict, enter a judgment of conviction on both counts, and proceed with sentencing DiCristina."[42] Interestingly, the appellate court reached its conclusion irrespective of its opinion on whether or not winners of the game of poker are predominantly determined based on skill or chance (a distinguishing factor that will be discussed thoroughly later in this chapter). Meanwhile, poker proponents have held on to the notion that the skill versus chance debate is an integral piece of the puzzle for legalized gambling on poker games. After the appellate court reversed the *DiCristina* decision, Poker Players Alliance executive director John Pappas stated: "The Second Circuit clearly did not dispute the district court's finding that poker is a game of skill. This is a key point distinguishing poker

---

41. *See* Donald Scarinci, *Will Gov. Christie Take a Gamble on the U.S. Supreme Court*, POLITICKER NJ, Dec. 18, 2013, *at* http://www.politickernj.com/dscarinci/70324/will-gov-chr istie-take-gamble-us-supreme-court.

42. *See* USA v. DiCristina, *at* http://theppa.org/ppa/2013/08/06/usa-v-lawrence-dicristi na-decision-08062013/.

from the types of gambling games that Congress and state legislatures have often tried to prohibit."[43]

Contest or Sweepstakes?

"When you are in any contest you should work as if there were—to the very last minute—a chance to lose it."[44]
—Dwight D. Eisenhower, U.S. president

Many state legislatures have expressed the intent to recognize certain exemptions to gambling prohibitions provided that the activities exempted from said restrictions are conducted in a manner that does not equate to gambling. For instance, Chapter 849 of the Florida Statutes, entitled "Gambling," proscribes a host of regulated activities including but not limited to playing a "game of chance." Because a pure drawing of chance is nothing more than a lottery consisting of the elements of prize, chance (the drawing of the winning ticket), and consideration (price paid for a chance), these statutory exemptions permit activities that appear to be a form of gambling conduct only if one of the aforementioned elements have been removed.[45]

In Florida, a game of chance in connection with the sale of consumer products or services, and in which the elements of chance and prize are present, qualifies as a game promotion. A sweepstakes may be considered a game of chance if the contestants simply register for the sweepstakes, without the obligation to pay for registration and for a chance to win a prize. It is distinguished from an illegal lottery through the elimination of consideration; however, a sweepstakes can require some form of consideration for the participant to enter as long as the sweepstakes also provides a free alternate method of entry. Further, those who choose to enter the sweepstakes

---

43. *See* Darren Heitner, *Online Poker May Be Considered Illegal Gambling Whether Based on Skill or Not*, Forbes, Aug. 6, 2013, *at* http://www.forbes.com/sites/darrenheitner/2013/08/06/online-poker-may-be-considered-illegal-gambling-whether-based-on-skill-or-not/.

44. http://freefamousquotes.net/dwight_d_eisenhower_when_you_are_in_any_contest_yo/.

45. Kent J. Perez, *Florida Statute S849.0935 Drawings by Chance*, Fla. B.J., Sec, 1996, at 63.

through the free alternate method of entry must be given an equal chance to win the prize(s), and the alternate method must not be too onerous to the point that it would deter people from taking the necessary steps to enter. The alternate method of entry should always be clearly disclosed.

The operator of such a sweepstakes cannot (1) predetermine a winner or allocate a winning game or part thereof to a particular geographic region; (2) arbitrarily remove, disqualify, disallow, or reject any entry; (3) fail to award the prize(s) advertised as being offered; (4) falsely, deceptively, or misleadingly advertise; and (5) require an entry fee, payment, or proof of purchase as a condition of entering a game promotion. Chance activities are clearly permitted; however, the element of consideration necessary to comprise a lottery is clearly and conspicuously prohibited. This concept is best recognized by the inclusion of the key phrase, "No purchase necessary."[46]

The posting of sweepstakes rules is also highly regulated by the states. First of all, a copy of the sweepstakes' rules typically must be filed with a state department a specific number of days prior to the commencement of the sweepstakes. It is common for the department to prohibit an operator from altering the sweepstakes' rules after submission of same. Additionally, in Florida, the sweepstakes operator must conspicuously post the sweepstake rules wherever such game promotion may be played or participated in by the public and in all advertising copy used in connection therewith. Any advertising copy shall include the following material terms in the sweepstakes' rules and regulations: (1) name of the operator and game promotion; (2) that no purchase is necessary to enter or play the game promotion; (3) start and end dates for entering the game promotion, consistent with the official full rules and regulations, including exact times if applicable; (4) who is eligible or not eligible to participate in the game promotion, with respect to age or geographic location; and (5) disclosure of where the game promotion is void.[47]

Upon completion of the sweepstakes, a winner or winners will be crowned and awarded in compliance with the sweepstakes' rules. Additionally, if the

---

46. *Id.*
47. 570.07(2), 849.094(8) FS. Law Implemented 849.094(3) FS. History-New 11-22-05.

prizes offered total an amount of money greater than a specified figure, certain states will require the sweepstakes operator to submit a list to an indicated state department of the names and addresses of all persons who have won prizes that have a value over another specified amount of money. In Florida, the operator shall provide a copy of the list of winners, without charge, to any person who requests it.

Whereas sweepstakes largely eliminate the element of consideration so as to steer clear from being labeled as an illegal lottery, contests eliminate the element of chance, and the winner is determined based on his or her level of skill. The main inquiry that contest regulators will focus on is whether an individual's skill truly determines the outcome, which is often a daunting question for sponsors to answer with sufficient proof.

Case Study

Scripps National Spelling Bee

The Scripps National Spelling Bee was established in 1925 as an annual contest held in Washington D.C., that challenges children 15 years old and younger on their ability to spell difficult words correctly. This event has gained national attention over the years, largely due to ESPN's around-the-clock coverage of the contestants sweating under the spotlight in an effort to win the competition. The 2013 winner received a $30,000 cash prize, an engraved trophy, a $2,500 U.S. savings bond, and a set of reference works from Encyclopedia Britannica worth $2,000. The competition has strict rules, including sections on eligibility, format, time constraints, and the judges' roles. Importantly, the competition establishes objective criteria for determining the winner. In 2013–2014, schools could enroll their students, teachers, and administrators in the competition for a total cost of $120 per school.[48] The Scripps National Spelling Bee is an excellent example of a legal contest based on skill. Resources for

---

48. *See* National Spelling Bee, *How Much Does It Cost to Enroll?* Spellingbee.com, *at* http://www.spellingbee.com/customer-service-center/enrollment/how-much-does-it-cost-enroll.

students and parents are freely available on the organization's web-site. The preparation is intense. People spend countless hours not only leaning difficult words and memorizing how to spell them, but also studying dead languages along with Greek and Latin root words.[49]

Fantasy Sports

Season-long fantasy sports games have been largely dominated by a few key players, including Yahoo!, Walt Disney Company (via its subsidiary ESPN), and CBS. A more recent phenomenon is the Internet-based "social" fantasy sports leagues that integrate a variety of "playing modes" for the benefit of interested sports fans and consumers. The companies that host such fantasy gaming formats typically derive profits from administering an entry fee and/or the purchase of a form of "credits" for users to continue to have access to particular features of the sites that are operated.

The legality of all fantasy sports games should be viewed against (1) the Unlawful Internet Gambling Enforcement Act (UIGEA) of 2006 (31 U.S.C. §§ 5361–5367) and (2) individual state laws. The majority of cases deal-ing with fantasy leagues have arisen out of intellectual property lawsuits (*see C.B.C. Distribution v. Marketing, Inc.* 505 F. 3d 818 (8th Cir. 2007), holding that the First Amendment protects the use of players' names and statistics by a producer of fantasy major league baseball) and thus do not deal with the general legality of these leagues vis-à-vis statutory gambling prohibitions.

The UIGEA of 2006 does carve out an exception to the typical illegal-ity attached to gambling for fantasy sports games, but it stipulates certain requirements that *must be met* for the exception to apply:

---

49. *See* Linette Lopez, *My Sister Was in the Scripps Spelling Bee, and Her Prep Was Intense,* Business Insider, May 31, 2013, *at* http://www.businessinsider.com.au/how-to-prep-for-the-scripps-spelling-bee-2013-5.

(E) does not include—...

(ix) participation in any fantasy or simulation sports game or educational game or contest in which (if the game or contest involves a team or teams) no fantasy or simulation sports team is based on the current membership of an actual team that is a member of an amateur or professional sports organization (as those terms are defined in Section 3701 of Title 28) and that meets the following conditions:

All prizes and awards offered to winning participants are established and made known to the participants in advance of the game or contest and their value is not determined by the number of participants or the amount of any fees paid by those participants.

All winning outcomes reflect the relative knowledge and skill of the participants and are determined predominantly by accumulated statistical results of the performance of individuals (athletes in the case of sports events) in multiple real-world sporting or other events.

(III) No winning outcome is based—

(aa) on the score, point-spread, or any performance or performances of any single real-world team or any combination of such teams; or

(bb) solely on any single performance of an individual athlete in any single real-world sporting or other event.

Although, as mentioned above, no completed cases have treated the fantasy games exception in depth, the UIGEA makes very clear the requirements that must be met by those seeking to fall within the fantasy league exception. According to the UIGEA, no fantasy or simulation sports team can be based on the current membership of an actual team, and no winning outcome can be based on the score or performance of any single real-world team or any combinations of such teams.

For example, consider the popular sports betting website "DraftStreet."[50] This website explicitly includes the following requirement in its rules, which, no doubt, the owners included in an attempt to avoid liability under the UIGEA: "No roster for any league can consist solely of players from one professional team."

Draft Styles

▾ Salary Cap Leagues

You can immediately select your roster upon joining a Salary Cap League. The combined fantasy salaries (as set by our DraftStreet team) of the players you select must not exceed the salary cap of $100,000. You can mix and match and save your selections up until the scoring period begins. If your roster is illegal at this time you will be disqualified and you will not receive a refund.

Illegal rosters either A) Exceed the set salary cap or B) Have one or more empty roster spots.

No roster for any league can consist solely of players from one professional team.

The rule makes perfect sense in light of the UIGEA's expressed purpose. The exception carved out for fantasy leagues was informed by a belief that winning in true fantasy leagues depends on the skill of the participants, not on chance (at least when viewed in accordance with the predominant factor test, which is a balancing test that focuses on whether skill predominates chance in a given scenario). Although seasonal and perennial fantasy sports leagues that allow users to select their players through an auction-style or allotted pick draft are likely to be deemed legal due to an inherent amount of skill and preparation required to understand each player's value, other forms of pay-to-play fantasy sports games will not necessarily pass the same legal muster.[51] Many daily fantasy sports games are operating in a space of legal uncertainty, picking up millions of dollars in investments nonetheless.[52] DraftStreet, for example, received roughly $3 million in venture

---

50. Found *at* www.Draftstreet.com.

51. Marc Edelman, *A Short Treatise on Fantasy Sports and the Law: How America Regulates Its New National Pastime*, HARVARD J. OF SPORTS & ENTM'T L., Vol. 3, January 2012.

52. *See* Darren Heitner, *Atlas Venture Delivers $7 Million to Daily Fantasy Sports Provider DraftKings, Inc.*, FORBES, May 6, 2013, *at* http://www.forbes.com/sites/darrenheitner/2013/05/06/atlas-venture-delivers-7-million-to-daily-fantasy-sports-provider-draftkings-inc/ (in June 2013, DraftKings, Inc. closed a $7 million Series A round of funding led by Atlas Venture); *see also* Darren Heitner, *Fantasy Sports Service, FanDuel, Secures $11 Million Investment; Includes Money from Comcast Ventures*, FORBES, Jan. 30, 2013, *at* http://www.forbes.com/sites/darrenheitner/2013/01/30/fantasy-sports-service-fanduel-secures-11-million-investment-includes-money-from-comcast-ventures/ (in January 2013, daily fantasy sports gaming leader FanDuel announced an $11 million round of financing led by Comcast Ventures).

capital from 2010 through 2012.[53] In late 2013, two-year-old daily fantasy sports operator DraftKings closed a $24 million Series B round of funding only six months after it closed a $7 million Series A round.[54] Because there is so much money being invested in this space, I felt the need to reach out to industry insiders to at least inquire whether there are any concerns that there are still pending legal issues to resolve. A high ranking individual at one of the most popular daily fantasy sports operators responded, "I can't speak to that right now, but I can tell you that there is an extraordinarily good chance that all legal issues will become moot in the near future." Perhaps time will tell.

Case Study

Humphrey v. Viacom

In 2006, Charles E. Humphrey Jr. filed a cause of action alleging that fantasy sports games in the United States are essentially an illegal form of gambling.[55] Humphrey filed the complaint against Viacom, Inc. (the owner of three main providers of online fantasy leagues) in the federal district court in New Jersey.[56] Humphrey sought relief under New Jersey's *Qui Tam* statute, which is intended to prevent gamblers from becoming "destitute due to gambling losses" by allowing them to recover from the winner of such illegal gambling activity.[57] Humphrey's argument was that Viacom's leagues all

---

53. *See* Peter Lauria, *Become a Millionaire Playing Fantasy Football*, Buzzfeed Business, Aug. 27, 2013, *at* http://www.buzzfeed.com/peterlauria/become-a-millionaire-playing-f antasy-football.

54. *See* Darren Heitner, *$24 Million Investment In DraftKings Should Shake Up The Daily Fantasy Sports Space*, Forbes, Nov. 26, 2013, *at* http://www.forbes.com/sites/darrenheitner /2013/11/26/daily-fantasy-sports-provider-draftkings-secures-substantial-amount-of-series-b -funding/.

55. *See* Humphrey v. Viacom, Inc., 06 2768 DMC, 2007 WL 1797648 (D.N.J. June 20, 2007).

56. *Id.*

57. *Id.* (The court stated that "although the specific elements of the *Qui Tam* statutes vary, they share a common origin and purpose. They were intended to prevent gamblers and their families from becoming destitute due to gambling losses—and thus becoming wards of the State—by providing a method for the gambler's spouse, parent or child to recover the lost money from the winner.")

required participants to "pay a set fee" for each team they entered and thus allowed Viacom to "win" based on its receipt of said entry fee.[58] The fee, however, is supported by consideration based on the paying player receiving "related support services" and the ability "to compete against other teams" within the league. The court ruled in favor of Viacom, concluding that "fantasy sports involve elements of both skill and chance, but the skill elements are dominant . . . as through research, intelligence, and skill, the participants can control the outcome of the contests."[59] This ruling became a huge victory for both Viacom and fantasy sports providers everywhere based on the court's ultimate decision that, as a matter of law, the entry fees paid by those wishing to participate in a fantasy league are *not* "bets" or "wagers."[60] The court gave three reasons for its decision: (1) the entry fees are paid unconditionally, (2) the prizes offered to fantasy sports contestants are for amounts certain and are guaranteed to be awarded, and (3) defendants do not compete for prizes.[61] The opinion went on to say that Viacom provides "substantial consideration, in the form of administration of the leagues and the provision of extensive statistical and analytical services, in exchange for the entry fees."[62] Viacom itself does not actually participate in any bet and for this reason cannot be considered a "winner" subject to liability under the *Qui Tam* statutes.[63]

---

58. *Id.*

59. *Id.*

60. *See* Matthew Heller, *All Bets Off for Fantasy Sports Anti-Gambling Suit*, ON POINT NEWS, June 22, 2007, *at* http://www.onpointnews.com/NEWS/all-bets-off-for-fantasy-sports-anti-gambling-suit.html. ("A first-of-its kind lawsuit against operators of fantasy sports leagues has turned out to be a bit of a fantasy itself as a New Jersey judge ruled that the leagues 'do not constitute gambling as a matter of law.'")

61. *Id.*

62. *Id.*

63. *See* Humphrey v. Viacom, Inc., 06 2768 DMC, 2007 WL 1797648 (D.N.J. June 20, 2007).

Although the UIGEA includes a carve-out for fantasy-style sports games, various states—Arizona, Iowa, Louisiana, Maryland, Montana, and Vermont—outlaw pay-to-play fantasy games. These states are commonly called chance states because they tend to restrict the exchange of money between competitors in games that rely on an outcome determined in some way by chance (thereby ignoring the previously discussed predominant factor test). The remaining nonchance states are either silent as to the legality of fantasy sports leagues or explicitly allow them. Confusion remains among the participating public because many state gaming laws are not necessarily clear when it comes to whether fantasy sports betting is legal. The State of Florida has expressly stated that it wants nothing to do with pay-to-play fantasy gaming, that it has "technically banned it," and that any Florida resident found to bet money on fantasy football leagues may be saddled with misdemeanor charges.[64] One Florida statute states in part:

> Whoever stakes, bets or wagers any money or other thing of value upon the result of any trial or contest of skill . . . or whoever receives in any manner whatsoever any money or other thing of value staked, bet or wagered, or offered for the purpose of being staked, bet or wagered, by or for any other person upon any such result, or who-ever knowingly becomes the custodian or depositary of any money or other thing of value so staked, bet, or wagered upon any such result, or whoever aids, or assists, or abets in any manner in any of such acts all of which are hereby forbidden, shall be guilty of a misdemeanor of the second degree.[65]

---

64. *See* Barnini Chakraborty, *Gaming Laws Could Pose Risk for Fantasy Football Craze,* Fox News, Aug. 31, 2013, *at* http://www.foxnews.com/politics/2013/08/31/gaming-laws -pose-risk-for-fantasy-football-craze/.

65. Fla. Stat. Sec. 849.14.

Chapter 6

Ethics

The vast majority of individuals who wish to practice law must take and receive a passing score on the Multistate Professional Responsibility Examination (MPRE). The exam contains 60 questions intended to quiz the potential lawyer's understanding of his or her duties to observe those established ethical standards that the National Conference of Bar Examiners deems to be relevant and necessary for practitioners to adopt. Some believe that the taking of this test, alone, requires those who are Sports Lawyers to adhere to a higher standard of ethics than their colleagues in sports business who are not practicing lawyers.

Ethics is an important, albeit dreaded, component of a lawyer's life. Beyond the chore of sitting to take the MPRE, lawyers are tasked with maintaining mandated levels of Continuing Legal Education (CLE) credits. Many jurisdictions require that a lawyer not only register for a certain number of general CLE credits in a specified span of time, but also obtain the necessary number of ethics-related CLE credits, which must be approved by the respective state bar in advance of receiving said credits. All of the aforementioned (in addition to stringent state rules of professional conduct) leads many to perceive lawyers as professionals who must stay true to a higher level of ethical conduct. Whether lawyers conform to said standards is a separate issue.

One of the largest ethical concerns in the world of sports is the notion that sports-related professionals inherently find themselves in serious situations wherein they have conflicts of interest. It may be a sports agent who represents both coaches and players within the same professional organization, financial planners who manage the money for both sports agents and their clients, or lawyers who serve as counsel for a company and an individual the company wishes to sign to an endorsement agreement. These are just a limited number of hypothetical situations where a conflict may occur. The best ways to avoid negative consequences from involving oneself in such a situation is to either inform the potentially conflicted clients of the situation and receive their written authorization to proceed representing both parties or simply refuse to engage in a representative capacity that is likely to lead to conflict. These situations are oftentimes easier to analyze after the fact as opposed to prior to performing services for clients who may have conflicting goals and aspirations.

Conflicts of Interest

"A marriage without conflicts is almost as inconceivable as a nation without crises."[1]
—Andre Maurois, French author

Sports Lawyers and agents typically do not marry their clients, although sometimes they may spend more time and act more emotionally with them than their spouses. Any successful Sports Lawyer or agent is going to run into his or her fair share of ethical quandaries, including those that involve a thorough analysis concerning whether or not the representation of an individual presents a conflict of interest for the practitioner. The smart agent/ attorney will disclose any and all potential conflicts of interest to his or her existing and potential future clients. The very prudent practitioner will make sure that such disclosures are in writing and confirmed as received by the intended recipients. Whenever in doubt, disclose.

Almost all major professional sports players' associations in the United States permit potential conflicts of interest through the representation of

---

1. *See Quotes by Andrew Maurois,* GAIAMlife, *at* http://blog.gaiam.com/quotes/authors /andre-maurois.

players and executives as long as the agents disclose those potential conflicts to their clients. The lone exception is the National Basketball Players Association (NBPA), which strictly prohibits

> [r]epresenting the General Manager or coach of any National Basketball Association [NBA] team (or any other management representative who participates in the team's deliberations or decision concerning what compensation is to be offered an individual player) in matters pertaining to his employment by or association with any NBA team; or any other matters in which he has any financial stake by or association with any NBA team.[2]

If an individual is an NBPA-certified player agent, it is assumed that the person wishes to represent basketball players who participate for NBA organizations. Thus, those certified player agents are prohibited from concurrently representing general managers, coaches, and/or other NBA-affiliated management personnel. Even this rule, which appears to be drafted in a way to avoid the potential for rampant conflicts of interest, is easily skirted by agencies that wish to maintain a vast representation portfolio composed of both players and management. For instance, in 2010, Creative Artists Agency began employing William Wesley (also known as "World Wide Wes," among other nicknames) to represent professional and college basketball coaches for the company.[3] Meanwhile, Creative Artists Agency employed other basketball agents, including Leon Rose, Henry Thomas, and Rich Paul, who represented some of the most well-known, profitable NBA players, such as LeBron James, Chris Bosh, and Dwyane Wade. William Wesley and Leon Rose may not have had conflicts of interest in their individual capacities, but the company that employed them certainly violated the NBPA rule against representing both players and coaches (at least the spirit of said rule). However, the NBPA does not certify companies; it

2. NBA Regulations Governing Players Agents § 3(B)(f).
3. Seth Davis, *Wesley to Become Rep for Coaches*, SPORTS ILLUSTRATED (Mar. 5, 2010, 7:06 p.m.), *at* http://sportsillustrated.cnn.com/2010/basketball/ncaa/03/05/wesley.agent/index.html.

only has jurisdiction over individual agents. Thus, Creative Artists Agency, like many other agencies, has been able to effectively circumvent the spirit of the rule concerning dual representation.

Case Study

Bob LaMonte

Sports agent Bob LaMonte has represented numerous football players and baseball players over decades of serving as a representative for athletes. He also created a lucrative practice in the representation of coaches and other higher-level management personnel in professional sport organizations. His clients include many current and former NFL head coaches, offensive coordinators, defensive coordinators, positional coaches, college coaches, and, of course, professional athletes. Representing such a wide array of individuals presents many challenges, including the ethical challenge of managing all the potential conflicts of interest in the representation of different classes of individuals who often find themselves subservient to one another and/or are a part of the negotiation process concerning a professional contract. LaMonte's most glaring conflict may have been present at the start of the 2012 NFL season when he represented Cleveland Browns president Mike Holmgren, executive vice president Bryan Wiedmeier, general manager Tom Hecker, head coach Pat Shurmur, and quarterbacks coach Mark Whipple.[4] Players' association rules and regulations aside, such widespread representation presented the opportunity for LaMonte to be highly conflicted as an agent for all the aforesaid individuals, especially because one of those individuals was the general manager, who is generally tasked with negotiating the contracts of those within the organization and being a major influence on whether those within the organization keep their jobs or receive promotions.

---

4. Darren A. Heitner and Jason B. Belzer, *An Offer They Should Refuse: Why Conflicts of Interest Raised by Dual Representation among Player Agents Is a Major Threat to the NCAA and Professional Leagues*, Ariz. St. Sports & Ent. L.J. (Dec. 2012).

Lawyers should be familiar with the American Bar Association's model rule concerning Client Conflicts of Interests (Rule 1.7), which states:

> A lawyer shall not represent a client if the representation involves a concurrent conflict of interest. A concurrent conflict of interest exists if . . . there is a significant risk that the representation of one or more clients will be materially limited by the lawyer's responsibilities to another client, a former client or a third person or by a personal interest of the lawyer.[5]

As an attorney who represents a variety of individuals and companies in the world of sport, including athletes, agents, publicists, brokers, and managers, I have a heightened obligation to run thorough conflict checks whenever a potential new client comes across my radar. Representing a smorgasbord of individuals and entities provides many advantages, especially when it comes to referrals, but it includes the additional burden of making sure that I am not jeopardizing my ability to competently represent my clients to the fullest extent possible. Potential perceived conflicts are almost unavoidable in what is the very small, incestuous business of sports; thus, it is vitally important that such potential conflicts are disclosed to all parties who may be affected by any new form of representation.

Sports agent Gary Uberstein, CEO of Premier Sports & Entertainment, is also a lawyer and author who wrote *Covering All the Bases: A Comprehensive Research Guide to Sports Law* and like me was a contributing author to a prior version of *An Athlete's Guide to Agents*. Uberstein is the agent of record for college football coaches Ed Orgeron and Steve Sarkisian, which meant that he was put into a difficult situation at the tail end of 2013. Uberstein's client Orgeron was the head coach of the University of Southern California and hoped to remain as a fixture in that position. Meanwhile, the school's athletic department was interviewing others, including Sarkisian, as a possible replacement for Orgeron. Was Uberstein able

---

5. Model Rules of Prof'l Conduct R. 1.7 (2013), *available at* http://www.americanbar.org /groups/professional_responsibility/publications/model_rules_of_professional_conduct/rule_1 _7_conflict_of_interest_current_clients.html.

to cure any perceived conflict among his clientele? In response to a line of questioning on that point, Uberstein said, "If a conflict develops at some point, you have a discussion about it. More often than not, they have a longstanding relationship and the client values that and believes the agent can represent them in an appropriate manner."[6] Sarkisian was eventually hired by USC, which led to Orgeron's departure.

Case Study

Pro Tect Management

In October 2013, a football agent who once represented linebacker Brandon Spikes, defensive end Allen Bailey, and cornerbacks Mike Harris and Chris Culliver, among many other players, was indicted on charges that he violated the State of North Carolina's Athlete Agent Act.[7] It was the culmination of a three-year investigation concerning possible rules violations surrounding agents, players, and even coaches at the University of North Carolina (UNC).[8] Part of that investigation related to former UNC associate head football coach John Blake, who had been accused of influencing players to sign with his friend and past business partner, Gary Wichard. It was said that Wichard, a National Football League Players Association (NFLPA) contract advisor, offered Blake an incentive to deliver players to Wichard's agency, Pro Tect Management. Blake denied receiving compensation in exchange for funneling players to Pro Tect Management and even denied having any previous working relationship with the company even though he had at one time been listed on the

---

6. *See* Paresh Dave, *Sports Agents Sometimes Have a Balancing Act with Clients*, L.A. Times, Dec. 25, 2013, *at* http://articles.latimes.com/2013/dec/25/sports/la-sp-1226-same-agent-20131226.

7. *See* Darren Heitner, *Football Agent Terry Watson Facing 14 Felony Counts For Violating North Carolina Athlete Agent Law*, Forbes, Oct. 9, 2013, *at* http://www.forbes.com/sites/darrenheitner/2013/10/09/football-agent-terry-watson-facing-14-felony-counts-for-violating-north-carolina-athlete-agent-law/.

8. *See* Darren Heitner, *The UNC Football Scandal*, Sports Agent Blog, Jul. 16, 2010, *at* http://www.sportsagentblog.com/2010/07/16/the-unc-football-scandal/.

agency's brochure as the "Vice President of Football Operations."[9] A former Pro Tect Management client, Brian Bosworth, nonetheless said that when he had played for Blake at Oklahoma in the 1980s, Blake had attempted to influence his agent selection decision and purposefully pushed him to sign with Wichard.[10] Perceived conflicts are a concern, but actual conflicts like the one Blake and Wichard engaged in are travesties.

Unauthorized Practice of Law Issues

"I would love to see the entire UPL [unauthorized practice of law] regime disappear. The accounting profession flourishes without such legal constraints, and consumers freely may choose from among certified public accountants and regular accountants, based on their needs and resources. Consumers are protected not by legal cartels but by choice, competition, transparency, and the enforcement of fiduciary relationships."[11]
—Clint Bolick, vice president for litigation at the Goldwater Institute

The American Bar Association (ABA) Center for Professional Responsibility provides Model Rules of Professional Conduct (MRPC) that individual state bar associations have the option of accepting in the form provided by the ABA or of instituting alternate codes of conduct. California remains the only state that has deviated from the ABA's professional conduct rules.[12]

---

9. Charles Robinson and Bryan Fischer, *Coach-Agent Ties Probed*, YAHOO! SPORTS, Aug. 9, 2010, *at* http://rivals.yahoo.com/ncaa/football/news?slug=ys-agentcoach080910.

10. Andy Staples, *The Case against John Blake*, SPORTS ILLUSTRATED, Oct. 26, 2011, *at* http://sportsillustrated.cnn.com/2011/writers/andy_staples/10/21/john.blake/1.html.

11. *See* Clint Bolick, *Access to Legal Services: The Market Provides*, THE LAST WORD, Oct. 2012, *at* http://www.myazbar.org/AZAttorney/PDF_Articles/1012LastWordBolick.pdf.

12. *See Model Rules of Professional Conduct*, AM. BAR ASS'N, *at* http://www.americanbar.org/groups/professional_responsibility/publications/model_rules_of_professional_conduct.html.

One of the many rules issued by the ABA is Rule 5.5: Unauthorized Practice of Law; Multijurisdictional Practice of Law.

Rule 5.5 of the MRPC is easily understandable when applied to attorneys who wish to litigate on behalf of individuals associated with sport. To serve as counsel for an individual or organization, draft and file pleadings, serve discovery, take depositions, and appear in court, one must be licensed by the appropriate state and/or federal bar, and Rule 5.5(a) reinforces that point. It states, "A lawyer shall not practice law in a jurisdiction in violation of the regulation of the legal profession in that jurisdiction, or assist another in doing so."[13] The rule is less clear when applied to lawyers engaged in transactional work on behalf of individuals and organizations associated with sport and located in jurisdictions where the lawyer is not licensed. Matters are further complicated when sports-related transactions are negotiated by those who are not licensed to practice law and have never attended law school.

Even though California does not follow the MRPC, it still has rules regarding the unauthorized practice of law. Because California hosts many professional franchises and serves as the home of numerous professional and amateur athletes, these rules are important to note. Section 6125 of California's Business and Professions Code provides that no person shall practice law in California unless that person is an active member of the state bar.[14] It has been held that the cited statute does not differentiate between attorneys and nonattorneys.[15] Many states have similar statutes, which aim to protect their constituents "against the dangers of legal representation and advice given by persons not trained, examined and licensed for such work, whether they be laymen or lawyers from other jurisdictions."[16]

The key question remains, what constitutes the practice of law? Does an NFLPA contract advisor who negotiates the terms of a uniform player contract with an NFL team engage in the practice of law? What about a

---

13. *Id.*

14. Bus. & Prof. Code, §§ 6125–6133.

15. See Birbrower, Montalbano, Condon, & Frank, P.C. v. Super. Ct. of Santa Clara County, 949 P.2d 1, 7 (Cal. 1998).

16. *Spivak v. Sachs*, 16 N.Y.2d 163, 168 [1965].

marketing agent who does not use a boilerplate contract provided pursuant to a collective bargaining agreement but instead drafts, redlines, and/or negotiates a contract with language that is not necessarily familiar to lay individuals? The ABA provides a thorough listing of the various state definitions of the "practice of law."[17] In Florida, the practice of law not only includes representing another in court, but also the providing of legal advice and counsel to others "and the preparation of legal instruments, including contracts, by which legal rights are either obtained, secured or given away, although such matters may not then or ever be the subject of proceedings in a court."[18] Additionally, the Florida Supreme Court has ruled that if the giving of advice

> affect[s] important rights of a person under the law, and if the reasonable protection of the rights and property of those advised and served requires that the persons giving such advice possess legal skill and a knowledge of the law greater than that possessed by the average citizen, then the giving of such advice . . . by one for another as a course of conduct constitute the practice of law.[19]

Case Study

Cuyahoga Cty. Bar Assn. v. Glenn

Even when attorneys wear the agent hat rather than the attorney hat, they are still subject to the lawyer code of ethics.[20] That particular stance is reinforced through the case of *Cuyahoga Cty. Bar Assn. v. Glenn*.[21] In 1992, Everett L. Glenn was acting in a sports agent

---

17. *See* American Bar Association, *State Definitions of the Practice of Law*, *at* http://www.americanbar.org/content/dam/aba/migrated/cpr/model-def/model_def_statutes.authcheckdam.pdf.

18. State *ex rel.* The Florida Bar v. Sperry, 140 So.2d 587, 591 (1962).

19. *Id.*

20. *See ABA Model Code of Professional Responsibility*, *at* http://www.americanbar.org/content/dam/aba/migrated/cpr/mrpc/mcpr.authcheckdam.pdf.

21. *See generally* Cuyahoga Cty. Bar Assn. v. Glenn, 1995-Ohio-35, 72 Ohio St. 3d 299, 649 N.E.2d 1213 (1995).

capacity while he renegotiated the terms in an NFL player's contract between his client, Richard Dent, and his client's team, the Chicago Bears.[22] After negotiating a deal between Dent and the Chicago Bears that entitled Dent to the amount of $200,000 in reporting bonuses, Glenn improperly represented to the treasurer of the Chicago Bears that he was entitled to $20,000 of the bonus amount.[23] Because the treasurer had dealt with Glenn under similar circumstances on prior occasions, the treasurer wired the money to Glenn with confidence that Dent had authorized the commission.[24] However, that was not the case, as Glenn never actually obtained Dent's authorization.[25] Additionally, Glenn was asked to provide an authorization form signed by Dent and to send it back to the treasurer once he received the wired funds, which he failed to do.[26] Glenn later refused to repay the money even after Dent objected to the payment, claiming that he was owed that amount (plus additional funds) for past services provided to Dent.[27] However, at a hearing, a panel credited Dent's testimony that he never authorized Glenn's receipt of the $20,000 sum in question, and the Chicago Bears refunded the amount to Dent.[28] As a result of Glenn's actions, the Ohio Bar Association ordered that Glenn be suspended from the practice of law in Ohio for a year, with the requirement that he make full restitution to the Chicago Bears for the amount in question in order to be readmitted once the one-year suspension ceased.[29]

---

22. *Id.*

23. *Id.*

24. *Id.* (The Chicago Bears' treasurer, who had knowledge of prior negotiations between the team and Glenn, "wired this money in the confidence.")

25. *Id.* (Glenn never actually "obtained Dent's signature on the authorization form.")

26. *Id.*

27. *Id.* (At a hearing, Glenn stated that "he was owed this money and more for past services.")

28. *Id.* (The Chicago Bears "subsequently refunded to Dent the difference between the present value of his advanced reporting bonuses and the $20,000" amount that was wired to Glenn.)

29. *Id.*

The State of Ohio has made it clear that it is taking what it views as unauthorized practice of law by sports agents very seriously. On May 29, 2012, the assistant general counsel at the MLBPA emailed all certified player agents about Ohio's charge that two baseball agents engaged in the unauthorized practice of law by (1) holding themselves out as attorneys representing professional athletes on professional teams within the State of Ohio, (2) traveling to Ohio to meet with an MLB team on behalf of a drafted college player and advising the player and his parents concerning such negotiations and compliance with NCAA rules, and (3) communicating with the MLB team on behalf of the player in connection with the offer of a contract to him by the team.[30] Although this isolated case currently only affects those operating their agency businesses in Ohio, it could serve as a significant threat to nonattorney agents and attorney agents not licensed in the states that they conduct business in if other states determine it to be in their best interests to follow Ohio's lead. After the charge made by the Ohio State Bar Association, the MLBPA sent an e-mail to player agents informing them that the association believed that the case "could represent a significant threat to the ability of Player Agents, who are not licensed to practice law in Ohio, to continue to represent athletes who reside or attend school in Ohio, or are employed, or wish to be employed by teams in Ohio."[31]

It appears that nonattorney agents and attorney agents who operate outside of the jurisdictions in which they are licensed may have cause for concern. However, there are no known decided cases that have made a clear determination as to whether said individuals are engaged in the unauthorized practice of law.[32] As discussed earlier, disputes between agents and their clients (or former clients) are quite common, with the athlete often doing whatever is possible to persuade an arbitrator (the disputes are typically

---

30. *See* Darren Heitner, *Detroit Tigers Pitcher Andrew Oliver's Former Advisors' Actions May Represent Significant Threat to Baseball Agents*, FORBES, June 6, 2012, at http://www .forbes.com/sites/darrenheitner/2012/06/06/detroit-tigers-pitcher-andrew-olivers-former -advisors-actions-may-represent-significant-threat-to-baseball-agents/.

31. *Id.*

32. Jeremy J. Geisel, *Disbarring Jerry Maguire: How Broadly Defining "Unauthorized Practice of Law" Could Take the "Lawyer" Out of "LawyerAgent" Despite the Current State of Athlete Agent Legislation*, 18 MARQ. SPORTS L.J. 225, 242 (2007).

handled through mandatory binding arbitration promulgated by the players' association) that no fee is owed to the agent. It may not be long before some athletes begin to opt for the claim that their agents were engaging in the unauthorized practice of law (in addition to some type of professional malpractice) in an attempt to avoid the payment of agent fees.

Chapter 7

Drug Testing and Use

In September 2013, I was asked to moderate a roundtable discussion in New York City about performance-enhancing drugs (PEDs). The roundtable was put together by PureSport, an anti-doping initiative backed by chairman of Skins International Jaimie Fuller and Canadian former sprinter Ben Johnson, who earned a gold medal and set a world record when he beat Carl Lewis and Linford Christie at the 1988 Seoul Olympic Games. The panel also included former Major League Baseball (MLB) player Jose Canseco, Bay Area Laboratory Co-Operative (largely recognized by the acronym BALCO) defense attorney Troy Ellerman, Olympic gold medalist sailor and professional CrossFit athlete Anna Tunnicliffe, and clinical psychologist Stan Teitelbaum. If the names gracing the panel were not enough to indicate the significance of the event, the heavy discussion and admissions in 2013 concerning the widespread use of PEDs demonstrated just how pressing the issue remained among those competing in amateur and professional sports. The professional leagues, the National Collegiate Athletic Association, and international governing bodies have been criticized and/or praised (depending on who is doing the speaking) for efforts to curb the use of PEDs and/or educate athletes on what is and is not permissible to ingest. This chapter will specifically focus on MLB, the National Football League (NFL), and cyclist Lance Armstrong in an effort to reveal some of the issues that exist in the 21st century concerning PEDs. MLB and the NFL have received the most scrutiny of the major professional leagues, but how can one speak about PEDs without a mention of Armstrong and the United States Anti-Doping Agency (USADA)?

Major League Baseball

"The guys that are cheating or whatever are taking something away from the other players. They're lying to the fans, they're lying to their teammates, they're lying to their GMs, their owners, and they're going to get caught."[1]
—Los Angeles Angels of Anaheim pitcher C. J. Wilson

Baseball, the most scrutinized major American professional sport for the widespread use of PEDs among its players, is also home to the league that has been at the lead of implementing changes to curb such habits. MLB's current drug-testing policy, which is actually a joint agreement between MLB and the Major League Baseball Players Association (MLBPA) (and is referred to as the Joint Drug Agreement), first became effective for the 2006 championship season. Its stated purposes are to educate players concerning the risk of using prohibited substances (as defined in the policy), deter players' use of prohibited substances, and provide for a proper resolution procedure in case a dispute may arise regarding the existence, interpretation, or application of the drug-testing program.[2]

Case Study

Melky Cabrera

In 2012, San Francisco Giants left fielder Melky Cabrera was suspended for 50 games after it was determined that he tested positive for having elevated levels of testosterone. According to MLB's drug-testing policy, testosterone is deemed to be a PED. Instead of simply accepting the punishment or filing an appeal based on a more traditional claim such as attacking the sanctity of the testing process, Cabrera was found to have enlisted a "paid consultant" of his agency (ACES Baseball) to create a fictitious website promoting

---

1. *See Quotes: Ryan Braun Suspended by MLB*, Associated Press, Jul. 23, 2013, *at* http://sports.espn.go.com/espn/wire?section=mlb&id=9501571.
2. Major League Baseball's Joint Drug Prevention and Treatment Program, Preamble, Page 1, MLB.com, *at* http://mlb.mlb.com/pa/pdf/jda.pdf.

a nonexistent product that Cabrera was then going to claim was the reason behind his failed test.[3] The theory was that Cabrera would persuade others that he ingested the product without knowledge that it contained a prohibited substance under MLB's drug program and that the story would lead to his eventual exoneration. The fake website cost approximately $10,000 to develop, but the fallout for Cabrera and his advisors when the scheme was discovered was ostensibly much larger. Although Cabrera's agents voluntarily spoke to the media in an effort to distance themselves from the "paid consultant," many high-profile baseball players moved to different agencies after the Cabrera news broke.[4] However, the MLBPA investigated the matter and concluded that the principals of ACES Baseball were not involved in and had no knowledge of the Cabrera scheme prior to the *New York Daily News* article that initially exposed the player and the "paid consultant."

MLB's current drug-testing policy is largely the result of a very public scandal that ended up involving the federal government. It began with the investigation of BALCO, a medical supplement company. There was a belief that BALCO and its principal Victor Conte were responsible for supplying PEDs to many prominent athletes, the most noteworthy being San Francisco Giants outfielder Barry Bonds.[5] After the conclusion of a federal investigation, BALCO's office was raided. Months later, Conte and other BALCO executives (along with Barry Bonds's trainer, Greg Anderson) were charged with conspiracy to distribute PEDs, including anabolic steroids. The House Government Reform Committee eventually became involved in the affair and questioned MLB

3. *See* Teri Thompson, *Exclusive: Daily News Uncovers Bizarre Plot by San Francisco Giants' Melky Cabrera to Use Fake Website and Duck Drug Suspension*, N.Y. DAILY NEWS, Aug. 19, 2012, *at* http://www.nydailynews.com/sports/baseball/exclusive-daily-news-uncovers-bizarre-plot-melky-cabrera-fake-website-duck-drug-suspension-article-1.1139623.

4. *See* Darren Heitner, *How the Melky Cabrera Chaos Is Affecting ACES Baseball Agency*, SPORTS AGENT BLOG, Oct. 17, 2012, *at* http://www.sportsagentblog.com/2012/10/17/how-the-melky-cabrera-chaos-is-affecting-aces-baseball-agency/.

5. *What Is the Balco Scandal*, THE TELEGRAPH (Mar. 21, 2011), *at* http://www.telegraph.co.uk/sport/othersports/drugsinsport/8396065/What-is-the-Balco-scandal.html.

officials and players concerning their use of PEDs.[6] At the hearings conducted by the House Government Reform Committee, former MLB player Rafael Palmeiro testified that he never used PEDs,[7] a testimony that was debunked when Palmeiro tested positive for steroid use later that same year.[8]

Baseball's drug-testing policy in the wake of BALCO (sometimes referred to as the post-steroid era) and the congressional hearings may be championed by many, including MLB and the MLBPA. However, it has not served as a veil to shield the sport of baseball from scrutiny due to the abuse of PEDs. The major PED scandal in 2013 involved a Miami-based company named Biogenesis, which was alleged to have provided PEDs to a plethora of prominent baseball players, including New York Yankees third baseman Alex Rodriguez and Milwaukee Brewers left fielder Ryan Braun.[9] Whereas Conte was the face of BALCO, Anthony Bosch was the principal under scrutiny at Biogenesis. MLB filed a lawsuit against Bosch, but has appeared to be willing to let it die (although perhaps also using it to obtain additional testimony) in exchange for Bosch's cooperation in the investigation concerning players who allegedly received PEDs from his operation. Because the Biogenesis scandal has been covered by practically every major media outlet and the names of those implicated for taking PEDs have been read by most people who follow professional baseball, those players who received a suspension will not be able to enjoy the level of confidentiality typically expected by players under the microscope for potentially violating the Joint Drug Agreement.[10] That agreement allowed MLB to announce

6. *ALCO Investigation Timeline*, USA Today (last updated Nov. 26, 2007), *at* http://usatoday30.usatoday.com/sports/balco-timeline.htm.

7. Testimony of Rafael Palmeiro before the Committee on Government Reform, Bizofbaseball.com (Mar. 17, 2005), *at* http://www.bizofbaseball.com/steroidhearings/PalmeiroTestimony.pdf.

8. 1 Jorge Arangure Jr., *Palmeiro Suspended for Steroid Violation*, Wash. Post (Aug. 2, 2005), *at* http://www.washingtonpost.com/wp-dyn/content/article/2005/08/01/AR2005080100739.html.

9. Tim Elfrink, *A Miami Clinic Supplies Drugs to Sports' Biggest Names*, MiamiNewTimes. Com (Jan. 31, 2013), *at* http://www.miaminewtimes.com/2013-01-31/news/a-rod-and-doping-a-miami-clinic-supplies-drugs-to-sports-biggest-names/.

10. *See* Ken Rosenthal, *PED Suspensions Could Be Announced before Appeals*, Fox Sports, June 23, 2013, *at* http://msn.foxsports.com/mlb/story/biogenesis-PED-suspensions-could-be-announced-before-appeals-ryan-braun-alex-rodriguez-melky-cabrera-062213.

said suspensions for more than ten players who were deemed to have violated MLB's drug policy as first-time offenders.[11] None of the players who received 50-game suspensions for their ties to Biogenesis decided to appeal the decision. Ryan Braun and Alex Rodriguez served as the exceptions: their suspensions were for more than 50 games.

In July 2013, Ryan Braun accepted a 65-game suspension, effectively keeping him away from competing for the Milwaukee Brewers for the remainder of the 2013 MLB championship season.[12] In front of the world, Braun stated: "I am not perfect. I realize now that I have made some mistakes. I am willing to accept the consequences of those actions."[13] In the wake of Braun's announcement, MLBPA executive director Michael Weiner responded: "I am deeply gratified to see Ryan taking this bold step. It vindicates the rights of all players under the Joint Drug Program. It is good for the game that Ryan will return soon to continue his great work both on and off the field."[14] The Joint Drug Agreement provides a formula for suspensions when a player is found to have failed a drug test. That formula applies a 50-game suspension for first-time offenders, a suspension of 100 games for second-time offenders, and a lifetime ban from MLB competitions upon the discovery of a third offense. Because Braun has not technically been found to have failed a drug test and because the suspension is justified by the commissioner's ability to suspend players for "just cause," Braun's suspension of 65 games is separate and apart from the Joint Drug Agreement's typical guidance concerning the length of a player's suspension.[15] The 60-game suspension may effectively be viewed as a settlement outside of the Joint Drug Agreement whereby Braun accepted a considerable pun-

---

11. *See* Christian Red, *Twelve Other MLB Players Accept 50-Game Suspension from Biogenesis Investigation*, N.Y. DAILY NEWS, Aug. 5, 2013, *at* http://www.nydailynews.com /sports/baseball/dirty-dozen-12-hit-a-rod-fights-article-1.1418464.

12. *See Ryan Braun Statement Text*, YAHOO! SPORTS, Aug. 23, 2013, *at* http://sports.yahoo .com/news/ryan-braun-statement-text-071956030—mlb.html.

13. *Id.*

14. *See* Darren Heitner, *Ryan Braun's Suspension Is the Least of His and the MLBPA's Concerns*, FORBES, July 23, 2013, *at* http://www.forbes.com/sites/darrenheitner/2013/07/23 /ryan-brauns-suspension-is-the-least-of-his-and-the-mlbpas-concerns/.

15. *See* Tom Verducci, *Answering Key Questions in Wake of Ryan Braun Suspension*, SI.COM, July 24, 2013, *at* http://sportsillustrated.cnn.com/mlb/news/20130723 /ryan-braun-suspended-biogenesis/.

ishment, but certainly not the worst possible discipline considering that he could have been deemed a second-time offender who would have also been required to sit out an additional 50 games for never serving time based on what should have been a first suspension after testing positive in October 2011. A 150-game suspension would have caused Braun to sit out a portion of the 2014 MLB championship season in addition to the remainder of the 2013 season and would have cost him an estimated $2 million above the $3.25 million that he forfeited for games lost in 2013.

In early August 2013, MLB informed Alex Rodriguez that his suspension would last a total of 211 games, keeping the New York Yankees third baseman off of the field for the remainder of the 2013 season and throughout the 2014 season. It would cost Alex Rodriguez more than $30 million in lost wages if held out of play for such a length of time. The number of days stipulated as part of the suspension does not fit naturally within the Joint Drug Agreement's stated disciplinary structure. As a first-time offender, Rodriguez should have been suspended only 50 games. However, MLB justified the extended suspension by stating that it was based not only on his violation of the Joint Drug Agreement, but also on a breach of the Basic Agreement due to his attempt to cover up violations "by engaging in a course of conduct intended to obstruct and frustrate the Office of the Commissioner's investigation."[16] Because Rodriguez quickly filed an appeal, the suspension was stayed. While awaiting a grievance hearing before the appointed arbitrator, he was able to continue to provide his services to the Yankees.

The media must be careful in the way that they report allegations concerning the (assumed) use of PEDs by professional baseball players. A failure to use caution and/or a proclivity to attach blame prior to any actual findings could attach liability to members of the media and their outlets based on the information that goes out to the public. Further, today, when blogging proliferates and journalists can reach the masses based on a single tweet, extra caution should be applied. A lack of adhering to basic journalistic principals may lead to defamation lawsuits filed by those whose reputations

---

16. *See* Tweet from MLB Public Relations, Aug. 5, 2013, *at* http://www.twitlonger.com /show/n_1rloqtu.

are harmed without justification. However, because it is a media entity publishing the potentially defamatory content and the subject is undoubtedly a public figure, the applicable standard required for defamation is "actual malice," which means that the speaker must have had knowledge of the falsity of the content or have displayed reckless disregard concerning its truth.[17]

The allegations that Los Angeles Angels first baseman Albert Pujols used PEDs serve as a good example of why media entities need to be careful about what they report and how they report it. In August 2013, sports radio host and former MLB player Jack Clark said on his radio show that he knew for a fact that Pujols was a "juicer" (used PEDs) based on what Clark had heard from Pujols's trainer.[18] Clark went so far as to say that Pujols's trainer "shot him up."[19] The trainer vehemently denied said allegations, saying that he would bet his life that Pujols would never use illegal drugs in any way.[20] Days after Clark's accusations, Pujols threatened to sue him; soon thereafter, Clark was fired from the radio station that hosted his show.[21] From a legal perspective, the worst of Clark's troubles may be in the form of a lawsuit filed by Pujols. Pujols would be able to claim that Clark's statements amounted to slander per se because the words concerned Pujols in his profession as a professional baseball player. Such a claim would allow Pujols to avoid the requirement of proving special damages because they would be assumed, as would Clark's malicious intent to harm Pujols. However, a lawsuit would also open the door to discovery, and if Pujols were be hiding anything (including results from prior drug tests), that information would

---

17. New York Times Co. v. Sullivan, 376 U.S. 254 (1964); Dun & Bradstreet, Inc. v. Greenmoss Builders, Inc., 472 U.S. 749 (1985); Philadelphia Newspapers, Inc. v. Hepps, 475 U.S. 767 (1986); Shari Albrecht, John P. Borger, Patrick L. Groshong, Ashley Kissinger, Joseph et. al., *Recent Developments in Media, Privacy, and Defamation Law*, 47 TORT TRIAL & INS. PRAC. L.J. 359, 382 (2011).

18. *See* Darren Heitner, *Albert Pujols Defends Clean Reputation by Threatening Legal Action against Radio Host*, FORBES, Aug. 10, 2013, *at* http://www.forbes.com/sites /darrenheitner/2013/08/10/albert-pujols-defends-clean-reputation-by-threatening-legal-action-against-radio-host/.

19. *Id.*

20. *Id.*

21. *See* Jim Salter, *Jack Clark Fired: PED Comment about Albert Pujols Costs Radio Host Job*, HUFFINGTON POST, Aug. 12, 2013, *at* http://www.huffingtonpost.com/2013/08/12 /jack-clark-fired-peds-albert-pujols-radio_n_3744598.html.

become available to Clark and his legal team. On October 4, 2013, Albert Pujols filed a lawsuit against Jack Clark in Circuit Court in St. Louis County, Missouri (the county in which Pujols resides).[22] After filing the lawsuit, Pujols said, "My lawyers have told me that the upcoming legal fight will not be an easy one, and that in cases like this even a liar can sometimes be protected under the law . . . I believe we are all accountable for the things we do and say, and it was important for me to stand up for what was right against those who would seek to drag me down to try and build themselves up."[23]

National Football League

"'For me, I'm happy,' Beason told NFL Network's 'NFL AM' on Tuesday. 'I don't take that stuff, so I'm more than happy to (take a test) because the guys who are taking it, if they get caught, now it's an even playing field. It's already hard enough to make it to the league, to stay in the league and to stay healthy in the league.'"[24]
—Carolina Panthers linebacker Jon Beason

If former NFL quarterback Boomer Esiason is correct, in 2013 approximately 60 to 70 percent of NFL players used human growth hormone (HGH) to gain a competitive advantage over their peers.[25] However, if that many NFL players were using the hormone, it appears that said players were simply taking it to remain competitive with the majority of their competitors. That high estimate lacks shock value simply because the NFL does not thoroughly test for the use of HGH, even though the NFL has

---

22. *See* Alan Scher Zagier, *Pujols Sues Jack Clark Over Steroid Comments*, ASSOCIATED PRESS, Oct. 5, 2013, *at* http://sports.yahoo.com/news/pujols-sues-jack-clark-over-171046504 --mlb.html.

23. *Id.*

24. *See* Marc Sessler, *Jon Beason of Panthers: I Look Forward to HGH Testing*, NFL.COM, July 23, 2013, *at* http://www.nfl.com/news/story/0ap1000000219781/article /jon-beason-of-panthers-i-look-forward-to-hgh-testing.

25. *See B&C Morning Show: Boomer Sounds Off on Perceived "Massive Growth" of HGH in NFL*, CBS NEW YORK, Sept. 25, 2012, *at* http://newyork.cbslocal.com/2012/09/25 /bc-morning-show-boomer-sounds-off-on-perceived-massive-growth-of-hgh-in-nfl/.

long desired to control the mechanisms by which players would be forced to undergo such testing.

The 2011 NFL collective bargaining agreement (CBA) includes a provision in Article 39, Section 7(b) that states that "[t]he parties confirm that the Program on Anabolic Steroids and Related Substances will include both annual blood testing and random blood testing for human growth hormone, with discipline for positive tests at the same level as for steroids."[26] The players and owners were supposed to develop a specific system to test for HGH within several weeks of signing the new CBA.[27] The understood goal was to implement such a system that included the safe and secure collection, transportation, and review of samples by the start of the 2011 NFL regular season.[28] Two years later, the players prepared for the start of the 2013 NFL preseason with no system in sight.

The National Football League Players Association (NFLPA), as the representative body of NFL professional football players, has long made it difficult for the NFL to implement any such HGH testing program. It has maintained that NFL players are a unique cross section of the general public and are indeed a different class of athlete compared with others. This position has led to a prolonged debate between the NFL and the NFLPA over the use of the World Anti-Doping Agency's (WADA) guidelines with regard to the implementation of HGH testing. However, in July 2013, the NFL and the NFLPA agreed to push the envelope and perhaps inch closer to the HGH testing system alluded to in the 2011 NFL CBA.

The agreement between the NFL and the NFLPA was to conduct a population study that would then provide insight as to the normal growth hormone levels among the group of NFL players.[29] The study's conclusion may allow the NFL and the NFLPA to reach an agreed-upon threshold in determining whether a player's future HGH test results lead to a suspension

---

26. *See* NFL, *Collective Bargaining Agreement, at* http://nfllabor.files.wordpress.com/2010/01/collective-bargaining-agreement-2011-2020.pdf.

27. *Id.*

28. *Id.*

29. *See* David Epstein, *A Step Toward HGH Testing—in the Wrong Direction*, THE MMQB, July 2013, *at* http://mmqb.si.com/2013/07/24/hgh-test/.

or clear a player for continued service to his team.[30] WADA has long provided such benchmarks for Olympic athletes, but the NFLPA has held that the athletes it represents need separate guidelines. The NFL may be concerned that if, as Esiason projects, as many as 60 to 70 percent of NFL players are using HGH, the population study could turn out to be severely skewed to represent a 2013 NFL player population full of HGH abusers.

Lance Armstrong's Battle with the USADA

"There is no limit to what [Lance Armstrong] would do to protect his secret, and not one word could come out of his mouth that would convince me to change his opinion of who he really is."[31]
—Kathy LeMond, wife of three-time Tour de France champion Greg LeMond

On January 17, 2013, seven-time Tour de France winner Lance Armstrong sat down with talk show host Oprah Winfrey as part of a two-night interview to discuss rampant allegations of Armstrong's PED use during his cycling career. The interview came long after the USADA had charged Armstrong with violating numerous anti-doping rules drafted and enforced by the agency, which brought disrepute to Armstrong's name and tarnished the many years of success that the cyclist enjoyed throughout his career.

The USADA claimed that beginning in January 1998, Armstrong took certain actions that violated the Union Cycliste Internationale (UCI), World Anti-Doping Agency (WADA), and USADA protocols. The alleged violations included (1) use and/or attempted use of prohibited substances and/or methods including Erythropoietin (also known as "EPO," which has an effect of increasing the number of red blood cells within one's circulatory system, enhancing an individual's capacity to carry oxygen), blood transfusions, testosterone, corticosteroids, and masking agents; (2) possession of prohibited

---

30. *Id.*
31. *See* Lance Pugmire, *Some Around Lance Armstrong View TV Confession with Skepticism*, L.A. Times, Jan. 17, 2013, *at* http://articles.latimes.com/2013/jan/17/sports/la-sp-lance-armstrong-20130117/.

substances and/or methods including EPO, blood transfusions and related equipment (such as needles, blood bags, storage containers, and other transfusion equipment and blood parameter measuring devices), testosterone, corticosteroids, and masking agents; (3) trafficking of EPO, testosterone, and corticosteroids; (4) administration and/or attempted administration to others of EPO, testosterone, and corticosteroids; (5) assisting, encouraging, aiding, abetting, covering up, and other complicity involving one or more anti-doping rule violations and/or attempted anti-doping rule violations; and (6) aggravating circumstances justifying a period of ineligibility greater than the standard sanction. The USADA indicated that multiple riders, team personnel, and others were willing to testify based on personal knowledge that Armstrong used EPO, blood transfusions, testosterone, and corticosteroids during the period in question and that he also provided and encouraged fellow riders to use doping products and/or methods during competition.

In June 2012, Armstrong was informed by the USADA that it was formally charging him with violating anti-doping rules. Soon thereafter, the World Triathlon Corporation suspended him from participating in its athletic events.

Armstrong quickly took legal action to challenge the USADA's jurisdiction to bring the aforementioned charges against him. Armstrong claimed that (1) the UCI had jurisdiction to determine whether to proceed against him, not the USADA; (2) prior to August 13, 2004, the UCI conferred no authority on the USADA; (3) the UCI discovered the information contained within the charges, not the USADA; and (4) the UCI did not delegate its jurisdiction to the USADA because "none of the requirements for a delegation of authority has been satisfied," including an independent conclusion by the UCI that a violation of its rules likely occurred. Armstrong's position was that even if the USADA had proper jurisdiction to bring the aforementioned charges against the cyclist, said charges would have still been insufficiently made because they were in violation of the USADA's own rules. To that end, Armstrong alleged that (1) the USADA's eight-year limitation time period barred many of the agency's charges; (2) improper inducements were afforded to potential witnesses who intended to testify against Armstrong; and (3) the USADA's review board was biased, was influenced by one-sided evidence, and failed to give meaningful consideration to Armstrong's version of the facts. In addition to his jurisdictional challenges, Armstrong also highlighted the USADA's arbitration procedures, calling into question whether said procedures comport with due process. Among his many issues with the arbitration process were the facts that Armstrong was not provided with an adequate charging document, he had no right to cross-examine or confront witnesses, and he had no right to an impartial arbitration panel.

The USADA moved to dismiss Armstrong's complaint, which was granted by the U.S. District Court for the Western District of Texas (Austin Division). Although the court noted that there were troubling aspects of the case, it determined that such matters are best resolved internally. The order contained a noteworthy footnote that reads as follows:

> Indeed, it is hard to imagine a situation more illustrative of Judge Posner's famous words, that "there can be few less suitable bodies than the federal courts for determining the eligibility, or the procedures for determining the eligibility, of athletes to participate in the Olympic Games." *Michels v. US. Olympic Comm.*, 741 F.2d 155, 159 (7th Cir. 1984) (Posner, J., concurring). By the same token, this Court simply has no business telling national and international amateur athletic organizations how to regulate their respective sports.

Armstrong agreed to arbitrate with the USADA, and the court deemed that the USADA's arbitration rules were sufficient to satisfy due process. The court stated that it *cannot* interfere on the basis of speculative injury.

Chapter 8

Contract Drafting and Negotiation

Sports Lawyers make a living by charging their clients fees; otherwise they would not last very long as able and willing practitioners. The most common form of compensation for those negotiating contracts on behalf of professional athletes and with professional organizations is based on a commission structure (with the range of acceptable percentages of the contract oftentimes regulated by a players' association). Unfortunately for these sports agents, their commissions are rather low (a maximum of 3 percent on an NFL contract and 4 percent on an NBA contract). However, the actual contract drafting and negotiation conducted by said professionals is somewhat limited; they engage in discussions surrounding "uniform player contracts" (agreements that leave little room to negotiate a large amount of the provisions contained therein) and oftentimes are bound by strict or looser salary guidelines (i.e., the NBA's rookie wage scale that dictates what a first-round selection will be entitled to at each pick [with the ability to negotiate as high as 120 percent or as low as 80 percent of that value]).

In an effort to become more competitive among the plethora of others fighting to represent the same players, some sports agents have diverted from the common model and opted to charge clients an hourly fee for the time spent negotiating contracts between their clients and professional clubs. This mimics a more regular practice of lawyers working on transactional matters wherein the lawyer hedges the risk of not receiving any commission should the client not sign a contract and the client ends up pocketing more money, because he or she is paying closer to the true value of the lawyer's services as opposed to some arbitrary percentage. Such an hourly fee is deemed acceptable by the players' associations as long as the total amount paid in hourly fees is less than the amount of money the agent would have expected to receive under the highest possible contingency fee arrangement.

While contingency fee arrangements between sports agents and their clients remain the most common form of fee model for both team-related contracts and endorsement deals, Sports Lawyers who operate outside the realm of agency are better known for charging their clients an hourly or flat fee to draft, negotiate, review, and revise contracts. A flat fee is an amount of money that the lawyer quotes his or her client to fully perform an obligation. It is typically an estimate comprised of the attorney's hourly fee multiplied by the amount of time estimated to be needed to complete the responsibility. Clients typically enjoy these arrangements; they know how much money they will be paying their counsel at the outset of representation. Lawyers are also fond of flat fees, since they too have a clear understanding that they will be compensated for the work they perform. Where flat fees become a pain is when lengthy negotiations may be anticipated. In those situations, it is hard for a lawyer and client to agree on an amount of money to be paid, since the amount of time spent on the representation may be unknown.

One provision that has become a point of contention in negotiations is the "morals clause." That clause is discussed at length, below.

Morals Clauses

"I haven't read [my contract] . . . I don't think it covers, 'Let me totally dominate and interfere with your personal life.'"[1]
—Charlie Sheen, former star of the CBS hit sitcom *Two and a Half Men*

In the 21st century, morals clauses have become integral instruments for endorsement contracts between brands and athletes. Around-the-clock

---

1. *See* Scott Collins, *Morals Clause in Contract Unlikely for Charlie Sheen*, L.A. Times, Feb. 22, 2011, *at* http://www.dallasnews.com/entertainment/television/headlines/20110221-morals-clause-in-contract-unlikely-for-charlie-sheen.ece.

coverage of sports on television, the addition of cable networks dedicated to the delivery of sports content, and above all, the instantaneous dissemination of content directly from the mouths and fingertips of athletes (via social media including, but not limited to Twitter, Facebook, and Instagram) have sufficiently and sensibly scared brands into protecting themselves in case an athlete endorser acts in a way that contravenes the essence and/or image of the contracting entity. In the past few years, seven-time Tour de France champion Lance Armstrong admitted to using performance-enhancing drugs during his cycling career,[2] Tiger Woods was found to have cheated on his wife,[3] National Football League (NFL) quarterback Ben Roethlisberger was accused of assaulting a 20-year-old woman,[4] and Rashard Mendenhall fired off tweets questioning the terrorist attacks of September 11, 2001.

Armstrong lost his endorsement contract with Nike, while Nike maintained support for Livestrong initiatives, and Nike used a broadly crafted morals clause to escape the terms of the agreement without having to pay a penalty.[5] The company released a statement that said, in part, "Due to the seemingly insurmountable evidence that Lance Armstrong participated in doping and misled Nike for more than a decade, it is with great sadness that we have terminated our contract with him."[6] Armstrong did not put up much of a fight; however, when Hanesbrands decided to invoke its morals clause to get out of a contract with Rashard Mendenhall, the running back fought back.

---

2. *See* Darren Heitner, *Livestrong's Challenges as a Consequence of Lance Armstrong's Confessions*, FORBES, Jan. 18, 2013, *at* http://www.forbes.com/sites/darrenheitner/2013/01/18/livestrongs-challenges-as-a-consequence-of-lance-armstrongs-confession/.

3. *See* Emily Friedman, *Tiger Woods Apologizes after Alleged Mistress Jaimee Grubbs Releases Texts, Voicemail*, ABC NEWS, Dec. 2, 2009, *at* http://abcnews.go.com/Entertainment/tiger-woods-apologizes-alleged-mistress-jaimee-grubbs-releases/story?id=9228059.

4. *See* Chris Mortensen, *Ben Roethlisberger Gets Six-Game Ban*, ESPN.COM, Apr. 22, 2010, *at* http://sports.espn.go.com/nfl/news/story?id=5121614.

5. *See* Darren Heitner, *Nike's Disassociation from Lance Armstrong Makes Nike a Stronger Brand*, FORBES, Oct. 17, 2012, *at* http://www.forbes.com/sites/darrenheitner/2012/10/17/nikes-disassociation-from-lance-armstrong-makes-nike-a-stronger-brand/.

6. *Id.*

Case Study

Rashard Mendenhall, NFL Running Back

In May 2011, in the immediate wake of the announcement that Osama bin Laden had been killed, NFL running back Rashard Mendenhall tweeted[7] the following statements: "What kind of person celebrates death? It's amazing how people can HATE a man they have never even heard speak. We've only heard one side . . ." and "We'll never know what really happened. I just have a hard time believing a plane could take a skyscraper down demolition style."[8] In response to Mendenhall's public statements, which were instantaneously pushed to his 13,000-plus followers and covered by a variety of media outlets, Hanesbrands, which owns the Champion manufacturer of athletic apparel, terminated its endorsement contract with Mendenhall.[9] Hanesbrands justified its termination of the agreement by referring to the morals clause contained therein, which explained that Hanesbrands had a right to terminate if Mendenhall: "[Became] involved in any situation or occurrence . . . tending to bring Mendenhall into public disrepute, contempt, scandal, or ridicule, or tending to shock, insult, or offend the majority of the consuming public. . . . [Hanesbrands'] decision on all matters arising under [this section] shall be conclusive."[10] Mendenhall fired back with a $1 million lawsuit against Hanesbrands, which alleged that Mendenhall's tweets did not amount to a violation of the morals clause and that Hanesbrands's unilateral action to terminate the agreement was a breach that damaged the NFL running back.[11] Hanesbrands filed a motion to dismiss Mendenhall's complaint, but was denied by the court based on a finding that

---

7. Rashard Mendenhall's official Twitter account is at https://twitter.com/r_mendenhall.

8. *See Rashard Mendenhall Doesn't Hold Back*, ESPN, May 4, 2011, *at* http://sports.espn.go.com/nfl/news/story?id=6471433.

9. *See* Venkat Balasubramani, *Technology and Marketing Law Blog: Terminating an NFL Player's Endorsement Agreement for Polemic Tweets May Be Contract Breach—Mendenhall v. Hanes*, EricGoldman.org, Apr. 16, 2012, *at* http://blog.ericgoldman.org/archives/2012/04/factual_dispute.htm.

10. *Id.*

11. *Id.*

"Hanesbrands had an implied covenant of good faith and fair dealing not to act arbitrarily, irrationally or unreasonably in exercising discretion to execute its termination rights under the morals clause of the contract with Mendenhall" and that the determination of same should be left for a trier of fact.[12] Ultimately, the lawsuit settled out of court for an undisclosed amount of money, but not before Mendenhall's counsel brought out that Hanesbrands "hired Mr. Mendenhall as an endorser *after* he had gone public to challenge the United States government's explanation for the attacks of Sept. 11."[13]

Although it settled prior to reaching trial, the *Mendenhall v. Hanesbrands* litigation brings to surface a lingering worry regarding the drafting of morals clauses in contracts for considerable compensation. Morals clauses tend to be written in an ambiguous fashion by brands in an effort to provide a wide scope of available justifications for an early termination of an endorsement agreement. However, brands need be concerned that their counsel draft morals clauses to be overbroad and/or vague because courts commonly construe ambiguous contractual language against the party that drafted it.[14] Had *Mendenhall v. Hanesbrands* been decided by a trier of fact adhering to a jury instruction that included reference to the common-law rule that any ambiguous language in the morals clause of the endorsement agreement be construed against Hanesbrands, what would the verdict have read? As is the case with most brands, Hanesbrands purposefully did not provide specific actions on the part of Mendenhall that would allow the company to terminate the endorsement agreement. A jury would have likely had to weigh the right of Hanesbrands to protect its image pursuant to the

---

12. *See* Benjamin Haynes, *Athletes, Morality Clauses, and Social Media*, SPORT IN LAW, Jan. 22, 2013, *at* http://sportinlaw.com/2013/01/22/athletes-morality-clauses-and-social-media/.

13. *See* Eriq Gardner, *Settlement Reached in Lawsuit by NFL Star Fired as Pitchman for 9/11 Conspiracy Tweets*, HOLLYWOOD REPORTER, Jan. 15, 2013, *at* http://www.hollywoodreporter.com/thr-esq/settlement-reached-lawsuit-filed-by-412750.

14. *See, e.g.*, United States Fire Ins. Co. v. Schnackenberg, 88 Ill. 2d 1, 4, 57 Ill. Dec. 840, 842, 429 N.E.2d 1203, 1205 (1981); Graff v. Billet, 64 N.Y.2d 899, 902, 487 N.Y.S.2d 733, 734–35, 477 N.E.2d 212, 213–14 (1984); Restatement (Second) of Contracts § 206; United States v. Seckinger, 397 U.S. 203, 210, 90 S. Ct. 880, 884–85, 25 L.Ed.2d 224 (1970).

morals clause against Mendenhall's allegation that Hanesbrands was not acting in good faith, in conjunction with the risk that Hanesbrands inured by drafting such a loose morals clause.

Sports Lawyers representing brands and athletes must consider the positives and negatives of a broadly drafted morals clause in endorsement contracts and, additionally, the consequences of negotiating same. If the athlete's attorney engages in negotiations with the brand's attorney concerning the specific language of the morals clause and/or if any of the drafter's original language is modified, any advantage the athlete may have had with regards to ambiguities could be ameliorated. Brands' attorneys should also consider the changing media landscape by including provisions concerning athletes' use of social media and providing a termination option should the athlete denigrate the brand through his or her actions therein.

Naming Rights Deals

"Naming rights, in the end, inhabit a quirky corner of the sports universe. Stadium and arena names change as companies go out of business, merge, are acquired or land in legal trouble."[15]
—Richard Sandomir, TV sports and business reporter for the *New York Times*

The first stadium named for a corporation in the United States is believed to be Wrigley Field, named after Wrigley chewing gum, which was owned by William Wrigley (who also owned the Chicago Cubs).[16] Since 1926, when the Cubs officially began playing in Wrigley Field, the cost to acquire naming rights has dramatically risen around the world. To get its name on the facility where the New York Giants and New York Jets play their games, insurance provider MetLife agreed to pay $400 million over a 25-year

---

15. *See* Richard Sandomir, *Arena Names Can Spell Embarrassment*, N.Y. Times, July 4, 2012, *at* http://www.nytimes.com/2012/07/05/sports/arena-names-can-spell-embarra ssment.html?_r=0.

16. *See* Darren Heitner, *Why Jerry Jones Still Hasn't Sold Naming Rights to Cowboys Stadium*, Forbes, Nov. 9, 2012, *at* http://www.forbes.com/sites/darrenheitner/2012/11/09 /why-jerry-jones-still-hasnt-sold-naming-rights-to-cowboys-stadium/.

span.[17] The most lucrative NFL naming rights deal prior to the MetLife arrangement was between the Houston Texans and Texas-based Reliant, an electricity company, for $320 million over a 32-year span.[18] In 2013, Dallas-based AT&T purchased the right to rename Cowboys Stadium to AT&T Stadium for a reported $17 million to $19 million per year.[19]

Naming rights deals typically revolve around the terms of compensation and rarely are based on how wholesome the sponsor may be. Compensation is a chief concern because the grant of naming rights typically generates a substantial amount of revenue for the operator of the facility. Common naming rights sponsors are in the financial services and/or insurance industries (e.g., MetLife, Farmers, Citi), and are often companies that are not exactly perceived as the bastion of wholesomeness. These companies tend to be naming rights sponsors because they are often willing to put forth a substantial portion of the money sought by the owner of the naming rights at the negotiating table. The reputation of the sponsor affiliated with the facility often does not matter as much to the facility as the compensation provision embedded within the naming rights deal. There may, however, be consequences for facilities that neglect to seriously consider how an association with a poorly perceived sponsor can negatively affect the reputation of the facility that joins with a non-family-friendly corporation.

Case Study

Florida Atlantic University in Shackles

In February 2013, Florida Atlantic University (FAU) found a naming rights sponsor for its football stadium, which had been unnamed

---

17. *Id.*
18. *See* Brian Finkel, *NFL Stadiums with the Most-Expensive Naming Rights—MetLife Stadium's $400 Million Deal*, BLOOMBERG BUSINESSWEEK, Aug. 23, 2011, *at* http://images.businessweek.com/slideshows/20110822/nfl-stadiums-with-the-most-expensive-naming-rights.html#slide20.
19. *See* Candace Carlisle, *AT&T Buys Naming Rights to Cowboys Stadium*, DALLAS BUS. J., July 25, 2013, *at* http://www.bizjournals.com/dallas/blog/2013/07/att-buys-naming-rights-to-cowboys.html?page=all.

since its creation in 2011.[20] However, the grant of naming rights was not delivered to the sponsor without controversy and protest. The recipient of the grant was a corporation named GEO Group, Inc., "the world's leading provider of correctional, detention, and community reentry services with 101 facilities, approximately 73,000 beds, and 18,000 employees around the globe."[21] GEO Group reportedly paid $6 million for a 12-year term, which promised the corporation that FAU's football stadium would be renamed GEO Group Stadium.[22] The issue with the deal was that GEO Group had been under scrutiny for purportedly detaining individuals labeled as the lowest immigration enforcement priorities, treating detainees in a shocking manner, and losing lawsuits regarding the mistreatment of inmates.[23] It is impossible to determine whether the risk of associating with GEO Group was worth the $6 million in compensation, without an understanding of the FAU Athletic Department's financial situation and the best alternative it may have had to a negotiated deal with the company. Perhaps FAU could have signed a marginally smaller deal with an airline or food chain, but the public was not privy to that proprietary information. As such, on the outside looking in, it is tough to say whether FAU's decision was worthwhile for the university. However, the university had to confront formidable opposition and a protest movement that included participants calling FAU's stadium "Owlcatraz."[24]

---

20. *See* Jerry Hinnen, *Report: FAU Stadium Name Rights Bought by Private Prison Group*, CBSS-PORTS.COM, Feb. 19, 2013, *at* http://www.cbssports.com/collegefootball/eye-on-college-football/21732438/report-fau-stadium-name-rights-bought-by-geo-group.

21. *See* Paul Myerberg, *FAU Sells Stadium Naming Rights to For-Profit Prison Operator*, USA TODAY, Feb. 20, 2013, *at* http://www.usatoday.com/story/gameon/2013/02/20/florida-atlantic-geo-group-stadium-naming-rights/1933013/; *see also* http://www.geogroup.com/.

22. *Id.*

23. *Id.* (A letter from 26 members of Congress provided an example of a female detainee being returned to her cell "on the same day she had emergency ovarian surgery and that she suffered bleeding and inadequate follow-up care.")

24. *See* Dave Zirin, *A Football Stadium Becomes Ground Zero in the Fight against the New Jim Crow*, THE NATION, Mar. 3, 2013, *at* http://www.thenation.com/blog/173166/football-stadium-becomes-ground-zero-fight-against-new-jim-crow#.

The facility can protect itself from a sponsor who threatens to reflect poorly upon the facility by including a termination right in the naming rights agreement in the case that the company goes through a material adverse change, such as being found guilty in a civil action. Based on some finding that negatively affects the reputation of the sponsor, the facility will likely want a clause that allows it to terminate the naming rights deal due to a decrease in the quality of the sponsor and a desire to immediately cease any association. Such a clause enables the facility to limit its liability should the sponsor threaten legal action based on a breach of contract cause of action. A perfect example of a sponsor undergoing a material adverse change is the fate of Enron, an energy trader that signed a naming rights deal with the Houston Astros in 2000 only to go bankrupt one year later after being found to have been fudging its finances and overstating its profits.[25]

The sponsor may also wish to exit the naming rights deal if it suffers a material adverse change, especially if based on financial reasons, as it may no longer be able to justify the expense of continuing the obligation with the compensation provision in the agreement. Similarly, the sponsor should bargain for a termination right in the case that the team suffers a material adverse change.

Although most facilities that house professional and amateur sports teams and matches choose to exploit their prized names by granting same to corporations, there are those that remain "unbranded" because of the legacy of the name (i.e., Lambeau Field, home of the NFL's Green Bay Packers), delusions of grandeur (i.e., Cowboys Stadium, home of the NFL's Dallas Cowboys, which now has a deal with AT&T), or the rare instance where a facility is unable to find a sponsor willing to shell out the money to get its name prominently displayed. Upon the grant of rights concerning Cleveland Browns Stadium to FirstEnergy in early 2013, only eight stadiums hosting NFL teams remained without naming

---

25. *See* Richard Sandomir, *supra* note 15

deals.[26] The Browns' deal with FirstEnergy was reported as nine years and $100 million.[27]

Facilities always gauge the market to determine the vast array of opportunities they have regarding potential naming rights sponsors. It is common for facilities to also retain third-party corporations that have extensive experience and contacts in the space to provide thorough penetration and analysis of corporations seeking to gain prominence in the world of sports. For instance, in early 2013, the Portland Trail Blazers of the National Basketball Association (NBA) signed up with a sports sales and advisory firm, Premier Partnerships, to seek a naming rights sponsor for the iconic Rose Garden facility.[28] Prior to being engaged by the Trail Blazers, Premier Partnerships had proven its success through the sale of naming rights to the Oakland A's and Raiders' O.co Coliseum, the Philadelphia Union's PPL Park, and San Diego State University's Viejas Arena, among other facilities.[29]

Artful Negotiation

"We make a living by what we get, we make a life by what we give."[30]
—Sir Winston Churchill, British politician and prime minister

26. *See* Curtis Crabtree, *Cleveland Browns to Sell Naming Rights to Stadium*, NBC Sports, Jan. 15, 2013, *at* http://profootballtalk.nbcsports.com/2013/01/15/cleveland -browns-to-sell-naming-rights-to-stadium/. (The eight stadiums and the teams affiliated with them were Arrowhead Stadium (Kansas City Chiefs), Candlestick Park (San Francisco 49ers), Cowboys Stadium (Dallas Cowboys), Georgia Dome (Atlanta Falcons), Lambeau Field (Green Bay Packers), Paul Brown Stadium (Cincinnati Bengals), Ralph Wilson Stadium (Buffalo Bills), and Soldier Field (Chicago Bears)).

27. *See* Bill Sheil, *Source: FirstEnergy Stadium a $100 Million Deal*, FOX8.com, Jan. 17, 2013, *at* http://fox8.com/2013/01/17/source-firstenergy-stadium-a-9-figure-deal/.

28. *See Trail Blazers Team Up with Premier Partnerships to Pursue the Sale of Rose Garden Naming Rights*, Premier Partnerships, Jan. 14, 2013, *at* http://www.premierpartnerships .com/trail-blazers-team-up-with-premier-partnerships-to-pursue-the-sale-of-rose-garden -naming-rights/.

29. *Id.*

30. *Quote Details: Sir Winston Churchill*, The Quotations Page, http://www .quotationspage.com/quote/2236.html.

Any good, experienced negotiator will agree that negotiation is an art. It is a craft developed over time and always modified, depending on the characters and circumstance of the occasion. No one method of negotiating is proper for all occasions; the best negotiators are those who put in the time and effort to conduct ample research on the underlying issues surrounding the negotiation and the positions of those at the bargaining table. Transactional attorneys base their practices on negotiations. Sports agents dedicate a large amount of time to negotiating their clients' team and endorsement contracts. Even litigators must learn to be good negotiators; almost all cases settle prior to trial, and a good negotiator knows his or her clients' priorities and will do what is necessary to arrange a prejudgment deal to satisfy those clients' interests.

There are two general negotiation styles: competitive and cooperative. Competitive negotiations are typically relegated to the litigators. They are the types of negotiations that start with lofty demands and conclude with statements like, "Please govern yourself accordingly." The discussions are adversarial by nature; there is commonly a dispute (often highly emotional), and both sides insist that they are correct in their positions to the point that they will stubbornly refuse to budge from their stances until a mediator steps in attempting to bridge the gap. There is nothing inherently wrong with competitive negotiations, but they should be restricted to only those situations where they are warranted. For instance, a contentious case between a divorced couple in a fight over alimony will likely turn (at least initially) into a competitive argument over distributions. That is normal. However, a negotiation between a baseball player and an equipment manufacturer over the amount of product to be distributed to the player throughout the term of the agreement has no place in the realm of competition. That negotiation is better suited for a cooperative debate.

Cooperative negotiations occur when both sides appreciate that there are divergent desires, but also the existence (or potential) of common ground. Tones of the negotiators are tempered, statements tend to stay away from being inflammatory, and communication is frequent and fluid. A cooperative negotiation is enhanced when the negotiators acknowledge the feelings and emotions of the counterparties, keep interruptions at bay, effectively articulate their positions and interests without insulting the other side, and openly recognize the need to make concessions so as to progress the negotiation to its eventual conclusion.

Case Study

Scott Boras

Scott Boras is the king of baseball contracts. He and his company, Boras Corp., are largely responsible for the extravagant growth of baseball player salaries in the recent past. Boras was the first baseball agent to negotiate $50-plus million, $100-plus million, and $200-plus million multi-year contracts for Major League Baseball players and was responsible for putting together San Francisco Giants pitcher Barry Zito's deal for a whopping $126 million.[31] Boras is sometimes praised (mostly by his clients and sometimes by other agents) for the hard work he has put forth to help baseball players earn more money across the board. However, he is often chastised by the media and baseball executives for his no-nonsense ultracompetitive style of negotiating. When you negotiate with Scott Boras, it is either his way or the highway. When Boras was negotiating with the Atlanta Braves on behalf of his client, outfielder Andruw Jones, Braves general manager and team president John Schuerholz said: "When he presented us with that kind of offer with Andruw Jones, we found it so ridiculous and obnoxious we didn't even respond. It didn't even rise to the level of requiring a response. It's just idiotic."[32] Los Angeles Angels owner Arte Moreno will not even use Boras's name when answering questions about him in public.[33] Expert negotiator and baseball agent Ron Shapiro said of Boras, "His approach to negotiation ignores the human factor. I respect Scott for getting the

---

31. *See* Jeffrey Anderson, *The Boras Factor*, LA WEEKLY, May 22, 2007, *at* http://www.laweekly.com/2007-05-24/news/the-boras-factor/.

32. *Quote: $30 M per Year Is Idiotic*, Oct. 16, 2007, METSBLOG, *at* http://metsblog.com/metsblog/quote-30-m-per-year-is-idiotic/.

33. *See* Bill Shaikin, *Arte Moreno Cool on Scott Boras, but Boras Salutes Angels*, L.A. TIMES, Jan. 27, 2011, *at* http://latimesblogs.latimes.com/sports_blog/2011/01/scott-boras-arte-moreno-angels-jered-weaver.html.

most money, but I'll take any contract that I've negotiated where someone did not flee to get the money . . . and I will say it's at least as good if not better than any contract he's gotten for his clients."[34] Boras is able to manufacture great deals for some of his clients, but at what long-term cost?

A negotiated deal is the ultimate goal in any negotiation, but sometimes negotiations take a while to even begin. That is because people often hesitate to even make an offer. A valid contract is made up of an offer, acceptance, and consideration. A key part of the equation is the initial offer, which sets the tone for the negotiation to follow. Many experienced negotiators use the line, "Never make the first offer." That is only half-true. In most circumstances, it is to one's benefit to wait on the other party to make the first offer. If, however, it appears that the other side will definitely not budge, insists that you make the first offer, and has leverage going into the negotiation, but it is perceived that you have more to gain from an eventual deal and you have a firm grasp on the true value of the deal, it makes perfect sense to stick your neck out there and put forth initial proposed terms of an eventual agreement.

It is also common for a deal to die soon after the initial offer is presented. If the offer is out of the zone of reasonableness, it may lead the other party to simply walk away instead of dedicating time to a worthless pursuit. That is why it is important for the parties to have a good sense of the positions and interests of each other before any tangible terms are discussed. Additionally, it is a good idea for the parties to assess their own positions and interests and realize what is their best alternative to a negotiated agreement (BATNA) before discussions commence. At what point is it better for you to walk away from a deal instead of agreeing to terms that are simply not suitable?

---

34. *See* Darren Heitner, *Joe Mauer's Multi-Million Dollar Minnesota Twins Contract Negotiation Revealed In Impending Book*, FORBES, Nov. 12, 2013, *at* http://www.forbes.com /sites/darrenheitner/2013/11/12/joe-mauers-multi-million-dollar-minnesota-twins-contract -negotiation-revealed-in-impending-book/.

I got a good taste of what BATNAs are all about when I represented former NBA referee Tim Donaghy in a potential deal to license his life rights for the creation of a movie. The negotiation occurred between the producer's attorney and me, with the producer wanting to secure Donaghy's life rights to depict him throughout the film, which was to largely focus on the controversy surrounding him betting on games that he officiated. My client had many (reasonable) demands, including the involvement of his confidant on a consulting basis, receipt of an advance script for the movie, and some amount of quality control over the final product. After weeks of negotiating the lengthy life rights contract, the deal fell apart, and Donaghy decided that the BATNA (walking away) was a better idea than entering into a contract that he did not appreciate. Thereafter, we put the producer on notice that he did not have permission to depict Donaghy in a false and negative light and that deciding to do so would likely result in litigation.

Finally, negotiations are aided by thoughtful, open questions. Far too often, people believe that they are making progress by doing the bulk of the speaking. Another problem occurs when individuals fall far too in love with their own voice. Making numerous arguments (while they may be logical and rational) may not be the most effective form of persuasion. Instead, open-ended questions that do not call for a simple yes-or-no answer can help the parties get a better sense of the true positions and interests of the parties as well as the necessary concessions that must be made to reach an eventual agreement. Additionally, when possible, it is best to stay away from compound questions, which typically serve to frustrate the other party or result in the individual asking the question to only receive a partial response to the inquiry.

Chapter 9

Antitrust

No book on Sports Law would be complete without a chapter on antitrust, even though it is commonly considered one of the more dry topics in the field. Antitrust is undoubtedly a very complex, complicated area of law. However, it has played an important role in shaping Sports Law since the phrase was first coined as its own unique discipline and is therefore an area with which any aspiring agent or sports attorney should have at least a general understanding.

Perhaps one of the most well-known items of antitrust as it relates to the world of sports is the unique antitrust exemption of Major League Baseball (MLB). In a decision related to the city of San Jose, California's claim that MLB was operating an illegal monopoly due to its prohibition of the Oakland A's moving its location, U.S. District Judge Ronald M. Whyte recognized that the antitrust exemption seems illogical, but noted that he did not have the power to do anything about its existence.[1]

Under Section 1 of the Sherman Act, "[e]very contract, combination . . . or conspiracy in the restraint of trade or commerce . . . is declared to be illegal."[2] The main purpose of Section 1 is to disallow conspiracies between businesses that would ultimately harm consumers by causing higher prices in

---

1. *See* John Woolfolk, *San Jose vs. MLB: Judge splits decision on claims over A's South Bay plans*, SAN JOSE MERCURY NEWS, Oct. 11, 2013, *at* http://www.mercurynews.com/politics-government/ci_24290747/judge-dismisses-san-jose-antitrust-claims-against-mlb.

2. *See* Marc Edelman, *Upon Further Review: Will the NFL's Trademark Licensing Practices Survive Full Antitrust Scrutiny? The Remand of American Needle v. Nat'l Football League*, 16 STAN. J.L. BUS. & FIN. 183, 188 (2011) (quoting Sherman Act, 15 U.S.C. §§ 1–7).

connection with goods and services and the creation and dissemination of inferior products and services that result from illegal restraints of trade.

Antitrust Threshold Issues

"A significant piece of the wealth that the NFL owners garner is a result of the enormous TV revenues they get—and those revenues are supported by a legislatively granted exemption from the antitrust laws that has been made applicable to sports leagues, primarily the NFL."[3]
—Eliot Spitzer, former governor of New York

Before determining whether a given activity can be challenged under Antitrust Law, two threshold issues must be met. First, because antitrust is governed under federal law, the initial step to any antitrust analysis should begin with a determination that the issue in question involves interstate commerce.[4] The reason behind such a starting point is that Congress is not at liberty to regulate activities that take place solely within the borders of one state.[5] Thus, the alleged violation must involve acts that involve two or more states. This first issue is not particularly difficult to meet because historically courts take a liberal approach in determining the type of activity that crosses state lines.[6] For example, a sporting event televised in multiple states would constitute interstate commerce.

The second step is to show that there are two or more parties involved with the alleged antitrust violation.[7] Antitrust Law exists to prevent

---

3. *See* Eliot Spitzer, *The NFL Referee Lockout Shows How Congress Rigged the Game*, Slate, Sept. 26, 2012, *at* http://www.slate.com/blogs/spitzer/2012/09/26/the_nfl_referee_lockout _owners_benefit_from_unfair_labor_practices_and_a_congressionally_rigged_game_.html.

4. *See supra* note 2.

5. *See* U.S.C.A. Const. Art. 1, § 8, cl. 3.

6. *See, e.g.*, Wickard v. Filburn, 317 U.S. 111, 63 S. Ct. 82, 87 L. Ed. 122 (1942). (In this case, the Supreme Court gave very broad limits to the government's regulation under the commerce clause. The court found that a farmer who was growing an excess of wheat on his personal farmland reduced the amount of wheat he would buy in the open market, and because wheat is traded nationally, the farmer's wheat production affected interstate commerce and could be regulated by the federal government.)

7. *See supra* note 2

organizations from colluding to create a state of unfair competition harmful to consumers. However, it is impossible for one company to collude with itself; thus, any type of scenario in which it may seem as though the company is restraining trade with its own subsidiary will not be considered to be a potential violation of Antitrust Law.[8] It was an unresolved question as to whether the teams that make up the National Football League (NFL) were one entity or 32 separate entities until the landmark case of *American Needle, Inc. v. National Football League.*[9] Because the *American Needle* court ruled that each team is a single entity, it became clear that each NFL team is subject to antitrust laws, just as any other collection of businesses.[10]

Types of Antitrust Violations

The acts prohibited under Section 1 that have come up in Sports Law have largely involved wage fixing[11] and group boycotts.[12] Group boycotts by employers (or in the context of sports, teams) that refuse to deal with certain workers (players) "have long been held to be forbidden" under Antitrust Law.[13] For example, this particular violation was the underlying issue in the case of *Mackey v. National Football League.*[14] In 1976, San Diego Chargers player John Mackey and a group of other players brought suit against the NFL challenging the Rozelle Rule, alleging that it was an illegal form of a

---

8. *See* Copperweld Corp. v. Independence Tube Corp., 467 U.S. 752, 104 S. Ct. 2731, 81 L. Ed. 2d 628 (1984). (The Supreme Court ruled that a parent corporation and its wholly owned subsidiary were not legally capable of conspiring with each other under Section 1 of the Sherman Act.)

9. *See* Am. Needle, Inc. v. Nat'l Football League, 560 U.S. 183, 130 S. Ct. 2201, 176 L. Ed. 2d 947 (2010). (The Supreme Court recognized that the teams within the NFL could not be treated as a single entity under the Sherman Act.)

10. *Id.*

11. *See generally* Brown v. Pro Football, Inc., 518 U.S. 231 (1996).

12. *See, e.g.,* Mackey v. National Football League, 543 F.2d 606 (1976).

13. *See* Klor's, Inc. v. Broadway-Hale Stores, Inc., 359 U.S. 207, 212, 79 S. Ct. 705, 709, 3 L. Ed. 2d 741 (1959). (The court recognized that group boycotts "have long been held to be in the forbidden category" under antitrust laws.)

14. *See supra* note 12.

group boycott prohibited by Section 1.[15] The Rozelle Rule (named as such based on NFL commissioner Pete Rozelle, who led the NFL when the rule was first enacted) implemented a compensation structure whereby teams that lost free agent players to their competitors would typically receive draft picks from the teams that signed the free agent players. It served as a disincentive for teams to sign free agent players because the NFL commissioner could then take from the signing team what he believed to be equal value.

Mackey argued that although the Rozelle Rule was not the cause of a typical group boycott, it created a similar situation because the chilling effect simulated a group boycott.[16] Although it did not actually prevent teams from signing players designated as free agents, it discouraged them from such transactions because under the rule the new team was obligated to pay some sort of compensation to the free agent's former team.[17] The court ruled in favor of Mackey and the players, finding the NFL's "implementation of the Rozelle Rule constitutes a per se violation of Section 1 of the Sherman Act."[18]

Wage fixing is a different type of concern that has received attention in the world of sports. Wage fixing occurs when two or more employers conspire to set the employee compensation rate at a certain amount.[19] In the past, courts have found wage fixing to be illegal because it harms not only the employees, but society as a whole, by potentially driving the workers (or athletes) into another line of work and damaging the quality of the product.

---

15. *See* Alvin Dominique, *NFL History: The Road to Free Agency*, Bleacher Report, Apr. 17, 2008, *at* http://bleacherreport.com/articles/18183-nfl-history-the-road-to-free-agency. (The author explains that under the Rozelle Rule, "whenever a team lost a free agent, the team signing that free agent had to compensate his former team.")

16. *Id.* (explaining that "most teams found that it was better not to sign free agents under the Rozelle Rule").

17. *Id.* (as is evident because "from 1963–1974, only 34 players signed with new teams").

18. *See supra* note 12.

19. *See* Arizona v. Maricopa Cnty. Med. Soc., 457 U.S. 332, 102 S. Ct. 2466, 73 L. Ed. 2d 48 (1982). (The Supreme Court ruled that the practice of physicians setting maximum fees for insurance purposes was an illegal restraint of trade under Section 1 of the Sherman Act.)

Case Study

Brown v. Pro Football, Inc.

Until 1989, developmental squad players in the NFL were able to negotiate their own salary, and teams could have as many developmental squad players as they desired.[20] However, when the collective bargaining agreement expired that year, the NFL teams got together and attempted to place a salary cap on the practice squad players in the amount of $1,000 per week.[21] As a result, 235 of those practice squad players brought suit against the NFL team owners under Antitrust Law, claiming that the owners were conspiring to restrain trade by attempting to fix their wages.[22] The players ultimately lost their case at the U.S. Supreme Court level, but it was strictly due to the nonstatutory labor exemption being successfully invoked by the defendant team owners. At the Federal District Court level, however, a jury found for the players and awarded them a treble-damages award that exceeded $30 million.[23] This case makes it clear that absent a valid defense, placing a salary cap on a group of players is indeed wage fixing, prohibited under Antitrust Law.

20. *See* Brown v. Pro Football, Inc., 518 U.S. 231, 234, 116 S. Ct. 2116, 2119, 135 L. Ed. 2d 521 (1996). (In 1987, the collective-bargaining agreement between the NFL and the teams expired. In April 1989, for the first time, the NFL "proposed a squad player salary of $1,000 per week.")

21. *See* Linda Greenhouse, *Supreme Court Considers Antitrust Case against NFL*, N.Y. Times, Apr. 5, 1996, *at* http://www.nytimes.com/1996/04/05/sports/pro-football-supreme-court-considers-antitrust-case-against-nfl.html. (The author stated that the $1,000/week salary cap would have meant a pay cut for "roughly 75 percent" of the practice squad players.")

22. *See supra* note 20.

23. *See id.* at 235. (At the federal level, the court "denied the employers' claim of exemption from the antitrust laws; it permitted the case to reach the jury; and it subsequently entered judgment on a jury treble-damages award that exceeded $30 million." The NFL and its member clubs then appealed, and the case went all the way to the Supreme Court.)

Brady v. NFL and the Nonstatutory Labor Defense

Perhaps one of the most important antitrust disputes to occur in the Sports Law world in recent history was the case of *Brady v. NFL*, the suit brought against the NFL by NFL players as a result of the institution of the 2011 NFL lockout.[24] The case involved one of the most commonly invoked defenses used by defendants in Sports Law antitrust cases: the nonstatutory labor exemption.

The nonstatutory labor exemption came into play with the passing of the National Labor Relations Act (NLRA), 45 years after Congress passed Section 1 of the Sherman Act.[25] The NLRA was intended to give employees, who would not normally have much bargaining power, the ability to bargain effectively against employers.[26] It was the NLRA that gave employees the right to form unions to bargain with their employers over hours, wages, and working conditions (discussed in Chapter 1).

A sort of "catch-22" was developed with the passing of the NLRA and the existence of Section 1 of the Sherman Act. For instance, assume that employees of McDonald's, Burger King, and Wendy's came together to form a single union. After forming the union, the employees attempt to bargain with each of their employers to set their wages at $10.00 per hour. This scenario may sound like it would be a wage-fixing violation under Antitrust Law. However, if McDonald's, Burger King, and Wendy's refuse to bargain with the union over the proposed salary, it seems to be more like an NLRA violation. In this type of situation, courts have said that Labor Law trumps Antitrust Law, and the nonstatutory labor exemption comes into play.[27]

---

24. *See* Brady v. Nat'l Football League, 640 F.3d 785 (8th Cir. 2011).
25. *See* National Labor Relations Act of 1935, 29 U.S.C. §§ 151–169.
26. *See Summary of the National Labor Relations Act*, USW.org, *at* http://usw.org /districts/new/page?district=9&type=organizing&id=0005. (The purpose of the NLRA is "to define and protect the rights of employees and employers, to encourage collective bargaining, and to eliminate certain practices on the part of labor and management that are harmful to the general welfare.")
27. *See* Michael Tannenbaum, *A Comprehensive Analysis of Recent Antitrust and Labor Litigation Affecting the NBA and NFL*, 3 Sports L. J. 205, 207–8 (1996) (stating that most courts "have used labor law and labor law principles to trump antitrust").

How does this relate to the *Brady* case? At the time when the NFL's Collective Bargaining Agreement (CBA) was formed, all the players belonged to a union, the NFL Players Association (NFLPA).[28] Thus, the NFL teams and players were able to bargain over hours, wages, and working conditions without violating Antitrust Law. However, at the midnight hour before the CBA expired in 2011, the NFL players filed paperwork to decertify the union, giving them the option to challenge the NFL's planned lockout under Antitrust Law and disallowing the NFL to invoke the nonstatutory labor exemption.[29]

The NFL argued that the union's decertification was a "sham," executed by the players with the sole purpose of invalidating the nonstatutory labor defense so as to successfully bring suit against the league under Antitrust Law.[30] Although the court did not actually address this argument, it ultimately ruled in favor of the teams. Although the ruling did not determine whether the lockout was legal or not, the court found that irrespective of whether a union exists, it cannot get involved with a labor dispute under the Norris Laguardia Act and therefore could not issue an injunction to end the lockout.[31]

The court did not determine that a lockout could *never* be overturned. Although the court system could not issue an injunction to end the NFL lockout, based on the opinion, the National Labor Review Board (NLRB) theoretically could have stepped in. However, the teams and players ended up returning to the bargaining table and settled the issue.[32] Thus, it remains a question as to whether players in a sports league can legally decertify at the conclusion of a CBA and prevent the league from holding a lockout; there is a possibility that the Sports Law world will see similar litigation regarding the issue in the future.

---

28. *See* John Clayton, *NFL Owners Vote Unanimously to Opt Out of Labor Deal*, ESPN .COM, May 20, 2008, *at* http://sports.espn.go.com/nfl/news/story?id=3404596.

29. *See* Lester Munson, *The NFLPA's Power Play: Cease to Exist*, ESPN.COM, Mar. 2, 2011, *at* http://sports.espn.go.com/espn/commentary/news/story?page=munson/110302.

30. *See supra* note 24.

31. *See id.* (The court ruled that "the Norris–LaGuardia Act does not apply in a situation where the Players are no longer represented by the union.")

32. *See* Adam Schefter, *Sources: Deal to End Lockout Reached*, ESPN.COM, July 25, 2011, *at* http://espn.go.com/nfl/story/_/id/6797238/2011-nfl-lockout-owners-players-come-deal-all -points-sources-say.

Afterword

The title of this book is *How to Play the Game: What Every Sports Attorney Needs to Know*. It is my hope that you feel further empowered to assist others in a fiduciary capacity now that you have finished reading the chapters contained here. Whether you wish to be a litigator who focuses on representing athletes and agents in fee disputes, a transactional attorney who protects sports-related individuals' and organizations' intellectual property, or a sports agent who specializes in the representation of baseball players, this book should have given you at least a little bit of advice concerning how to play the game.

In April 2007, without any real experience (other than an internship between my sophomore and junior years at the University of Florida), I formed a sports agency with someone I had never even met in person. Two years before, I had created SportsAgentBlog.com, which developed into the most respected source for sports agency industry-related news and information. It was through my writing on SportsAgentBlog.com that I virtually met the person who eventually became my partner at this new sports agency venture, which we agreed to call Dynasty Athlete Representation, LLC. My business partner was the same age as me, but lived many miles away. I was finishing up my undergraduate degree at the University of Florida with plans to continue my education and strive to obtain a Juris Doctor degree at the University of Florida Levin College of Law, while he was doing the same at the University of Illinois and also wanted to attend law school. I vividly recall the first time that I met him in person, on a not very fruitful trip to Illinois as we met with an athlete whom we wished to represent but who barely gave us the time of day. I remained partners with the person I first met through SportsAgentBlog.com for two years before we realized that we had divergent interests. I then purchased his units of the company and continued to operate the business for another two years. After four years of grinding it out as a sports agent, I moved on to focus my talents in different arenas, including as a lawyer, a writer, and a professor. However, I "quit" being an agent after learning quite a few things about the profession and what it takes to succeed. Here I share some my wisdom, from one former sports agent to you, who may want to represent athletes in some shape or form.

1. **Be unique.** In November 2012, there were a total of 714 NFLPA certified contract advisors representing 1,800 NFL players.[1] Approximately 300 of those certified contract advisors failed to have any clients active on NFL rosters at the time,[2] largely because a select few agents and agencies represent the bulk of those players performing on the field. In late 2013, Drew Rosenhaus had 104 clients on active NFL rosters, followed by Joel Segal with 60, Tom Condon and his colleague Ben Dogra with 45 each, David Dunn with 42, and Todd France with 42.[3] That is a total of 348 NFL players represented by seven agents. The point of highlighting the vast number of players represented by those agents is to further demonstrate how power in the world of sports agency is locked up in the hands of a select few. Further, even though it is widely known that a handful of agents run the show in every major sports league, there are still hundreds of new agent applicants per year. Want to compete against these interested individuals? You must bring something unique to the table. Most of the agents have degrees from impressive universities, are smooth talkers and savvy with numbers, and are able to look the part. To break through the noise, one has to truly have a unique skill set and offering. That is the biggest challenge for newcomers in this profession.

2. **Follow the money.** Perhaps the biggest barrier to competing in the industry effectively is a lack of funding. The barrier of entry is ridiculously high. There are the standard costs incurred with starting up your

---

1. *See* Andrew Brandt, *An Agent's Life Isn't All Glamour*, ESPN, Nov. 27, 2012, *at* http://espn.go.com/nfl/story/_/id/8681968/nfl-agent-life-all-glamour.

2. *Id.*

3. *See* Neil Stratton, *ITL Notebook: Agents by Total Clients 9.27.13*, INSIDE THE LEAGUE, Sept. 27, 2013, *at* http://www.insidetheleague.com/reports2.asp?IDReports=2332.

own business (if you choose to go that route as opposed to working for an established agency), but those are just the beginning. Thereafter, an agent must become licensed in each state in which he or she wishes to recruit student-athletes (a select few states do not have any type of athlete agent law in effect). Each state license application has an associated fee and states require that certifications be kept current (extra costs). Further, players' associations have their own licensing processes, which require payment of application fees and then yearly certification fees. The real costs are established when one hits the recruiting trail and is spending money on travel and making other expenditures just to have a chance of signing a player. It culminates with the signing of clients and actually paying for their training, housing, meals, and so forth before they even make a dime (and before you receive any commissions). Thus, if you do not have the capital to go on your own, find someone who will provide the financial backing or find an existing, established agency willing to take a chance on you (but pay you a starting salary).

3. **Sleep is for the weak.** Expect to leave sleep for at least two reasons. First, clients have no concept of time. Their schedules are crazy and change depending on whether they are in-season or enjoying their time off. Either way, expect late-night calls for anything from girlfriend advice to much more serious issues. Sometimes, you may be asked to accompany them to certain events that last until the break of dawn. If you do not go, many of your competitors will gladly fill your shoes. Second, you will always be concerned that your competitors (whether it be those who represent no active clients or those at the top of the game) have their eyes set on your clients. It is easy to say that you are not concerned about losing your clients—"I know these guys, and they are good people, are loyal, and would never leave me"—until they do. Expect these thoughts to keep you up at night from time to time.

4. **It's about who knows you.** You will undoubtedly put in a lot of time on the recruiting trail doing whatever is necessary to get your first few clients. The recruiting effort never ends, but it should naturally change in scope. At some point, you should expect your practice to grow organically through referrals. Those referrals should come not

only from your existing clientele who believe that you are a competent agent and the right person for the job, but also from professionals who service athletes in a nonagent capacity. For instance, financial planners and accountants can be great referral sources. It is not good enough that you know these individuals on a first-name basis; you should be one of the first people they think of when they hear that a player is in the market for an agent. Create relationships with respected individuals who are on many athletes' business teams. That is the key to long-term success.

5. **Expect failure.** Due to the sheer number of competitors and the fickle nature of many athletes, it is impossible that you will score every player you recruit and also improbable that you will make it throughout your career without losing a single client to a competitor (unless the term of your career is prohibitively short). A key to surviving in this industry is to expect but not accept failure in the form of losing out to your competitors and having some clients that you will not be able to keep forever. It just happens to be the nature of this particular game and not a quality of a certain class of individuals that you will be able to change on the whole. The caveat to the rule of expecting failure is that you need to know when to hold them and know when to fold them. If you suddenly see all your clients leave you in some sort of mass migration, it may be time to reconsider whether this career path is the right one for you.

6. **Follow the law.** The sports agent industry is one that is heavily regulated; however, until recently, those laws have not been widely enforced. You do not want to be made into the example that any one state uses to scare others into adhering to that state's athlete agent law. In October 2013, football agent Terry Watson was charged with violating the North Carolina Athlete Agent Act and obstruction of justice.[4] Watson is a man who represented many high-draft picks,

---

4. Darren Heitner, *Football Agent Terry Watson Facing 14 Felony Counts For Violating North Carolina Athlete Agent Law*, FORBES.COM, Oct. 9, 2013, http://www.forbes.com/sites/darrenheitner/2013/10/09/football-agent-terry-watson-facing-14-felony-counts-for-violating-north-carolina-athlete-agent-law/.

including former Florida Gators and current New England Patriots linebacker Brandon Spikes.[5] Watson was indicted for allegedly providing benefits (in the form of money, hotel rooms, and travel expenses) to former University of North Carolina football players in violation of the state's law. Providing any sort of monetary benefit to a student-athlete in any state with an athlete agent law is known by all agents to be an impermissible action. Potential civil and criminal penalties follow for one who is convicted and found to have violated an athlete agent act. Skirting the law may lead to impressive short term gains, but in the long run it is never worth it. It is better to fail in your attempt to be a sports agent than to risk ending up in a cell.

7. **Go big, but not too soon.** Before I split from my partner, he informed me that his major critique of my plan and execution was that I was trying to do too much at any given time. He wanted our agency to focus on building our baseball division first and foremost. I was too busy just trying to get our feet wet, taking on what I believed to be interesting projects when the opportunities presented themselves. For instance, if a basketball player with potential came across the radar, I would try to place him with an overseas team. A very successful and marketable bowler needed representation? Sure, I would give it a try. Looking back, it probably was not the best idea to spread myself too thin. Although it served as a great learning experience, it was likely not the greatest business plan. Thus, my advice is to focus on a particular sport and become a master in that field. Understand the rules, regulations, and key players inside and out, and build up a sterling reputation before expanding to other disciplines.

8. **Geography is gold.** The most successful agents put together a thorough game plan and recruit according to a strategy based on geography. Sometimes that means focusing on a specific region close to home, but more often than not, it is based on honing in on where your relationships and affiliations lie. A tried-and-true tactic is to recruit your alma mater. This strategy can be a major advantage if you went to a

---

5. *Id.*

university that is not a traditional powerhouse (i.e., a Fresno State) and is not heavily recruited by your competition. Should that school have a blue-chip athlete, you may be able to capture the opportunity to represent the player and thus amass future commissions. It was less effective for me, a graduate of the University of Florida and its law school. A hotbed for talent, my alma mater was heavily recruited by the most well-known and connected agents in the business. As a newcomer with little experience, it was difficult to use geography to my advantage. However, it is a strategy that is worth exploring for those wishing to play the game to the best of their ability.

9. **Get a postgraduate degree.** Many practitioners will take issue with this advice, but it is my opinion that a postgraduate degree is valuable in this industry and elsewhere. The National Football League Players Association (NFLPA) is the only players' association that currently requires a postgraduate degree to gain certification to represent players (the exception being that a candidate has sufficient negotiating experience, which is a highly subjective criteria), but that does not mean that a postgraduate degree is only valuable for those who wish to represent professional football players. I can only speak from my experience of going to law school, and I believe that the material learned and the thinking process inherited from the experience is almost invaluable. Further, a postgraduate degree will separate you from many of your peers (remember that uniqueness is vital) and give you options should the sports agent field not work out in the long run. It is possible that other players' associations may follow the NFLPA's lead and make it a requirement that applicants obtain a postgraduate degree before being admitted to represent players that the unions protect. Either way, I believe that the attainment of a postgraduate degree is a worthy pursuit.

10. **Understand *The Dip*.** I was given a book called *The Dip* by blogger and author Seth Godin near the final days of my career as a sports agent. It was probably the best and most timely piece of property I could inherit. The premise of the book is that the most successful people know when they are simply in a natural bind but will eventually achieve success, and they are able to separate that from instances when

it is just best to quit and move on to a different path. Many people get stuck in situations in which they invest a lot of time, money, and passion into a pursuit and fear the process of quitting. The agent business simply is not for everyone. I determined that instead of continuing to pump my efforts and economy into being an agent, my talents were better suited for law, teaching, and writing. Give being a sports agent a try and put all your energy into being the best that you can be. If the cards do not fall in your favor, have the courage and humility to move on. There are hundreds of others who will absorb the vacuum you leave behind.

Acknowledgments

The easiest part in drafting these acknowledgments was determining the first three people to thank. Without the meaningful and appreciated influence of my mother, Gloria Heitner, my father, Phil Heitner, and my stepfather, Perry Blank, this book would likely have never come to fruition. Their support throughout my life has been instrumental in building my confidence to the point where I do not fear failure and fail to accept "no" as an answer. Individually, my mother has been my biggest fan and has always been by my side. She has supported me in my endeavors, but has never been afraid to provide her opinion when she believed that I was better suited to take an alternative course of action. I like to think that her brilliance has rubbed off on me; even a modicum of her intelligence would be more than enough to satiate my brain. My father is also proud of my accomplishments, and I am thankful that he has remained an integral part of my life. My knowledge and connection to sports was fostered through him, and he still believes that I would make one hell of a second baseman for some Major League Baseball–affiliated organization. My stepfather also deserves a lot of credit for who I am today. He has cherished me since the moment he entered my life and has continuously shown affection and care for my mother. For that, I will always be grateful.

I have been fortunate to be nurtured by many distinguished professionals in my limited career as a Sports Lawyer. Sports Law professors Marc Edelman, Michael McCann, Warren Zola, and Gabe Feldman, among others, have served as mentors as I continue to grow as a legal practitioner in the world of sports. My partner, Richard Wolfe, at Wolfe Law Miami, P.A. deserves more than I will ever be able to repay him. After a year of practicing in Fort Lauderdale and spending much of my time churning through property insurance matters, Richard offered me a job as his associate. A year later, I became his partner. He has helped me become a better litigator and has shown me what it means to be a strong advocate for clients from all walks of life. I like to think that as a team, Richard and I have become a formidable force in the world of sports and entertainment and have established our practice as one of the best in those particular fields.

Many sports-related clients put their trust in me despite my young age and childish looks. Those individuals and companies include football agents Drew Rosenhaus and Cleodis Floyd, basketball agent David Sugarman, NFL player Atari Bigby, NHL player Jack Johnson, former Miami Hurricanes football player Dyron Dye, BMX stars Mike Spinner and Tyler Faoro, former NBA referee Tim Donaghy, professional boxer Yuandale Evans, Sure Sports Lending, Miami Sports Consulting, 4th Quarter Sports Group, Athlete Originals, Moves Magazine, FanHold, NPM Public Relations, and NCLUSIVE, Inc. There are countless other individuals and companies outside of the sports world that I must thank for pushing me to become the professional I am today. I cherish each of those professional relationships and look forward to continuing to solve problems and create value for my clients for the rest of my life.

I must also express deep gratitude to Kristen Chiger, who went from being a client to a valuable assistant as I neared completion on this project. I likely would have never complied with my contractual obligations in submitting the initial draft of the manuscript (especially concerning the tedious task of providing detailed footnotes) for this book without her relief as deadlines approached. In addition to my wonderful clients who have given me the opportunity to grow as a practitioner while representing their interests, I also thank those who were bold enough to write scholarly articles concerning Sports Law prior to the publication of this book. They include Bob Ruxin, Andrew Delaney, Jeffrey Levine, Jason Wolf, Jason Belzer, and my former professor Thomas Baker. Many thanks are also sent to the wonderful people at Forbes, who provided me a platform to grow my brand by giving me an expanded audience with whom I could share my sports business knowledge. I will never forget that May 3, 2012, e-mail with the subject line, "from Forbes" and the message stating that I had "a few fans here in the editorial dept." before concluding with an offer to become a contributor for the publication.

I hope that this book will be the first of many. With the support of those mentioned herein, in addition to the many others who have provided support for many years, I will undoubtedly remain driven to provide more content to the masses.

APPENDIX A

Form Sponsorship Agreement

SPONSORSHIP AGREEMENT

THIS SPONSORSHIP AGREEMENT ("Agreement") is made and entered into as of the _____ day of _____, 20___, by and among _____ and _____ ("Team"), _____("Arena Manager") and _____ _____ ("Sponsor").

RECITALS:

WHEREAS, Arena Manager has the right to manage and operate a sports and entertainment facility known currently as _____ Arena, ("Arena"), including the right to sell space in the Arena for commercial sponsorships and other advertising;

WHEREAS, Team has the right to operate a franchise in the National Basketball Association ("NBA") which shall play its home games at the Arena; and

WHEREAS, Sponsor desires to display advertisements in the Arena and/or to be a sponsor of Team for promotional purposes.

NOW, THEREFORE, for and in consideration of the mutual covenants and promises contained herein, and other good valuable consideration, the receipt, adequacy, and sufficiency of which is hereby acknowledged, the Arena Manager, Team and Sponsor agree and covenant as follows:

AGREEMENT

1. TERM

The term of this Agreement (hereinafter "Term") shall begin upon the date of signature and shall expire at midnight exactly one year from that date, unless terminated earlier pursuant to the terms hereof. Notwithstanding the fact that this Agreement may contemplate that the Term shall commence on a date subsequent to the execution hereof, in such case, Arena Manager, Team and Sponsor intend that each shall have vested rights immediately upon the execution of this Agreement, and that this Agreement shall be fully binding and in full force and effect from and after the date of execution.

2. ARENA MANAGER AND TEAM OBLIGATIONS; CONDITIONS AND LIMITATIONS

a. The Arena Manager and/or Team shall furnish to or for the benefit of the Sponsor the inventory described in **Schedule A**, attached hereto and hereby made a part of this Agreement; *provided, however,* that provision of such inventory to Sponsor is subject to the conditions and limitations set forth herein. If Sponsor's rights hereunder are to be exclusive, then such rights and any conditions or limitations thereon are set forth in **Schedule B**, attached hereto and hereby made a part of this Agreement.

3. SIGNAGE/SPONSORSHIP CONDITIONS AND LIMITATIONS

Arena Manager's and/or Team's obligation to furnish the inventory described in **Schedule A** shall be conditioned or otherwise limited as follows:

a. All of Sponsor's advertising and promotional materials are subject to the prior written approval of Arena Manager, Team and/or any other relevant parties, including, but not limited to, the NBA. Such approval, if given, will be given in a reasonable and timely manner and will not be unreasonably withheld. Arena Manager or Team shall have the right to inspect and require change or deletion of advertising and promotional copy or material that Arena Manager or Team deems, in its sole discretion, to be contrary to: (i) its rules, policies or best interests, or those of the NBA, (ii) generally-accepted community standards of good taste, or (iii) any applicable laws, ordinances or other public regulations. Such requirements will

not be unreasonably imposed, and the foregoing approvals and requirements will be consistently given and imposed on all sponsors.

b. Sponsor shall be responsible for the cost of all design and artwork
relating to advertising inventory to be displayed hereunder. Arena Manager
and/or Team shall be responsible for the costs associated with the initial
fabrication, installation or programming of such advertising inventory to
be displayed hereunder; provided, however, that Sponsor agrees to provide
Arena Manager and/or Team with such design or artwork within production and installation schedules as reasonably set by Arena Manager and/or
Team, failing which Sponsor shall be responsible for any reasonable costs
incurred by Arena Manager and/or Team resulting from such failure.

c. Following the initial fabrication, installation and programming of
Sponsor's advertising inventory to be displayed hereunder, Sponsor may alter
the appearance of such advertising inventory: (i) at Sponsor's sole expense,
(ii) upon thirty (30) days' prior written notice to Arena Manager, and
(iii) subject to all approvals and requirements as set forth herein.

d. Arena Manager, acting in good faith and upon due consultation with
Sponsor, may dim illumination, fail to illuminate, cover up, or otherwise
preclude the view any of Sponsor's advertisements displayed in the Arena
under the following conditions:

  (i) safety of guests and patrons: if such action is appropriate for
  the safe and orderly operation of the Arena, as determined by Arena
  Manager, in its reasonable discretion;

  (ii) non-public events: if specific Sponsor advertisements are incon-
  sistent with the nature of such an event in the Arena, such as private
  collegiate, religious, political or professional conventions or trade
  shows, provided that the organizer, promoter, governing body or sponsor of such event requests that such action be taken;

  (iii) private event sponsored by a competitor: if the only guests at
  an event in the Arena will be the employees or customers of a competitor of Sponsor, or non-paying patrons;

  (iv) special events: if such action is required under the terms of
  Arena Manager's agreement with a sponsor of such a special event
  (including, by way of example only and without limitation, tournament,

playoff or other championship events of the National Collegiate Athletic Association, Atlantic Coast Conference, Southeastern Conference, or other similar intercollegiate athletic governing body or organization, "All-Star" events of the NBA, the National Hockey League or other similar professional league or organization, events associated with the Olympic movement or organizations, or musical concerts). Arena Manager will use its best efforts to provide Sponsor with prior written notice of any such special events; or

(v) staging of an event: if the staging requirements of a specific event in the Arena, including by way of example only and without limitation a musical concert, exhibit, movie, or television broadcast, necessitate such action, and such action is required for all similarly located advertisements.

e. All of the terms, conditions, rights and obligations herein are subject to the Constitution and By-Laws and all rules, regulations and agreements of the NBA as they presently exist or as they may, from time to time, be entered into, amended or adopted.

4. SPONSOR'S OBLIGATIONS
In consideration of Arena Manager's and/or Team's provision of the inventory described in **Schedule A**, the Sponsor shall make the payments ("Sponsorship Fees") set forth in **Schedule C**, attached hereto and herby made part of this Agreement, and perform any other obligations set forth therein.

5. REPRESENTATIONS AND WARRANTIES
a. Arena Manager and Team represent and warrant to Sponsor, as follows: (i) This Agreement has been duly authorized, executed and delivered by Arena Manager and Team, and constitutes the legal, valid and binding obligation of them, enforceable against them, in accordance with the terms hereof, except to the extent enforceability is limited by bankruptcy, reorganization and other similar laws affecting the rights of creditors generally and by general principles of equity.

(ii) The execution, delivery and performance of this Agreement by Arena Manager and Team does not conflict with, nor will it result in, a breach or violation of any material agreement to which either of them is a party.

(iii) Both Arena Manager and Team are duly organized and validly existing limited liability companies under the laws of the State of Delaware, and have all requisite power and authority to execute, deliver and perform their obligations under this Agreement.

b. Sponsor represents and warrants to Arena Manager and Team as follows:

(i) This Agreement has been duly authorized, executed and delivered by Sponsor and constitutes the legal, valid and binding obligation of it, enforceable against it, in accordance with the terms hereof, except to the extent enforceability is limited by bankruptcy, reorganization and other similar laws affecting the rights of creditors generally and by general principles of equity.

(ii) The execution, delivery and performance of this Agreement by Sponsor does not conflict with, nor will it result in, a breach or violation of any material agreement to which it is a party.

(iii) Sponsor is duly organized, validly existing, and in good standing under the laws of all appropriate States, and has all requisite legal power and authority to execute, deliver and perform its obligations under this Agreement.

(iv) Sponsor possesses all rights necessary to allow display of its advertisements in the Arena and use of its name or logos in connection with sponsorship of the Team, including without limitation all necessary copyrights and trademarks.

6. NBA RULES

This Agreement is subject to the Constitution and By-Laws and all rules, regulations and agreements of the NBA as they presently exist or as they may, from time to time, be entered into, amended or adopted.

7. BROADCAST RIGHTS AND COPYRIGHT RETENTION

Any provision herein to the contrary notwithstanding, the Team, and/or NBA shall be regarded for all purposes, including without limitation for the purposes of federal copyright law, as the holder of all rights in and to all broadcast or rebroadcast of all, or any portion of, any of the Team's games, play-by-play descriptions, pregame, or postgame shows, in which the Sponsor participates or advertises hereunder, together with all rights and obligations resulting therefrom, and the Team and/or NBA shall have the exclusive right to authorize, consent, and control any and all replaying, rebroadcasting, or other use of such broadcasts. Such authorization or consent of the Team and/or the NBA may be withheld for any reason or no reason, in the sole discretion of the Team and/or the NBA.

8. GOVERNMENT REGULATIONS AND BROADCAST ACKNOWLEDGEMENT

a. This Agreement is subject to the terms of licenses held by radio and television broadcasters of Team's games and to applicable federal, state, and municipal laws, regulations and decisions either presently in existence or thereafter enacted, made or enforced, including regulations and actions of governmental administrative agencies and commissions; and Sponsor specifically acknowledges and agrees that Team shall be entitled to modify the goods and services to be provided for the benefit of Sponsor in accordance with section 2 above to conform with such licenses and/or laws, regulations, and decisions.

b. Sponsor agrees and acknowledges that Team shall use its best efforts to arrange for television broadcasts through licensed television and radio broadcasters and that Team's ability to provide the commercial time set forth herein is subject to the terms and conditions of the Team's agreement with its radio and television broadcasters and to the performance of such radio and television broadcasters and to the performances of such radio and television broadcasters.

9. USE OF TRADEMARKS AND SERVICE MARKS

a. Sponsor recognizes and acknowledges the Team's and/or NBA's exclusive ownership, right, title, and interest to the Team's trademarks, logos, and service marks ("Team Marks"). Any rights granted to Sponsor to use the Team Marks are subject to the control of the Team and shall cease immediately upon the expiration or earlier termination of this Agreement.

Sponsor shall not have the right to use or the right to authorize the use by third parties of any of the Team Marks, except as expressly permitted under this Agreement.

b. Sponsor agrees that it shall not, during the term of this Agreement or thereafter, directly or indirectly: (i) contest the validity of the Team Marks or any of the Team's or the NBA's registrations pertaining thereto, in the United States or elsewhere; or (ii) adopt the Team Marks or any term, word, mark or designation which is in any aspect confusingly similar to the Team Marks. Sponsor specifically acknowledges and agrees that any use of the Team Marks pursuant to this Agreement shall not create in Sponsor any right, title or interest in the Team Marks. Sponsor further agrees that it will not at any time do or cause to be done any act or thing, directly or indirectly, which contests, clouds or otherwise impairs any right, title and/or interest of Team or NBA in the Team Marks. Sponsor shall not represent, in any manner, that it has any ownership right or interest in the Team Marks or the registrations thereof.

10. TERMINATION

This Agreement may be terminated by either party upon the other party's breach of any of its material covenants and agreements in this Agreement or the breach of any of its representations or warranties under this Agreement, if such breach is not cured or remedied by the breaching party to the aggrieved party's reasonable satisfaction within thirty (30) days after delivery of written notice to the breaching party specifying the nature of the breach. If Arena Manager and/or Team terminates this Agreement pursuant to this section, no portion of any Sponsorship Fees paid by Sponsor prior to the date of such termination shall be refundable. If this Agreement is terminated by Arena Manager or Team due to Sponsor's uncured breach, as set forth in the immediately preceding paragraph, then Sponsor's obligation to pay the Sponsorship Fees as set forth in Schedule C shall survive such termination, and shall continue in full force and effect, subject to Arena Manager's and/or Team's mitigate its damages in a commercially reasonable manner.

11. RELOCATION

This Agreement will terminate automatically if the Team's NBA franchise is permanently relocated more than fifty (50) miles from the _____, _____ city limits during the Term. In the event that this Agreement is terminated pursuant to this subsection 11, then Sponsor shall be entitled to a refund of prepaid Sponsorship Fees which are unearned as of the date of such termination.

12. FORCE MAJEURE; LABOR DISPUTES

a. Subject to the terms of the following subsection, in the event compliance with any of each party's obligations under this Agreement is impractical or impossible due to any unforeseen circumstance or emergency, including, but not limited to, player strikes, management lockouts, or other labor disputes, embargoes, flood, earthquake, storm, lightning, fire epidemic, acts of God, war, national emergency, civil disturbance or disobedience, riot, sabotage, terrorism, threats of sabotage or terrorism, restraint by court order or order of public authority, failure of machinery or equipment or any other occurrence beyond such party's reasonable control (each occurrence being an "Event of Force Majeure"), then such party shall not be in breach or default of its obligations under this Agreement, but instead the time for performance of such obligations shall be extended for a period equal to the duration of the Event of Force Majeure.

b. Notwithstanding the remedy set forth in the preceding subsection, in the event that one or more regular season Team home games are not played as the result of a strike by or a lockout of the NBA Players Association or the members thereof, and such home games are not rescheduled and played at the Arena, then Arena Manager and/or Team shall either: (i) provide Sponsor with substitute advertising inventory or other benefits or consideration reasonably equivalent in value to the amount by which the value of Sponsor's advertising inventory provided hereunder decreased as a result of such cancelled games, or (ii) to extend the length of the Term for a period equal to the duration of the strike or lockout. The choice of remedy pursuant to this subsection 12(b) shall be in the reasonable discretion of Arena Manager and/or Team.

13. TAXES

Sponsor shall be responsible for the payment of all applicable taxes arising out of the sale, assignment or other transfer of Sponsor's rights, obligations, duties or responsibilities pursuant to this Agreement.

14. NOTICES

All notices, demands and other communications between the parties required hereunder shall be in writing and deemed given upon personal delivery, confirmed facsimile transmission ("fax"), or if mailed, postage prepaid, to the respective addresses and fax numbers as set forth below. Any party may specify another address or fax number, from the one set forth below, by notice to the other as provided herein.

If to Arena Manager:

_____

_____

_____

Attn: _____

Fax: (___) _____

If to Sponsor:

_____

_____

_____

Attn: _____

Fax: (___) _____

15. CHOICE OF LAW

This Agreement shall be construed and enforced in accordance with the laws of the State of _____, without regard to the conflicts of laws principles thereof.

16. RESERVATION OF RIGHTS

Any and all rights not granted herein are expressly reserved to Arena Manager and Team. Nothing herein contained shall be deemed a commitment by either Arena Manager or Team on behalf of any of its managerial, coaching, or player employees, with the exception of any specific provisions or obligations contained in **Schedule A** of this Agreement.

17. DISPUTE RESOLUTION

a. Any controversy, claim or dispute arising out of or relating to this Agreement or the breach, termination, enforceability or validity hereof, including without limitation the determination of the scope or applicability of the agreement to arbitrate set forth in this subsection 17(a), which cannot be resolved following good faith mutual efforts of the parties hereto, shall be determined exclusively by binding arbitration in _____ County of the State of _____. There shall be three arbitrators, one to be chosen by Arena Manager and/or Team, one to be chosen by Sponsor and a third to be selected by the two arbitrators so chosen. The arbitration shall be governed by the American Arbitration Association (the "AAA") under its Commercial Arbitration Rules.

b. Judgment upon the award rendered may be entered in any court having jurisdiction. The parties hereby expressly consent to the nonexclusive jurisdiction of the state and federal courts situated in _____County of the State of _____ for this purpose and waive objection to the venue of any proceeding in such court or that such court provides an inconvenient forum.

c. Each of the parties shall, subject to the award of the arbitrators, pay an equal share of the arbitrators' fees. The arbitrators shall have the power to award recovery of all costs (including attorneys' fees, administrative fees, arbitrators' fees and court costs) to the prevailing party.

18. WAIVER

No waiver by any party hereto of any covenant or condition of this Agreement shall constitute a waiver by such party of any subsequent breach of such covenant or condition or authorize the breach or nonobservance on any other occasion of the same or any other covenant or condition of this Agreement.

19. BINDING EFFECT AND ASSIGNMENT

a. This Agreement shall be binding upon and shall inure to the benefit of the parties hereto and their respective successors and assigns.

b. Sponsor shall not sell, assign or otherwise transfer its rights and obligations hereunder without the prior written consent of Arena Manager and Team. Either Arena Manager or Team may transfer its rights and obligations hereunder without the consent of Sponsor; *provided, however*, that in such instance the transferee agrees to be bound by either Arena Manager's and/or Team's obligations to Sponsor hereunder. Notwithstanding the foregoing, either Arena Manager or Team shall have the right to assign this Agreement and their right to receive payments from Sponsor hereunder to any bank, lending or financial institution to secure any indebtedness of Arena Manager, Team and their affiliates. If Arena Manager or Team notifies Sponsor of any such assignment to any bank, lending or financial institution, then Sponsor shall, if and when requested by such bank, lending or financial institution in writing, pay all amounts payable by Sponsor hereunder directly to such bank, lending or financial institution, as the case may be.

20. ENTIRE AGREEMENT; MODIFICATIONS

This Agreement is an integrated contract which contains all agreements of the parties with respect to the subject hereof. No other prior or contemporaneous agreement or understanding pertaining to the subject shall be effective. This Agreement may be modified in writing only, signed by the parties hereto. There are no oral or written statements, representations, agreements or understandings which modify, amend or vary any of the terms of this Agreement. Unless the context requires otherwise, reference such as or similar to "hereof" refer to this Agreement and the Schedules hereto as a whole and not merely to the paragraph, section or other subdivision in which such words appear. The singular shall include the plural and the masculine gender shall include the feminine and the neuter, unless the context otherwise requires. The captions and headings throughout this Agreement are for convenience and reference only, and they shall not be deemed to define, modify or add to the meaning, scope or intent of any provision of this Agreement. In the event that any one or more of the phrases, sentences, clauses, or paragraphs contained in this Agreement shall be declared invalid, this Agreement shall be construed as if it did not contain such phrase, clause or paragraph.

21. CONFIDENTIALITY

Arena Manager, Team and Sponsor agree that they will hold the terms and conditions of this Agreement in strict confidence and shall not make any disclosure, publicly or privately, of the terms and conditions hereof (including any initial public announcement of the existence or terms of this Agreement), other than as agreed mutually by the parties, and except as otherwise required by law.

IN WITNESS WHEREOF, the parties hereto have caused this Agreement to be executed as of the date first above written.

_____

_____

[Name]
[Title]

_____

[Name]
[Title]
[SPONSOR]
By:_____
[Name]
[Title]

SCHEDULE A—INVENTORY
SCHEDULE B—EXCLUSIVITY

1.   During the term of this Agreement, and for so long as Sponsor is not in default of this Agreement, neither Arena Manager nor Team shall not display any signage or other advertisements in the Arena nor engage in any sponsorship activities other than those of or concerning Sponsor in the [_____] category ("Exclusive Category").

2.   Sponsor shall not display (or cause or authorize the display of) signage or other advertisements in the Arena, nor engage in sponsorship activities for or concerning products or services other than products or

services within the Exclusive Category without the prior written consent of Arena Manager and Team, which consent may be withheld by Arena Manager and Team in their sole discretion.

3.   Sponsor agrees and understands that the exclusivity noted in this **Schedule B** is limited as follows:

a. Arena Manager and/or Team shall not be precluded from temporary display of advertising or sponsorship activities concerning products in the Exclusive Category (other than those of Sponsor) if required pursuant to a contract with the promoter, organizer, governing body or sponsor of a non-public event, private event sponsored by a competitor or a special event, as those events are described in section 3(d) herein. Arena Manager and/or Team will use its best efforts to provide Sponsor with prior written notice of any such events;

b. Arena Manager shall not be precluded from contracting for events in the Arena which are title-sponsored by a third party, even if such third party or its products are within the Exclusive Category. Sponsor agrees and understands that promoters or organizers of such events may require display of signage or other advertisements other than those of Sponsor which are within the Exclusive Category, and/ or removal or other obstruction of Sponsor's signage or other advertisements. Arena Manager will use its best efforts to provide Sponsor with prior written notice of any such events;

c. Sponsor acknowledges that sports teams other than the Team may utilize the Arena as their primary "home" venue for their events. Such users shall include, by way of example and without limitation, a professional hockey, football, soccer or lacrosse team, or a college basketball team. Moreover, Sponsor acknowledges that such sports teams may possess "temporary" advertising rights in the arena, for display of advertisements during and in conjunction with such teams' events. Such temporary advertising may include advertisements of competitors of Sponsor in the Exclusive Category. In such case, Sponsor's exclusivity as noted herein shall not apply; provided, however, that Arena Manager shall use its best efforts to secure for Sponsor a right of first refusal to become the exclusive sponsor of such other sports teams in the Exclusive Category;

d. Arena Manager shall not be precluded from selling advertising within the Exclusive Category outside of the Arena premises, or in game-day promotions or scorecards, including those distributed inside the Arena;

e. Arena Manager shall not be precluded from advertising events sponsored by competitors of Sponsor; and

f. Sponsor acknowledges that its exclusivity may not apply: (i) in the case of NBA league sponsors advertising during broadcasts of Team games pursuant to the NBA's national broadcasting agreements, or (ii) as mandated by any other NBA rules, regulations and agreements.

Student-Athlete Statement, NCAA Division I

Form 13-3a Academic Year 2013–2014

For: Student-athletes.
Action: Sign and return to your director of athletics.
Due date: Before you first compete each year.
Required by: NCAA Constitution 3.2.4.6 and NCAA Bylaw 14.1.3.
Purpose: To assist in certifying eligibility.
Effective Date: This NCAA Division I Student-Athlete Statement/Drug-Testing Consent form shall be in effect from the date this document is signed and shall remain in effect until a subsequent Division I

Student-Athlete Statement/Drug-Testing Consent form is executed.
Student-Athlete: _____
(Please print name)
Name of your institution: _____

This form has seven parts:

1. A statement concerning eligibility;
2. A Buckley Amendment consent;
3. An affirmation of status as an amateur athlete;
4. A statement concerning the promotion of NCAA championships and other NCAA events;
5. Results of drug tests;

6. Previous involvement in NCAA rules violation(s); and

7. An affirmation of valid and accurate information provided to the NCAA Eligibility Center and admissions office, including ACT or SAT scores, high school attendance, completion of coursework and high school grades. If you are an incoming freshman, you must complete and sign Parts I, II, III, IV, V and VII to participate in intercollegiate competition.

If you are an incoming transfer student or a continuing student, you must complete and sign Parts I, II, III, IV, V and VI to participate in intercollegiate competition.

Before you sign this form, you should read the Summary of NCAA Regulations, or another outline or summary of NCAA legislation, provided by your director of athletics or his or her designee or read the bylaws of the NCAA Division I Manual that deal with your eligibility. You are responsible for knowing and understanding the application of all NCAA Division I bylaws related to your eligibility. If you have any questions, you should discuss them with your director of athletics or your institution's compliance officer, or you may contact the NCAA at 317/917–6222.

The conditions that you must meet to be eligible and the requirement that you sign this form are indicated in the following bylaws of the Division I Manual:

• Bylaws 10, 12, 13, 14, 15, 16, 18.4 and 31.2.3.

Part I: Statement Concerning Eligibility.

By signing this part of the form, you affirm that, to the best of your knowledge, you are eligible to compete in intercollegiate competition.

You affirm that your institution has provided you a copy of the Summary of NCAA Regulations, or another outline or summary of NCAA legislation, or the relevant sections of the Division I Manual and that your director of athletics (or his or her designee) gave you the opportunity to ask questions about them.

You affirm that you have knowledge of and understand the application of NCAA Division I bylaws related to your eligibility.

You affirm that you meet the NCAA regulations for student-athletes regarding eligibility, recruitment, financial aid, amateur status and involvement in gambling activities.

You affirm that you are aware of the NCAA drug-testing program and that you have signed the current NCAA Drug Testing Consent Form.

You affirm that all information provided to the NCAA, the NCAA Eligibility Center and the institution's admissions office is accurate and valid, including ACT or SAT scores, high school attendance, completion of coursework and high school grades, as well as your amateur status.

You affirm that you have reported to the director of athletics or his or her designee of your institution any violations of NCAA regulations involving you and your institution.

You affirm that you understand that if you sign this statement falsely or erroneously, you violate NCAA legislation on ethical conduct and you will further jeopardize your eligibility.

Name (please print)	Date of birth	Age
Signature of student-athlete	Home address (street or P.O. Box)	
Date	Home city, state, and zip code	
Sport(s)		

Part II: Buckley Amendment Consent.

By signing this part of the form, you certify that you agree to disclose your education records.

You understand that this entire form and the results of any NCAA drug test you may take are part of your education records. These records are protected by the Family Educational Rights and Privacy Act of 1974 and they may not be disclosed without your consent.

You give your consent to disclose only to authorized representatives of this institution, its athletics conference (if any) and the NCAA, except as permitted in the Drug-Testing Consent form, the following documents:

1. This form;
2. Results of NCAA drug tests and related information and correspondence;
3. Results of positive drug tests administered by a non-NCAA national or international sports governing body;
4. Any transcript from your high school, this institution, or any junior college or any other four-year institution you have attended;
5. Precollege test scores, appropriately related information and correspondence (e.g., testing sites, dates and letters of test-score certification or appeal), and where applicable, information relating to eligibility for or conduct of nonstandard testing;
6. Graduation status;
7. Your social security number and/or student identification number;
8. Race and gender identification;
9. Diagnosis of any education-impact disabilities;
10. Accommodations provided or approved and other information related to any education-impact disabilities in all secondary and postsecondary schools;
11. Records concerning your financial aid; and
12. Any other papers or information pertaining to your NCAA eligibility.

You agree to disclose these records only to determine your eligibility for intercollegiate athletics, your eligibility for athletically related financial aid, for evaluation of school and team academic success, for awards and recognition programs highlighting student-athlete academic success (e.g. Elite 89), for purposes of inclusion in summary institutional information reported to the NCAA (and which may be publicly released by it), for NCAA longitudinal research studies and for activities related to NCAA compliance reviews and athletics certification. You will not be identified by name by the NCAA in any such published or distributed information. This consent shall remain in effect as long as any issues regarding the purposes listed above exist.

You also agree that information regarding any infractions matter in which you may be involved may be published or distributed to third parties as required by NCAA policies, bylaws or procedures.

_____   _____
Date   Signature of student-athlete

Part III: Affirmation of Status as an Amateur Athlete.

You affirm that you have read and understand the NCAA amateurism rules.

By signing this part of the form, you affirm that, to the best of your knowledge, you have not violated any amateurism rules since you requested a final certification from the NCAA Eligibility Center or since the last time you signed a Division I student-athlete statement, whichever occurred later.

You affirm that since requesting a final certification from the NCAA Eligibility Center, you have not provided false or misleading information concerning your amateur status to the NCAA, the NCAA Eligibility Center and the institution's athletics department, including administrative personnel and the coaching staff.

_____   _____
Name (please print)   Date

_____
Signature of student-athlete

Part IV: Promotion of NCAA Championships, Events, Activities or Programs

You authorize the NCAA [or a third party acting on behalf of the NCAA (e.g., host institution, conference, local organizing committee)] to use your name or picture in accordance with NCAA Bylaw 12.5, including to promote NCAA championships or other NCAA events, activities or programs.

_____   _____
Name (please print)   Date

_____
Signature of student-athlete

Part V: Results of Drug Tests.

1. Future positive test—all student-athletes sign.

Should I test positive for a substance banned by the NCAA and/or by a non-NCAA national or international sports governing body; violate their drug-testing protocol; or fail to show for their drug test, at any time after I sign this statement, I acknowledge I must report the results to my director of athletics.

_____   _____
Name (please print)   Date

_____
Signature of student-athlete

1. **Positive test by NCAA or other sports governing body—sign either A or B.**
   A. No positive drug test.
I affirm that I have never tested positive for a substance banned by the NCAA and/or by a non-NCAA national or international sports governing body; or violated their drug-testing protocol; or failed to show for their drug test.

_____   _____
Name (please print)   Date

_____
Signature of student-athlete

B. Positive drug test.
I have tested positive for a substance banned by the NCAA and/or by a non-NCAA national or international sports governing body; or violated their drug-testing protocol; or failed to show for their drug test. Should I subsequently transfer, I am obligated to report this to the transferring institution.

_____
Name (please print)

_____
Signature of student-athlete

_____   _____   _____
Date of test   Organization conducting test   Substance
Are you currently under such a drug-testing suspension?
Yes _____ No _____

Part VI: Incoming Transfers—Previous Involvement in NCAA Rules Violation(s)

Have you previously attended a four-year NCAA Divisions I, II or III institution?

Yes _____ No _____

If yes, what is the name(s) of the institution(s)? _____

Are you aware of any NCAA violations you were involved in while previously attending an NCAA institution?

Yes _____ No _____

If yes, did this violation result in your being withheld from competition while attending your previous institution?

Yes _____ No _____

If you answered yes to either of the above questions, please provide an explanation.

_____

_____

_____

_____

Part VII: Incoming Freshmen—Affirmation of Valid ACT or SAT Score.

You affirm that, to the best of your knowledge, you have received a validated ACT and/or SAT score. You agree that, in the event you are or have been notified by ACT or SAT of the possibility of an invalidated test score, you will immediately notify the director of athletics of your institution. You affirm that all information provided to the NCAA, the NCAA Eligibility Center and institution's admissions office is valid and accurate, including high school attendance, completion of coursework and high school grades. You affirm that you did not fraudulently earn your qualifying ACT or SAT score by having someone else take the test for you, copying answers from another person taking the test, etc.

_____   _____
Name (please print)   Date

_____
Signature of student-athlete

What to do with this form: Sign and return it to your director of athletics or his or her designee before you first compete. This form is to be kept in the director of athletics' office for **six years.**

Any questions regarding this form should be referred to your director of athletics or your institution's NCAA compliance staff, or you may contact the NCAA at 317/917–6222.

APPENDIX C

NFLPA Marketing Representation Notice

Date   _____

    Dexter Santos
    Vice President
    Player Services
    NFL PLAYERS
    ██████████████████
    ██████████████████

    Re: Marketing Representation Notice for

_____

(player's name)

Dear Dexter:

Please be informed that I have authorized _____
_____ (my "Marketing Representative") to seek and negotiate the
marketing opportunities identified below effective immediately and until
further notice. Accordingly, NFL PLAYERS, upon receipt of this letter, is
authorized and directed to correspond with my Marketing Representative
in connection with such opportunities.

Marketing Opportunities (*Check all that apply*):
- ❑ Endorsements
- ❑ Paid Appearances
- ❑ Non-Paid Appearances-Media /PR
- ❑ Non-Paid Appearances-Charitable

❑ Trading Card & Collectible Offers

❑ Other: (Please list): _____

My Marketing Representative's contact information is as below. I understand that NFL PLAYERS will only contact this individual for the opportunities above.

Name   _____
Company   _____
Mailing Address   _____
City, State, Zip   _____
Email Address   _____
Contact numbers Office: Fax: _____
 Mobile: _____ Other: _____

If you have any questions regarding this letter, I can be reached at _____ (player's primary telephone number) or via email at _____ (player's email address).
Thank you.

_____
Signature

Please mail the ORIGINAL of this Marketing Representation Notice to the address above. No faxes or photocopies will be accepted.

For NFL PLAYERS use only:
Date Received:

APPENDIX D

NFLPA Section 5 Grievance Filed by Agent John "JR" Rickert v. Audie Attar

Section 5 Grievance

Dispute Between Contract Advisor and Contract Advisor
John W. Rickert Grievant

And
Audie A. Attar Respondent

Matters Concerning:
Tortious Interference
Violation of Restrictive Covenant and Non-compete Agreement
Failure to Comply with NFLPA Regulations
Failure to Recognize the Jurisdiction and Authority of the NFLPA
Served:
Via Facsimile and Certified Mail
Action Required:
Please serve a response upon me within 20 days of receipt with a copy to the NFLPA legal department.

BEFORE ARBITRATOR ROGER KAPLAN

In the Matter of Arbitration Between:)
) Motion for Arbitration Order and
) Request for Relief
)
John W. Rickert   )
Grievant;   )
)
and   )
)
Audie A. Attar   Respondent   )
)

John W. Rickert, ("Rickert"), a registered and Certified Contract Advisor since 2003, hereby filed a Complaint and Demand for Relief from Respondent, Audie A. Attar, ("Attar"), also a Certified Contract Advisor. The Grievance was received by Attar and the NFLPA, on or about October 3, 2011.

The Grievance was based upon the following facts:

On or about the months of February, March, and April of 2011, Attar interfered with the contractual relationship with Rickert and players: Matt Ware of the Arizona Cardinals, Aaron Berry of the Detroit Lions, and Roberto Wallace of the Miami Dolphins. As a result the 3 above mentioned players were provided an email address by Attar and enticed to terminate their Standard Representation Agreements with Rickert.

On or about the months of February 2011 to the present, Attar has attempted to encourage Chris Ogbannaya of the Cleveland Browns and Cam Morrah of the Seattle Seahawks to terminate their respective Standard Representation Agreements with Rickert as well.

At some point in the year 2011, Attar signed Pierre Allen to a Standard Representation Agreement and went on to execute a contract on Allen's behalf with the Seattle Seahawks. This is a clear violation of the restrictive covenant and agreement not to compete pursuant to the agreement executed with Rickert.

On or about September 30, 2011, Attar served Rickert with a notice of claim in United States District Court for a breach of contract between

2 certified contract advisors. The agreement clearly states that the NFLPA shall have original jurisdiction over any and all disputes regarding said agreement. Therefore, Attar has failed to recognize the jurisdiction and authority of the NFLPA, which is a blatant violation for any certified contract advisor.

Attar received commissions from clients in 2009 and 2010 who he did not have a Standard Representation Agreement with, and he failed to report these commissions to Rickert.

REQUEST FOR RELIEF

WHEREFORE, Grievant petitions and applies to the Arbitrator for:

Order which requires payment from Attar to Rickert for one-half of the commissions received for the duration of the careers of the 3 players that Attar improperly induced to terminate Rickert.

Order which requires payment from Attar to Rickert for one-half of any and all revenues earned by Pierre Allen.

A directive from the NFLPA to cease attempts at tortious interference with any and all clients of other contract advisors.

Compensatory Damages as seen as appropriate by this tribunal Attar's damaging of Rickert's professional reputation by inducing the said terminations and attempting 2 additional terminations.

Discipline and/or referral of Attar to CARD for significant violations of regulations that govern certified contract advisors.

Suspension and/or monetary fines for Attar's willful and blatant disregard for the legitimate authority and jurisdiction of the NFLPA.

Any other damages this tribunal deems necessary and appropriate, including, but not limited to costs and attorney's fees for pursuing this claim.

Respectfully Submitted,

John W. Rickert
16 Brendan Lane
Niskayuna, New York 12309

Certificate of Service

I hereby certify that a copy of the forgoing was served upon Audie A. Attar at his current legal address, 2203 Watermark Place, Irvine, California 92612, and by mail and electronic mail to Tom DePaso, Esq. Staff Counsel of the National Football League Players Association, this 3rd day of October, 2011.

_____

APPENDIX E

PABLO SANDOVAL PRELIMINARY REPORT 11/5/11

Numbers operate as indicators of players' value in baseball more than probably all other professional sports. Statistical breakdowns tend to be vital in contract negotiations between players and teams, and agents rely heavily on analyses of same in order to persuade executives and ownership that their clients are worth the amount of dollars they are pushing. Alternatively, in salary arbitration, agents and players seek to use statistics to win over a panel of arbitrators. Oftentimes they are assisted by outside specialists involved in the crafting of in-depth arbitration reports that are used as integral exhibits at the arbitration hearings. Below is an example of one such report that was created to support San Francisco Giants third baseman, Pablo Sandoval as he was getting ready to approach the arbitrators.

A SIGNIFICANT COMP for PABLO relative to a 1-year arbitration contract is the

$3.65 million NELSON CRUZ contract signed 1/18/11;

$3.4 million STEPHEN DREW contract 1/19/10 would be insufficient

In fact a very REVEALING CASE is KCR BILLY BUTLER who filed at $4.3m, team filed @ $3.4m and they ended up with a 4 year $30 million agreement 1/22/11;

Another is RYAN ZIMMERMAN filing at $3.9m, team @ only $2.75; they SETTLED at MIDPOINT $3.325m on 2/19/09. . . . ONLY TWO MONTHS LATER 4/20/09 they agreed on 5-year $45 million contract!

And so for a MULTI-year deal look to

The 2-year $11 million contract MATT KEMP signed 1/15/10 (E ENCARNACION 2y, $7.6m; 2/17/09

May get mentioned BUT 801 OPS only)

A 3-year $19.15 m contract is what DREW ended up with upon signing 1/18/11 2yrs, $15.75m

The 4-year $30 million contract ROBINSON CANO signed 2/08

The 6-year $66 million contract MARKAKIS signed 1/21/09 is intriguing for he FILED @ $5m; team only $2.9m . . . agreement provided for $3m in arb1 year + $1m BONUS payout as well . . .

This MARKAKIS contract as well as the KEMP & BUTLER ones makes it clear we'll be looking for $4m PLUS!!!

PLAYER PAs BA OBP SLUG OPS AllStars WorldSeriesW HighMVP

SANDOVAL thru 2011 1,869 307 356 501 857 1 yes #7 in 09

N CRUZ thru 2010 1,570 273 334 502 836 1 no not high

S DREW thru 2009 2,103 270 324 445 769 0 no #26 in 08

B BUTLER thru 2010 2,188 298 360 455 815 0 no not high

R ZIMMERMAN to 2008 1,932 282 341 462 803 0 no not high

M KEMP thru 2009 1,801 299 345 479 824 0 no #10 in 09

R CANO thru 2007 1,728 313 345 489 834 1 no #22 in 06

MARKAKIS thru 2008 1,949 300 378 483 861 0 no not high

MCGEHEE thru 2011 1,689 265 320 426 746 0 no not high

Note on the chart above

PABLO the only guy in TOP 3 on each CRITERIA: BA, OBP, and SLUG%!!!!

DAVID WRIGHT's 6 year, $55 million contract was signed 8/06 PREarbitration BUT the last 5 years @ $53.75 million is similar ANNUAL money to the MARKAKIS CONTRACT, about $11m PER YEAR, which is a GOOD NEIGHBORHOOD for you to be in. . . . WRIGHT is key for MVP#19 in 2005 & MVP #9 in 2006

I fully expect PABLO to rank HIGH in MVP VOTING once more. . . . the only guy to do that is DAVID WRIGHT

5 years, $55m or 6 years, $66m

7 years, $80m matching the 1/11/11 CARLOS GONZALEZ contract is where you want to be.

* * *

PABLO has played 146+ games TWICE, in 2009 and 2010; as did MARKAKIS in 2007 and 08

And BILLY BUTLER in 2009 and 2010 as well as ZIMMERMAN in 2006 and 2007;

however DREW,KEMP & CANO & MCGEHEE each only ONCE; CRUZ NEVER!

PABLO as WINNER . . . GIANTS are 234–204, 534 in his STARTS vs 104–106,495 in his SITS; +39

D WRIGHT NYM 199–183, 521 in his STARTS vs 52–52,500 in his SITS; +21

MARKAKIS BAL 190–255, 427 in his STARTS vs 17–23,425 in his SITS; +2

CANO NYY 239–167, 589 in his STARTS vs 47–33,588 in his SITS; +1

M KEMP LAD 214–184, 538 in his STARTS vs 135–115,540 in his SITS; –2

B BUTLER KCR 216–295, 423 in his STARTS vs 60–77,440 in his SITS; –17

CRUZ TEX 182–189, 490 in his STARTS vs 229–210,522 in his SITS; –32

S DREW ARI 235–236, 499 in his STARTS vs 180–152,542 in his SITS; –43

R ZIMMERMAN WSH 184–251, 423 in his STARTS vs 100–112,472 in his SITS; –49

MCGEHEE MIL 193–188, 507 in his STARTS vs 60–45,571 in his SITS;-64

PABLO as DOMINANT FORCE ...

PABLO's 2011 909 OPS LED TEAM & was 35.5% BETTER than TEAM AVG OPS of 671, 15th in NL;

His sole teammate with 400+ PAs and decent OPS: C ROSS @ 730 only

PABLO's 2009 943 OPS LED TEAM & was 34.9% BETTER than TEAM AVG OPS of 699, 16th in NL

DREW's 2009 748 OPS 5th on TEAM and 0.8% BETTER than TEAM AVG OPS of 742, 9th in NL

DREW 4 teammates with 400+PAs and OPS 775+(JUPTON, REYN-OLDS, MONTERO, FLOPEZ)

CANO's 2007 841 OPS 4th on TEAM and 1.5% BETTER than TEAM AVG OPS of 829, 1st in AL;

CANO: 6 teammates with 400+ PAs and OPS 747+(AROD, POSADA, MATSUI, JETER, ABREU, DAMON)

So these 2 COMPS do NOT LEAD TEAM NOR are they MUCH ABOVE TEAM AVERAGE!!!

M KEMP 09 842 OPS 3rd on TEAM and 11.1% BETTER than TEAM AVG OPS of 758; 4th in NL

M KEMP: 6 teammates 400+PAs & OPS 756+ (MANNY, ETHIER, BLAKE, HUDSON, PIERRE, LONEY)

D WRIGHT 06 912 OPS 2nd on TEAM & 16.9% BETTER than TEAM AVG OPS of 780; 4th in NL

D WRIGHT: 5 teammates 400+PAs & OPS 783+(BELTRAN, DELGADO, REYES, VALENTIN, LODUCA)

CRUZ' 2010 950 OPS 2nd on TEAM and 25.5% BETTER than TEAM AVG OPS of 757; 5th in AL

CRUZ 5 teammates with 400+ PAs and OPS 774+ (HAMILTON, VLADDY, DMURPHY, KINSLER, YOUNG)

MARKAKIS' 08 897 OPS 2nd on TEAM and 17.7% BETTER than TEAM AVG OPS 762; 7th in AL

MARKAKIS has 4 teammates with 400+PAs and OPS 807+(HUFF, ROB-ERTS, MORA, SCOTT)

ZIMMERMAN 08 774 OPS 2nd on TEAM & 11.2% BETTER than TEAM AVG OPS 696; 16th in NL

ZIMMERMAN has 3 teammates with 400+PAs and OPS 731+ (GUZ-MAN, W HARRIS, MILLEDGE)

BBUTLER 2010 857 OPS LEADS TEAM and 17.4% BETTER than TEAM AVG OPS 730; 9th in AL;

BUTLER has 3 teammates with 400+PAs and OPS 743+ (PODSEDNIK, AVILES, J GUILLEN)

MCGEHEE 2011 626 OPS is 8th!!! And 16.5% WORSE!!! than TEAM AVG OPS 750; 2nd in NL

MCGEHEE has 5 teammates 400+PAs and OPS 778+ (BRAUN, FIELDER, HART, WEEKS, MORGAN)

Notes:

Among these COMPS ONLY BUTLER led his TEAM in OPS in PLATFORM YEAR

Among these COMPS . . .

CRUZ beat TEAM AVG by 25.5%

MARKAKIS did so 2nd most by 17.7%

In BOTH 2009 and 2011 PABLO BEAT TEAM AVG by about 35%!!!!

Among these COMPS everyone had at least 3 STRONG SUPPORT OPS mates . . .

In 2011 PABLO had ONE!!!

DOES this TALENTED TEAMMATE point really MATTER?

Consider in

3 games PABLO hit #3 & BELTRAN hit #4 (dates 8/3/11; 8/4/11; 8/31/11)

PABLO goes 5 for 13, 385 BA with 3 runs, 2 RBI, HR

33 gms PABLO hit #4 & BELTRAN #3 (dates: 7/28; 7/29;7/30; 7/31; 8/1; 8/2; 8/5; 8/6; 8/7;

8/24; 8/25;8/27; 8/28; 8/29; 8/30; 9/2; 9/3; 9/4;

9/7; 9/9; 9/10; 9/11; 9/12; 9/13; 9/14; 9/15; 9/16;

9/18; 9/22; 9/24; 9/25; 9/26; 9/27)

PABLO goes 43 for 119, 361 BA with 12 runs, 22 RBI, 8 HR, 8 2Bs, 2 3Bs

TOTAL: 36 games . . . 48 for 132 for 364 BA, 397 OBP, 659 SLUG, 1,056 OPS!!!!

So having BELTRAN around him in LINEUP was a BOON to PABLO!!!

PABLO's DEFENSE Page 4

What at one time might have been considered a LIABILITY has now become an ASSET, PABLO's RANGE and DEPENDABILITY at 3B . . . .

This was affirmed by his status as a FINALIST for NL GG AWARD . . . .

PABLO's RANGE FACTOR which was 2.32 and 2.36 in 2009 and 2010 SOARED to 2.84 in 2011;

PABLO's FIELD% has IMPROVED from 960 to 961 to 966 the past 3 years . . . .

PABLO's ABILITY to START DPs from 3B is NOW IMPRESSIVE . . . .

In 2009 he was involved in 13 DPs in 1,028 innings = 1 every 79.1 innings
By 2011 he was involved in 16 DPs in 905 innings = 1 every 56.5 innings
In 2011 YOUKILIS was in 15 DPs in 947 innings = 1 every 63.1 innings
In 2011 POLANCO was in 15 DPs in 1,044 innings =1 every 69.6 innings
PABLO in CLUTCH
PABLO's CAREER SPLITS:
838 OPS in 2 OUTS RUNNERS in SCORING POSITION and
882 OPS in TIE GAMES
Should speak to his ability in the CLUTCH; however his DISAPPOINT-
ING 2010 SEASON and PLAYOFFS are the ONLY VULNERABLE SPOT
that MANAGEMENT can TARGET and so here is AMMUNITION to
RESPOND to any criticism.

Sunday, 9/26/10 the GIANTS were UP 0.5 games on SDP with 88–68
record and 6 games to go; they went 4–2 in those remaining games to
HOLD OFF the PADRES.

In those 6 games 9/28/10 thru 10/3/10
SANDOVAL 7 for 18, 389 with 2B and HR
BURRELL 7 for 21, 333 with 2B and HR
URIBE 6 for 20, 300 with 2 2Bs and 2 HRs
HUFF 5 for 19, 263 with 2B and 5 BBs
TORRES 6 for 24, 250 with 3B and HR
FONTENOT 3 for 12, 250
F SANCHEZ 2 for 12,167
POSEY 3 for 24,125 with 2 HRs
J GUILLEN 1 for 13, 077
RENTERIA 0 for 3
C ROSS 0 for 2
Clearly PABLO was a HUGE CONTRIBUTOR down the
STRETCH . . . and DURING the SEASON

Page 5
APRIL, 2010 GIANTS go 13–9 and hover just 1.5 GB in 2nd largely
because
PABLO has 1,008 OPS for month including 3 HRs, 10 RBI, 12 runs
May 28 & 29 GIANTS win 1st 2 games of series vs ARI and remain
3rd, 2.5 GB @ 26–22

PABLO goes 5 for 8 with 4 runs, 4 RBI, 2B and HR in these 2 games

June 12 &13 GIANTS beat OAK twice to remain 3rd, 1.5 GB @ 35–27

PABLO goes 2 for 5 with 3 BBs, 4 runs, RBI, HR in these 2 games

July 7th & 8 GIANTS win last 2 games of 4 game sweep @ MILW . . .

Remain 4th, 5 GB @ 45–40; critical as it comes on heels of 7-gm LOS-ING streak

PABLO goes 4 for 10, scores run in these 2 games

July 17th GIANTS beat METS 8–4 to remain 2nd, 3.5 GB @ 50–41

PABLO goes 3 for 4, 2B, run, 3 RBI

July 19 & 20 GIANTS get 2 WINS @ LAD and @ 52–42 are 2nd, 3.0 GB

PABLO goes 3 for 9, 2 2Bs, BB, run, 3 RBI in these 2 games

Aug 11 & 12 GIANTS get 2 "one run" WINS vs CUBS to get to 66–50, 2nd, 2.5 GB

PABLO goes 4 for 8, with 2B, 3B, HR (cycle over 2 days), 2 runs, RBI

Aug 23&24 GIANTS get 2 WINS vs CINCY to get to 71–56, 2nd, 5.5 GB

PABLO goes 6 for 10, 2 2Bs, HR, 4 runs, 7 RBI in these 2 games

Sept 5th GIANTS WIN 3–0 @ LAD to move within 1.0 GB @ 76–61

PABLO goes 2 for 3, scores 1 of the 3 runs, and knocks one home on SF

So PABLO's CONSISTENT PLAY and CONTRIBUTIONs helped make the STORYBOOK 2010 POSTseason possible.

ATTENDANCE

PABLO has become the " everyday FACE of the FRANCHISE" and helped ERASE the STAIN upon the GIANTS organization brought on with the BONDS controversy.

In 2009 35,322 fans/game 10th in MLB

In 2010 37,499 fans/game 9th in MLB

In 2011 41,829 fans/game 3rd in MLB ... that's an 18.4% increase over 2009!!!

So in a DOWN ECONOMY the GIANTS franchise has NEVER been HEALTHIER FINANCIALLY . . . and to GIANTS EXECS please do NOT attribute this to the BALLPARK . . . BALTIMORE, CLEVELAND, NY METS, HOUSTON are just a few clubs where the LUSTRE of a NEW BALLPARK "EXPIRED" within a short period of time and ATTENDANCE PLUMMETED as FANS ABANDONED BAD TEAMS!!! PABLO's PRESENCE and POPULARITY should INSULATE SF from a similar fate!!!

Index